D0745112

AFTER EFFECTS FOR **FLASH**

FLASH FOR **AFTER EFFECTS**

DYNAMIC ANIMATION AND VIDEO
WITH ADOBE® AFTER EFFECTS® CS4 AND
ADOBE® FLASH® CS4 PROFESSIONAL

RICHARD HARRINGTON

MARCUS GEDULD

Adobe

After Effects for Flash | Flash for After Effects:
Dynamic Animation and Video with Adobe® After Effects® CS4 and Adobe® Flash® CS4 Professional

Richard Harrington and Marcus Geduld

This Adobe Press book is published by Peachpit. For information on Adobe Press books, contact:

Peachpit
1249 Eighth Street
Berkeley, CA 94710
510/524-2178
Fax: 510/524-2221
For the latest on Adobe Press books, go to www.adobepress.com.

To report errors, please send a note to errata@peachpit.com
Peachpit is a division of Pearson Education
Copyright © 2009 by Richard M. Harrington and Marcus Geduld

Acquisitions Editor: Victor Gavenda
Project Editor: Karyn Johnson
Development Editor: Anne Marie Walker
Production Editor: Cory Borman
Tech Editor: Alex Czetwertynski
Technical Quality Control: Megan Tytler
Compositor: David Van Ness
Proofreader: Rebecca Rider
Indexer: Jack Lewis
Interior and Cover Design: Mimi Heft
Cover illustration: Mike Campau, Seventh Street, www.seventhstreetstudio.com

Notice of Rights

All rights reserved. No part of this book may be reproduced or transmitted in any form by any means, electronic, mechanical, photocopying, recording, or otherwise, without the prior written permission of the publisher. For information on getting permission for reprints and excerpts, contact permissions@peachpit.com.

Notice of Liability

The information in this book is distributed on an "As Is" basis without warranty. While every precaution has been taken in the preparation of the book, neither the authors nor Peachpit shall have any liability to any person or entity with respect to any loss or damage caused or alleged to be caused directly or indirectly by the instructions contained in this book or by the computer software and hardware products described in it.

Trademarks

Adobe, After Effects, and Flash are registered trademarks of Adobe Systems, Inc. Many of the designations used by manufacturers and sellers to distinguish their products are claimed as trademarks. Where those designations appear in this book, and Peachpit was aware of a trademark claim, the designations appear as requested by the owner of the trademark. All other product names and services identified throughout this book are used in editorial fashion only and for the benefit of such companies with no intention of infringement of the trademark. No such use, or the use of any trade name, is intended to convey endorsement or other affiliation with this book.

ISBN-13: 978-0-321-60607-5
ISBN-10:   0-321-60607-8

9 8 7 6 5 4 3 2 1

Printed and bound in the United States of America

To my wife Meghan: Thank you for your love and support—without you this book would have never been written.

To my children: You inspire me to be a better man and to create new worlds for you to explore.

To my family: Your help through the years has made all things possible.

—Rich

To my brother Daniel who uses Flash. Let's see if we can get him to use After Effects, too!

To the good folks at Zeitbyte Digital Media and Future Media Concepts.

To the actors and staff at Folding Chair Classical Theatre.

And, as always, to my partner in crime, Lisa.

—Marcus

Acknowledgments

The authors of this book would like to acknowledge the following individuals for their contributions to this book and the techniques shared within:

Giles Baker

Corey Barker

Lee Brimelow

Michael Coleman

RC Concepcion

Alex Czetwertynski

Bob Donlon

Emmanuel Etim

Michelle Gallina

Rod Harlan

Karyn Johnson

Jim Kanter

Todd Kopriva

Ben Kozuch

Xi Lin

Ron & Kathlyn Lindeboom

Adam Martray

Chris Meyer

Trish Meyer

Ian Pullens

Mike Shaw

Colin Smith

Paul Temme

Megan Tytler

Paul Vogelzang

Anne Marie Walker

Mark Wesier

CONTENTS

INTRODUCTION

In this case, we truly hope that you can judge a book by its cover.

This book is about two great animation tools and how they can work together. It's about using Adobe Flash CS4 Professional (generally thought of as "just" a Web-animation program) and Adobe After Effects CS4 (which most regard as an animation/compositing program for film and video).

Over time the Web has become deeply integrated into the world of film and video. Similarly, Flash and After Effects have grown to become complementary and even codependent. Now that both tools are owned by Adobe, the emphasis has been on two important areas: making it easier to move assets between the two applications and developing the core strengths of each application to create a suite-based workflow that emphasizes the "toolbox" approach.

This book teaches you the wide range in which these programs can cooperate and assist each other. The goal of the book is to explore the essential techniques and workflow as well as some of the more advanced tools and skills. We use these tools every day to create projects for our clients. In this book, we share what we've learned about Flash and After Effects.

Why Flash and After Effects?

The professionals who create animation, video, and interactive content are always looking for new and better ways to do their job, driven by a deep desire to entertain and inform. Flash and After Effects started out worlds apart, with different mediums, different markets, and even different companies. It's funny how things change.

The land of video used to be far away from the land of the Web. But continents are drifting, and video professionals are now holding hands with Web developers. Often, video professionals *are* Web developers. Back when the world was simpler—when video was over *here* and the Web was over *there*—video professionals animated and composited in After Effects. Meanwhile, Web developers animated and added interactivity in Flash. But now it's common to stroll through video production offices and see people struggling with Flash; it's equally common to hear Web folks cursing at After Effects.

Why struggling and cursing? Because the programs have very different legacies. What looks similar at first becomes tricky in application. From design issues, like keyframes and composition, to technical challenges, like frame rates and non-square pixels, the two applications have subtle and dramatic differences—much like two languages that, while similar, can lead to misunderstandings and frustration. This book attempts to bridge the gaps and expose you to some very cool techniques along the way.

Nowadays, the best video, motion graphics, and Web professionals use both Flash and After Effects. They might use After Effects to finish a graphic-rich video and then add interactivity and deploy the video using Flash. Or they might create vector-based animation with Flash that is used on the Web and even on television. Each application has its treasures and its pitfalls. You need to learn how the applications behave and how they work with each other.

After Effects can import and display the SWF and QuickTime files that Flash creates and in fact can create those very formats. Flash can import rendered-video formats from After Effects, as well as After Effects generated SWFs. One new way to move from After Effects to Flash (with layers intact) is the powerful XFL exchange format. Once you understand that the two applications can exchange data, you'll begin to think of them less as two different programs and more as two tools in the same toolbox.

What Flash Does

Adobe Flash Professional is a hybrid application: It's 50 percent a design/animation tool and 50 percent a computer programming tool—programmable using the ActionScript language. In this book, we cover both sides of the application. We begin by explaining Flash's toolset and then use its animation tools, which offer different benefits than After Effects. In later chapters, we expose you to the essentials of ActionScript and teach you how to distribute video and animation via interactive Flash Video.

What After Effects Does

After Effects is a powerhouse tool for video animation and compositing. If you can imagine something, you can likely create it in After Effects. But with all that ability comes great complexity. After Effects has a ton of tools and a steep learning curve. For many Flash animators, the change to raster graphics and increase in render times is challenging. After Effects is a great animation tool, but on its own does not allow for the interactivity the Web demands.

How Can You Use Flash and After Effects Together?

Well, that's the question, isn't it? The answers are found between the front and back covers of this book. Ever since the two applications started shipping together in Adobe's Creative Suite bundles, new users are discovering Flash and After Effects—and they know there's more there than first meets the eye.

Are all the answers here? Of course not, but we put the coolest, most useful projects we could think of in this book. Sometimes we keep it simple; at other times we go really deep. You'll learn how to create transparency with a green screen background in After Effects, exporting the video to Flash. You'll learn how to use Flash's Bones tool to animate an object, move it into After Effects, and then finesse it with Photoshop-like effects. You'll learn how to create a video in After Effects and later add captions and searchable text to it in Flash, making it accessible. The list goes on.

The key is to learn from the journey and pick up good ideas and best practices along the way that you can adapt to your job and your projects.

Who This Book Is for

It's for After Effects users.

No, it's for Flash users.

Please, everyone! Keep calm. This book is for After Effects *and* Flash users. We show users of both applications how the other half lives by bridging the two different mediums and revealing the best features of each application.

We *do* expect you to have some experience with one of the two applications. But it's fine if you've never touched the other one. This book addresses professional motion-graphics artists, video professionals, and animators who have produced work for the big screen, the small screen, and anything in between.

How This Book Is Organized

This book is divided into four sections.

Part I: Technical Essentials starts by explaining the essentials of After Effects from a Flash user's point of view. Then it introduces Flash to After Effects users. Even if you feel comfortable with both applications, you're sure to pick up some shortcuts and new ideas. You then take a quick tour of the rest of the Production Premium CS4 bundle as we suggest ways you can use other Adobe applications like Photoshop, Soundbooth, and Premiere Pro to enhance your workflow.

Part II: Creating Content for Flash with After Effects explains everything you need to know if you're creating movies in After Effects that will one day wind up in Flash. This includes keying out green screen footage, creating dynamic-text effects, working with raster and vector graphics, and creating a cartoon look for video. This section ends with a tour of some of the power features of Flash and After Effects, such as After Effects' Puppet tools and Flash's Bones tool.

Part III: Enhancing Flash with After Effects travels to the third dimension, explaining how to use After Effect's 3D layers, lights, and cameras. We also share our knowledge about prepping Flash files for broadcast on television and DVD.

Part IV: Enhancing Video with Flash shows you how to create great looking Flash Video with small file sizes and clear images. You'll also dip your toes into Flash as a programming tool, using ActionScript to make video interactive. You then learn to use Adobe Soundbooth to transcribe video to make video clips searchable and more accessible.

On the DVD and Web

We've included a DVD at the back of the book that contains all the files you'll need to complete the exercises in the book. Not only that but you'll find a number of video tutorials on the DVD that go beyond the book. You'll also find some templates and bonus material to make working in Flash or After Effects easier. When you are ready to complete a lesson, just drag the chapter's Project Files folder to a hard drive.

In addition, we want you to keep up to date with the latest information. The tools discussed throughout the book will continue to evolve and get easier to integrate. As things change or we discover new workflows, you'll find out about them at www.peachpit.com/AEFlashCS4.

1 AFTER EFFECTS ESSENTIALS FOR THE FLASH USER

After Effects is a powerful animation software program that offers many tools for creative effects, dynamic animation, and excellent compositing. Although After Effects and Flash now share the same manufacturer, they evolved as very different programs. After Effects began its life with the Company of Science and Art (CoSA), and Flash was originally developed as FutureSplash Animator and renamed Flash after Macromedia purchased it in 1996.

Over time, both programs have grown significantly in their scope and capabilities. For a Flash user, the core principles of After Effects will seem similar. Elements are stacked from top to bottom in a timeline and then animated with keyframes. From there, the similarities pretty much end. Sure, the interfaces look similar, but Flash users may find themselves scratching their heads a bit due to the subtle intricacies of the two applications.

Let's jump into using After Effects with a crash course that shows the key tools as well as a standard workflow.

The After Effects Interface Tour

The After Effects interface provides several specialized tools and panes that assist in animation tasks. You'll explore most of these in depth throughout the book, but a quick introduction is necessary to lay the foundation for the chapters to come. Even though After Effects takes just a few days to learn, it takes years to master. Let's take a look at the essential areas of the program you'll use most often.

Configuring the Application with Workspaces

After Effects CS4 offers nine default workspaces to speed up specific animation and effects tasks. Each workspace configures the visibility and arrangement of specific panels to increase efficiency for particular tasks. In addition,
you can create custom workspaces based on user preferences. To ensure you
are working with the default workspace in After Effects (so the standard tools
and panels are easy to find), follow these steps.

1. From the book's DVD, copy the **Chapter_01 Project Files** folder to your
    computer.

2. If it's not already running, launch After Effects CS4. At the Welcome
    screen, click the Open Project button.

3. Navigate to the **Chapter_01 Project Files** folder and open the file **01_Com-
    pleted.aep**. A project with footage and a completed sequence for refer-
    ence opens. You'll build this project from scratch shortly.

4. In the upper-right corner, click the Workspace drop-down menu and
    choose Standard to reset the After Effects interface to the Standard view.
    If Standard is already selected, choose Reset "Standard" to ensure the
    workspace is at its default starting point, and then click Discard Changes.
    After Effects is now in its Standard view.

5. In the Project panel, double-click the composition named Bumper to load
    the project into the Timeline and Composition panels.

Standard Panels in After Effects CS4

After Effects CS4 offers 26 different panels to control or view elements of your
animation project. That can be a bit unwieldy. Let's take the most commonly
used panels that you will have visible most of the time when working.

Project

The Project panel contains all the elements within an After Effects project. It is
similar in functionality to the Library in Flash. Keeping the Project panel organized makes it easy to find elements and speeds up the animation process.
The project is already filled with several elements. Let's explore two ways to
find footage.

- To search for an item, just type its name or keyword into the search field
  at the top of the Project panel. Type the word chart in the search field to
  locate all files with the word chart in the name. To reset the search, click
  the X in the search field.

- If an item is already added to the Timeline, right-click the object and
  choose Reveal Layer Source in Project. Try revealing the file skyline.ai in
  the Timeline.

▲ **TIP Find Out More**

To see more informa-
tion about an item,
simply select it in
the Project panel. A
thumbnail image and
detailed information
are shown at the top
of the Project panel.

Composition

In Flash, you build an application and see its elements on the Stage. The closest analogy in After Effects is the composition and related Composition panel.

● NOTE **Composition to Comp**

The word composition is frequently shortened to comp in many tutorials and in everyday workflow.

After Effects allows you to create one or more compositions for a project. A composition can contain one or more footage items. Layers can be stacked in 2D space, or you can arrange them in 3D space. After Effects also offers masks, blending modes, and keying tools to composite or combine multiple layers.

Let's load a composition to view it.

1. Examine the numerous controls along the bottom of the Composition panel.

2. Click the Magnification ratio pop-up menu and choose Fit up to 100% to show the entire composition as large as possible in the Composition panel.

Timeline

Just like Flash, the Timeline panel is where most animation occurs. The Timeline provides easy access to core properties like Anchor Point (the equivalent of Flash's Registration Point), Position, Rotation, Scale, and Opacity. Additionally, effects and masks can contain keyframes to change them over time.

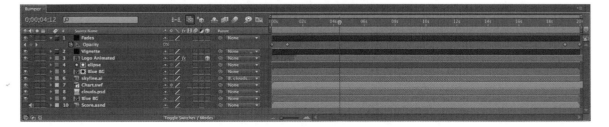

The Timeline and Composition panels are linked. The yellow Current Time Indicator (CTI) determines which frame is shown in the Composition panel. You can move this indicator by

- Clicking Play
- Invoking a Preview
- Using the Page Up or Page Down keys
- Dragging the Current Time Indicator
- Clicking the current time in the upper-left corner of the Timeline

Effects & Presets

The Effects & Presets panel is the easiest way to browse and apply effects and animation presets. While these options are all available via menus, it is much faster to browse and use effects with the panel.

1. Click the disclosure triangle next to the category * Animation Presets. Several options are now visible and are sorted by category.
2. Click the disclosure triangle next to the Image – Creative category.
3. In the Timeline, click the layer clouds.psd to select it.
4. In the Effects & Presets panel, double-click the preset Colorize – sky blue to enhance the color of the clouds.
5. Let's apply an effect to the line chart to further enhance it. Select the Chart.swf layer in the Timeline.
6. In the search field of the Effects & Preset panel, type Glow. Results containing the word glow are filtered.
7. Double-click the Glow effect in the Stylize group to apply it. The line chart is now enhanced with a distinct glow.

● NOTE Fun with Presets

Feel free to choose Edit > Undo and experiment with other Image presets.

Tools

After Effects offers several tools that you'll use during the design and animation process. These tools are located in the Tools panel across the top of the interface window. You'll fully explore most of these tools throughout the lessons in the book.

Info

The Info panel is a useful panel to leave open. It provides detailed information based on which tasks are being performed. When selecting items, it provides feedback on colors. When a layer is activated, the Info panel shows information about the active layer. Even during the rendering process the Info panel

displays information about progress. It is a good idea to keep the Info panel visible at all times so you can learn more about After Effects as you work.

Audio

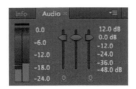

Audio will frequently play a key role in a motion graphics project, because you'll want to include music or narration into the final piece. After Effects fully supports the use of sound, but it is not designed to be a robust audio tool. Be sure to use Adobe Premiere Pro or Adobe Soundbooth if you need to perform major audio edits. In the Standard view, the Audio panel is docked with the Info panel.

1. Click the Audio tab to activate the Audio panel. When this panel is selected, you'll see three sliders.
   - The left slider controls just the left channel of audio output.
   - The right slider controls just the right channel of audio output.
   - The middle slider controls both channels of output for a stereo file.
2. Select track #10 Score.asnd in the Timeline panel.
3. Lower the middle audio slider to approximately -4.4. You can also click the yellow number to precisely enter a value.
4. To preview audio from the Current Time Indicator, choose Composition > Preview > Audio Preview (Here Forward) or press the period key (.) on the numeric keypad.

● **NOTE Digital Video Quality**

When creating animation for digital video, you'll want to make sure the audio settings match. Choose File > Project Settings and make sure the sample rate is set to 48.000 kHz.

Preview

The act of invoking a preview indicates to After Effects that you would like to see all the transformations and effects applied to a selected area of your composition. Depending on a variety of factors (including the speed of your machine and type of effects chosen) this process can take a while. The good news is that as machines and video cards get faster, so does After Effects.

To speed up the preview process, it is common practice to view previews at a low quality and a low frame rate. The Preview panel makes it easy to drop the quality of previews that only affect previews (as opposed to the final output of the animation file).

1. Click the Timeline panel and press the Home key to move the Current Time Indicator to the start of the composition.
2. Press B to mark the beginning of the work area (think **B**eginning). The work area defines which part of the animation you want to preview.
3. Move the Current Time Indicator to approximately 10:00. Then press N to mark the end of the work area (think e**N**d).
4. Click the Resolution/Down Sample Factor setting menu at the bottom of the Preview panel. Choose Half, which renders only every other pixel.

Because this option renders half the height and half the width for the preview, it is 75 percent faster than Full Quality.

5. Click the Skip drop-down menu and choose 1. This renders every other frame for the preview.

6. Click the RAM Preview button to invoke a RAM preview. The green bars indicate cached frames that are ready to preview. If you skip frames, the green line will be dashed. When all the frames are cached (or your system runs out of RAM), the file will begin to play back in realtime.

Panel Shortcuts

You can use the following keyboard shortcuts to quickly toggle the visibility for standard user interface items.

● NOTE **Know More About Rendering**

If you want details about renders and previews, choose Edit > Preferences > Display (Windows) or After Effects > Preferences > Display (Mac OS), and then select Show Rendering Progress In Info Panel And Flowchart.

Items	Windows	Mac OS
Project panel	Ctrl+0	Command+0
Render Queue panel	Ctrl+Alt+0	Command+Option+0
Tools panel	Ctrl+1	Command+1
Info panel	Ctrl+2	Command+2
Preview panel	Ctrl+3	Command+3
Audio panel	Ctrl+4	Command+4
Effects & Presets panel	Ctrl+5	Command+5
Character panel	Ctrl+6	Command+6
Paragraph panel	Ctrl+7	Command+7
Paint panel	Ctrl+8	Command+8
Open or Close Brushes panel	Ctrl+9	Command+9
Maximize or Restore panel under pointer	` (accent grave)	` (accent grave)

Creating a Project

Now that you have an overview of the After Effects interface, let's explore the production process by building a small project. This project utilizes all elements of the Production Premium suite. You won't necessarily need every one of these programs for each project, but it is useful to know how to import all the file types that After Effects supports.

1. If it's not running already, launch Adobe After Effects.

2. Choose File > New > New Project.

3. Choose File > Save As.

4. Navigate to the **Chapter_01 Project Files** folder and name the file 01_Bumper.aep.

5. Click Save to write the project file to disk.

Creating Compositions

▲ **TIP** Confused by Video Formats?

If you are befuddled by the many different flavors of video, be sure to read Chapter 11, "Converting Flash to Broadcast Standards."

In After Effects, the first step to creating animation is to make a composition. Creating a new composition is important because it defines the duration and technical specifications for the project. Knowing which settings to use can be difficult, but After Effects offers several presets to make composition creation easy.

1. Choose Composition > New Composition.

2. In the Composition Settings dialog, click the Preset list and choose HDV/HDTV 720 29.97. After Effects automatically enters the correct Width, Height, Pixel Aspect Ratio, and Frame Rate for the video format. Enter a Duration of 20;00. Enter the name Bumper in the Composition Name field.

3. Click OK to create a new composition.

Using Folders to Organize

The best way to organize files in the Project panel is with folders. Folders created within After Effects only exist in the Project panel. Footage on your hard drive is not moved or renamed by default. Let's create a new folder to help organize this project.

▲ **TIP** Changing a Name

Renaming items is a bit tricky. Instead of double-clicking, just select the item and press Return/ Enter to edit a name. You can also rename most items using a context menu. Simply right-click and choose Rename from the menu that appears.

1. Click the folder icon at the bottom of the Project panel. A new empty folder called Untitled 1 is added and ready to be named.

2. Name the folder Pre-comps and press Return (Enter). The folder is named.

Importing Assets

If you've organized media on your hard drive, you can import an entire folder of assets at one time. This makes it easy to translate organized files into an organized project.

1. Choose File > Import > File. In the Import File dialog, navigate to the **Chapter_01 Project Files** folder and open it. Double-click the **Sources** folder to open it. Then click the Import Folder button at the bottom of the panel. A new folder called Sources is added to the Project panel.

2. Click the disclosure triangle next to the Sources folder to reveal its contents. After Effects imports five subfolders and their respective contents

of footage and graphics. Then click the disclosure triangle next to the Illustrator Files folder. The folder contains three files, two of which need adjustment.

3. Select the logo.ai file and press the Delete key because you don't need this graphic. The file is removed from the project (but still exists on your hard drive).

4. The file logo start.ai also needs to be removed, not because it's unneeded, but because it was imported as a flattened file. Press the Delete key to remove the file.

5. Choose File > Import > File. Navigate to the **Chapter_01 Project Files** folder and open it. Open the nested folder **Sources**. Open the nested folder **Illustrator Files**.

6. Select the file **logo start.ai**. Set the Import As menu to Composition. Click Open. A new composition and a folder with several layers is imported into the project.

7. Drag the new composition and folder into the Illustrator Files folder in the Project panel. Choose File > Save to capture the current state of the project.

Animating in the Timeline

The Timeline in After Effects gives you access to several key animation parameters. You can visually access Transform properties (such as Rotation and Position) as well as animate effects. The After Effects Timeline is powerful but offers a refined interface to make it easy to get things done.

Organizing Layers

Before you can animate items, you need to add them to the composition (by dragging either the Composition panel or the Timeline panel). The stacking order of layers in the Timeline matters when you're working in 2D space. Layers are stacked from bottom to top (as in Flash or Photoshop).

1. Click the disclosure triangle next to each of the Sources folders so you can see all the files contained within.

2. Drag the following elements into the Timeline (be sure to drag in this order). Place each new layer on top of the previous in the Timeline.

- Score.asnd
- bg.mov
- clouds.psd
- Chart.swf
- skyline.ai
- logo start (composition)

The Timeline should contain six layers and match the following figure.

Trimming Layers

When working with layers in the Timeline panel, you'll often need to adjust their start and end points. The beginning of a layer is called its In point and the end of a layer is called its Out point. The duration of a layer is defined as the span between a layer's In and Out points.

When you trim a layer in After Effects, you modify its In or Out point (and therefore its duration). Let's explore trimming as well as adjust the In point for a layer.

1. Select the layer Chart.swf in the Timeline.

2. Press the End key or drag the Current Time Indicator to the end of the composition.

3. To make trimming easier, you can view the In and Out point controls. Right-click on the Source Name header and choose Columns > In. Repeat and choose Columns > Out.

4. Click the Out point text for the Chart.swf layer and enter 19:29 in the pop-up menu.

5. The layer's In and Out points have changed. This is not desired because the start of the animated SWF file now occurs before 0;00;00;00. While it may seem confusing, it is possible to set layers to occur before the first visible frame. This allows effects to pre-roll or start animating before they are visible. Choose Edit > Undo to reposition the layer.

6. To trim a layer, use the keyboard shortcuts. Press Option +] (Alt+]) to modify the layer's Out point.

7. Although you trimmed the Chart.swf layer, you need to extend the bg.mov layer. Unfortunately, this layer is a movie file with a duration of only 10 seconds. Before the layer can be trimmed, it needs to be looped. Select the bg.mov file in the Project panel.

8. Choose File > Interpret Footage > Main. The Interpret Footage dialog opens. In the Other Options area, enter a value of Loop: 2 Times. This particular footage is a looping background, which means it has been prepared to have identical first frames and last frames. Click OK to store the change. This process is very specialized, but many movie files sold by stock footage companies are prepared this way.

9. Select the file bg.mov in the Timeline. Press Option +] (Alt+]) to modify the layer's Out point (if you need to trim an In point, use the [key).

10. Drag the Current Time Indicator to 1:15 in the Timeline.

11. Select the layer logo start. Press the [key to move the selected layer's In point. By using just the bracket key, the layer is moved but not trimmed.

12. Choose File > Save to save your work so far.

▲ **TIP** Making Footage Loops

To learn how the bg.mov footage clip was prepared, you can download a handout at www.rhedpixel.com/handouts/theresources/conferencehandouts/DVExpo/DVDMENUS handout.pdf.

Pre-composing Layers

As your Timeline gets more and more full, it is a good idea to consider using pre-compositions. A pre-composition (or pre-comp) is essentially one composition nested inside another. There are many reasons to use a pre-comp; they range from technical decisions (such as forcing certain effects to render first) to organizational decisions (making repeated use of an element easier).

1. Click the eye icons next to all layers in the Timeline except the bg.mov layer to disable their visibility.

2. Select the layer bg.mov in the Timeline.

3. Choose Layer > Pre-compose. A new window opens prompting you to specify settings for the pre-composition.

4. Enter the name Blue BG into the New composition name field. Select the "Move all attributes into the new composition" option. This option will nest the selected layers inside the new pre-composition. Select the Open New Composition check box. Click OK to create and open the new pre-composition.

5. In the Project panel, drag the new pre-comp Blue BG into the Pre-comps folder you created earlier. This helps keep the project organized.

Using Adjustment Layers

An adjustment layer makes it easy to quickly stylize layers in a composition. Using adjustment layers is a useful way to apply effects to one or more layers. Let's add an adjustment layer to the current pre-composition.

1. Choose Layer > New > Adjustment Layer. An adjustment layer is added to the top of the Timeline.

2. In the Effects & Presets panel, type Colorama into the search field. The Colorama effect uses a range of colors to colorize the affected layer.

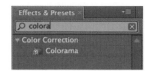

3. Drag the Colorama effect onto the adjustment layer. The footage is colorized with the default color map (which is pretty unattractive).

4. The Project panel now has the Effect Controls panel docked with it. This panel offers precise control over the applied effect. Click the disclosure triangle next to Output Cycle to view the applied color map.

5. Click the Use Preset Palette menu and experiment with the different options in the list. The circle indicates the color that is being applied to the image. The colors are mapped based on the luminance value of the footage.

6. Let's use a saved preset for the animation. The use of presets allows you to store settings for use again in the future or to exchange them with another user. Choose Animation > Apply Animation Preset.

7. A new dialog opens so you can navigate to the preset. Open the **Chapter_01 Project Files** folder.

8. Select the file **Sky_Blue.ffx** and click Open. The new settings for the effect are applied.

9. Select the adjustment layer in the Timeline.

10. Click the Toggle Switches/Modes button to access blending modes. You can use blending modes to change how two layers interact.

11. Change the mode for the adjustment layer to Color. The effect is now applied more "gently" based on the original color values in the underlying footage.

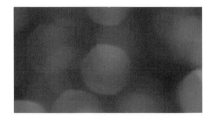

12. Close the pre-composition by choosing File > Close. The original

Bumper composition is now selected. Choose File > Save to save your work so far.

Transforming Layers

After Effects offers five Transform properties for layers. These properties can be adjusted to affect the appearance of a layer or keyframed to create animation:

- Anchor Point (A)
- Position (P)
- Rotation (R)
- Scale (S)
- Opacity (T)

Let's apply transformations to several layers to create changes to the composition's appearance.

Chart.swf layer

1. Select the Bumper Timeline, then select the Chart.swf layer in the Timeline and click the eye icon to enable its visibility.
2. Press S to access the Scale properties for the layer. Enter a value of 125% to enlarge the layer and press Return (Enter).
3. The SWF layer is a vector file, which means it can be scaled above 100%. You must enable a switch to preserve vector scaling and quality; otherwise, the image gets pixilated. Click the Toggle Switches and Modes button at the bottom of the Timeline, then click the Continuous Rasterize switch for the chart layer (click in the empty space for the layer in the "sun" column).

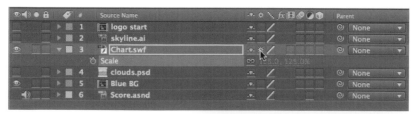

4. Press T to control the Opacity of the layer, enter 40%, and press Return (Enter).
5. Press P to control its Position, and enter 500 into the Y value (the second number) to lower the chart along the Y-axis.

Skyline.ai layer

1. Select the skyline.ai layer and click the eye icon to enable its visibility.

2. Press S for Scale, hold down the Shift key, and press P for Position. Scale the layer to 65%.

3. Drag the Y value for the Position property until the skyline is aligned with the bottom of the Composition panel. If needed, be sure to choose Fit from the Magnification ratio pop-up menu.

4. Set the X value for the Position property to 1350 and the Y value to 450.

Clouds.psd layer

1. Select the layer clouds.psd in the Timeline and click the eye icon to enable its visibility.

2. Press S to access the Scale properties for the layer. Enter a value of 80% and press Return (Enter).

3. Let's animate the layer so the clouds appear to drift. Hold down the Shift key and press A to add the Anchor Point controls.

4. Switch the cloud.psd layer to the Hard Light blending mode (if necessary, click the Toggle Switches/Modes button at the bottom of the Timeline).

5. Move the Current Time Indicator to the start of the Timeline.

Using Keyframes

If you want to animate a Transform property, you can use keyframes. The word keyframe has a long history in animation, dating back to the time of early hand-drawn animation where the lead animator would draw the major poses (or keyframes) and assistants would fill in the drawings in between. In modern computer animation, you set the keyframes and the computer fills in the rest (called interpolation or tweening).

1. Make sure the layer cloud.psd is selected.
2. Click the stopwatch next to Anchor Point to enable keyframing.
3. Enter a value of 850 into the X field for Anchor Point.
4. Press End to go to the end of the composition.
5. Enter a value of 1750 into the X field for Anchor Point. A new keyframe is added to the layer.

> ▲ TIP **What is the Anchor Point**
>
> The Anchor Point is similar to the Registration Point in Flash. It, however, is more flexible as it allows for animation in After Effects.

6. Click the RAM Preview button to see the results so far. Then choose File > Save to save your work.

Using Parenting

After Effects makes it easy to synchronize layers by establishing parent-child relationships. When you employ parenting, changes you make to one layer affect another. An easy way to think of parenting is to think of the relationship between your body and arms. When you move your body by turning at the waist, this causes your arms to turn. However, your arms can also move on their own (but they must still follow your body). The rest of the relationship persists throughout your arm: just think of the dependencies between the elbow, the wrist, and the individual fingers on your hand.

1. Move the Current Time Indicator to the start of the Timeline and select the layer skyline.ai.
2. In the Parent column, click the pickwhip and drag it to the layer clouds.psd. The new name appears in the parent column for the skyline. ai layer.

3. Click the RAM Preview button to see the results so far. The skyline layer now moves with the clouds layer and pans to the right. Then choose File > Save to save your work.

Compositing in the Timeline

One of After Effects' greatest strengths is its ability to composite elements. After Effects offers several powerful options including track mattes, layer masks, and 3D space. These options provide you with precise control on how the layers are mixed together in the Composition panel.

Using Track Mattes

Track mattes allow you to use one layer to create holes that allow another layer to show through. For example, you can use the shape of one layer (the matte) to define a pattern that the underlying layer (the fill) shows through.

Let's use a second instance of the Blue BG pre-comp to create a masked effect.

1. Select the Blue BG pre-composition in the Timeline panel.
2. Choose Edit > Duplicate to create a second instance of the pre-comp.
3. Drag the new copy so it is the second layer in the Timeline stack.
4. Choose Edit > Deselect All so no layers are active.
5. Click the Magnification ratio pop-up menu and choose 25% to see more of the canvas space.
6. Click in the toolbar and choose Ellipse Tool.

7. Drag with the Ellipse tool to create a shape.
8. Activate the Selection tool in the toolbar.

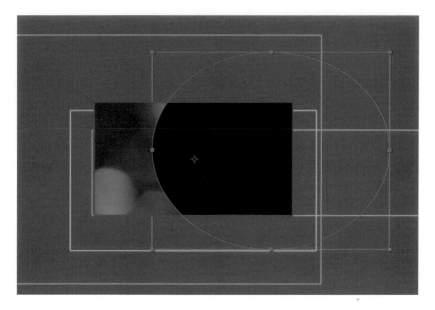

9. Click and drag the control handles to resize the shape layer as needed. You can click near a corner handle to rotate the shape layer.

10. Drag the shape layer so it is immediately above the top instance of Blue BG.

11. Click the Toggle Switches/Modes button to see blending modes.

12. For the Blue BG layer, click the TrkMat menu to access the track matte controls:

   • **No Track Matte.** No transparency is created; next layer above acts as a normal layer.

   • **Alpha Matte.** Opaque when alpha channel pixel value is 100%.

   • **Alpha Inverted Matte.** Opaque when alpha channel pixel value is 0%.

   • **Luma Matte.** Opaque when the luminance value of a pixel is 100%.

   • **Luma Inverted Matte.** Opaque when the luminance value of a pixel is 0%.

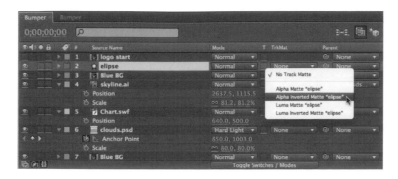

13. Choose Alpha Inverted Matte. The top copy of Blue BG only shows through where the ellipse shape does not exist. The mask layer automatically has its visibility turned off.

14. Click the Magnification ratio pop-up menu and choose Fit. Then choose File > Save to save your work.

Using Masks

Another way to apply selective transparency in After Effects is to use masks. A mask is essentially a vector-based path that can be applied to a layer. You can create masks using the Shape or Pen tools. Additionally, you can copy and paste paths from Illustrator to a selected layer in After Effects for even more options. Let's experiment with shapes by adding a vignette.

1. Click the topmost layer in the Timeline and press the Home key.

2. Choose Layer > New > Solid. The Solid Settings window opens.

3. Enter Vignette into the Name field. Click the color swatch at the bottom of the window. A new window opens. Set the color to black and click OK. Click OK again to create the solid layer.

4. Double-click the Ellipse tool to add an elliptical mask to the Vignette layer. The layer is masked, but it needs modification.

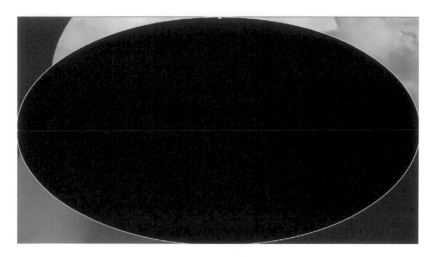

5. The basic Mask properties are visible. Press M to hide them.

6. Press MM to access the advanced Mask properties.

7. Select the Inverted check box to invert the mask.

8. Set Mask Feather to 250. Set Mask Opacity to 80%.

9. Click the RAM Preview button to see the results so far. Choose File > Save to save your work.

Using 3D Space

After Effects offers powerful support and several options for 3D space. These options allow for objects to be rotated or positioned along the X, Y, or Z axes. To work in 3D space, an object must be converted to a 3D layer.

1. Select logo start in the Timeline. Click its eye icon so it is active.

2. Click the Toggle Switches/Modes button.

3. Select the 3D column (it uses a cube-shaped icon).

4. Press P for Position. Set the layer to 775.0, 325.0, 0.0.

5. You want to animate the layer in 3D space so it swings into place. So you need to adjust the anchor point of the layer so it rotates around the left edge. Select the Pan Behind tool from the toolbar to adjust the layer's anchor point without changing the visible position of the layer.

6. Drag the anchor point of the layer so it lands just outside the logo.

Using the Pan Behind tool, drag the anchor point to the outside edge to the right of the logo. Since the layer was trimmed, be sure to move the Current Time Indicator to view the logo.

7. Press R for rotation to control the layer.

8. Press I to move to the layer's In point.

9. Click the stopwatch to add a rotation keyframe for the Y Rotation. Enter a starting value of 60.0°.

10. Click the time display (at the bottom of the Composition panel or in the upper-left corner of the Timeline). Enter 2:25, and press Return (Enter).

11. Set the Y Rotation to 0.0°.

12. Click the RAM Preview button to see the results so far. Choose File > Save to save your work.

Using Animation Presets

To speed up tasks, After Effects offers several animation presets that you can apply to layers. Included with After Effects are several options for Backgrounds, Shapes, Text, and Transitions. Additionally, more can be downloaded from Adobe's Web site at www.adobe.com/cfusion/exchange.

Let's apply one of the presets as a transition.

1. Select the layer logo start in the Timeline.

2. Press I to go to the layer's In point.

3. Click the Effects & Presets panel.

4. Click the disclosure triangle next to * Animation Presets.

5. Click the triangle next to Transitions – Dissolves. There are several options available.

6. Knowing what each effect does by simply looking at its name is difficult. Fortunately, After Effects makes browsing easy. Click the submenu in the Effects & Presets panel and choose Browse Presets.

7. Bridge opens with a folder for each category. Double-click the Transitions – Dissolves category to view the previews.

8. Click a thumbnail to preview the Animation Preset.

9. Let's use the Dissolve – vapor.ffx on the logo layer. Double-click to apply the effect to the selected layer. Bridge is hidden and After Effects becomes the active application.

10. Click the RAM Preview button and review the effect. The two transitions applied have different durations. Let's confirm this by examining the keyframes applied to the layer.

▲ **TIP Learn More About Expressions**

Expressions are a bit tough to the uninitiated. Here are a few resources to check out:

- Visit Dan Ebbert's scripting Web site at www. motionscript.com.
- Read The AE Enhancers forum at www.aenhancers. com.
- Check out the book *After Effects Expressions* by Marcus Geduld.

11. With the logo start layer selected, press U to see all the user added keyframes. If the keyframes are hidden, press U again to reveal them. This is a useful shortcut to quickly access animation controls. You now see two sets of keyframes and two expressions that are controlling the animation. Expressions are small computer programs written in a language called Javascript—a language similar to Flash's ActionScript.

12. Closely examine the sets of keyframes. Notice how the first two frames line up, but the second set does not.

13. Click the second keyframe, hold down the Shift key, and drag the second keyframe for the Transition Completion property. As you get near the next keyframe, it snaps into place.

▲ **TIP Jump Between Keyframes**

Two useful shortcuts you can use to navigate keyframes are J and K. J moves to the previous keyframe and K moves to the next.

14. Click the RAM Preview button to see the results so far. Choose File > Save to save your work.

Replacing Content

During the animation process, you may decide to replace certain elements in a project, perhaps because the footage or logo file has been updated or to encompass changes requested by a client. In this case, another artist has already animated the logo used in this bumper animation. After Effects allows multiple users to collaborate by making it easy to import a project into an existing project.

1. Click the Project panel to select it.

2. Choose File > Import > File.

3. In the Import File dialog, navigate to the **Chapter_01 Project Files** folder. Open the folder **Logo Animation**. Select the file **Logo_Animation.aep** and click Open. A new folder with the same name is added to your project. It contains one composition and the source footage used. Drag these two new items into the Pre-comps folder.

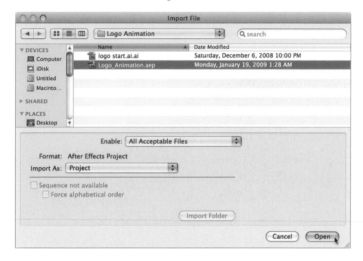

4. Click the disclosure triangle next to the folder Logo_Animation.aep.

5. In the Timeline, click to select the layer logo start, and then press I to move to its In point.

6. While holding down the Option (Alt) key, drag the composition Logo Animated onto the layer logo start. The new layer is swapped for the old layer.

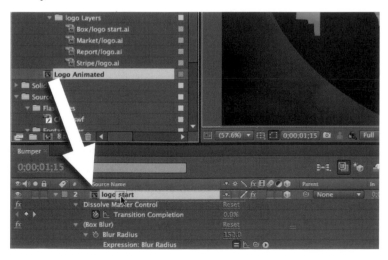

Drag the layer from the Project panel to the Timeline while holding down the Option (Alt) key.

▲ **TIP A Different Swap**

You can also swap items in the Project panel. This works for imported footage (but not compositions). Simply select the item you want to replace and choose File > Replace Footage > File or press Command+H (Ctrl+H).

● **NOTE Memory Overload**

To edit a footage layer, you must have the application installed on the same system. Additionally, there must be adequate RAM and scratch disk space to open the files.

7. Invoke a RAM Preview. Notice that the swapped layer still preserves the animation and transition of the original. Only the contents of the layer were swapped but all applied effects and keyframes remain. This is a useful way to swap content. Choose File > Save to save your work.

Edit Original Command

After Effects intelligently handles imported files. It is quite capable of detecting which application created the file and allows you to open the file using that program for changes. Simply modify, close, and save the file. After Effects then updates the instance in your project. This particular workflow is very handy, especially when using the Creative Suite applications.

Let's use the Edit Original command to update a graphic in the bumper.

1. Double-click the layer Logo Animated in the Timeline to open it. The new file loads into the Composition panel and Timeline.

2. Select the bottommost layer called Box in the Timeline.

3. Chose Edit > Edit Original or press Command+E (Ctrl+E).

4. Adobe Illustrator opens and reveals the layered file. Activate the Selection tool in the toolbar.

5. Click the green box one time to activate it.

6. At the bottom of the toolbar, click the color swatch and pick a deep red. The box updates.

7. Click on the word REPORT to select it.

8. In the options bar, click the color swatch and pick a warm yellow. The text updates.

9. Choose File > Close and click Save. Switch back to After Effects where the composition updates.

10. Switch to the Bumper tab in the Timeline and invoke a RAM Preview. Review your work so far.

11. Let's add a fade in and out for the composition. Press the Home key.

12. Choose Layer > New > Solid. Name the Solid Fades, make sure it is set to black, and click OK.

13. With the layer Fades selected, press T to access the Opacity Transform controls.

14. Add the following opacity keyframes:
    - 00:00:00   100%
    - 00:01:00   0%
    - 00:19:00   0%
    - 00:19:29   100%

15. Invoke a RAM Preview. Review your work so far. Choose File > Save to save your work.

Rendering Animations

When you are satisfied with an animation, you'll need to render it at final quality. Most users create RAM Previews at a lower quality to save time. The final rendering process usually takes longer due to the improvements in output quality. The process of rendering can be time-consuming depending on the complexity of effects chosen as well as the speed of the machine. As such, rendering is often run as an unsupervised task.

The Render Queue

The primary way of rendering and exporting motion content from After Effects is to use the Render Queue panel. The key advantage of using the Render Queue is that you can add multiple files into it for processing. Additionally, you can render a file once but encode, compress, and output multiple versions.

1. Choose Composition add to Render Queue.
2. The active composition is added to the panel for processing.

Video and Motion Formats

The following file types can be created with After Effects CS4 on both Mac and Windows platforms:

- 3GPP
- Adobe Clip Notes
- Animated GIF
- Cineon
- Electric Image
- Filmstrip
- FLV, F4V
- H.264 and H.264 Blu-ray

- MPEG-2, MPEG-2 DVD, and MPEG-2 Blu-ray
- MPEG-4
- QuickTime
- SWF
- Video for Windows
- Image Sequence (IFF, JPEG, PICT, PNG, PSD, Radiance, SGI, TIFF, or Targa)

Render Settings

The Render Settings specify the quality that After Effects uses when processing the animation file. Click the small triangles to access several different Render Settings templates. You can also click the underlined text for a template name to customize the settings. For now, use the default value of Best Settings.

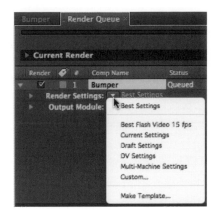

Output Module

The Output Module determines which type of file is written to disk. After Effects offers multiple output modules to choose from. Simply click the small triangle next to Output Module to access the Presets lists. These modules can be further customized by clicking the underlined text. You'll explore creating custom output modules in upcoming chapters. For now, choose Lossless.

Setting a Destination

The final step to setting up a render is to target a destination drive. This is where you want the files to render to. Rendering out a Lossless file creates a big file on your hard drive. But this file can always be recompressed to other specific formats as needed using the Adobe Media Encoder (more on this in Chapter 12, "Professional Encoding of Flash Video").

1. Click the text *Not yet specified* to target a location for the file. For this example, be sure you have at least 1 GB of free disk space. (Alternately, click the triangle next to the Output To heading and choose a preset naming convention.)

2. In the Navigation dialog, enter a name in the Save As field.

3. Specify a location for output and click Save.

4. Choose File > Save to capture the current state of your project.

5. With your mouse pointer over the Render Queue, press the Accent Grave key (`) to maximize the panel. Hiding the Composition panel can speed up the final render because the computer screen doesn't need to load and refresh the processed frames for viewing.

6. Click Render.

> ▲ **TIP** Render Once, Output Many
>
> You do not need to render a movie multiple times to create multiple formats. Simply choose Composition > Add Output Module to add additional formats to the Render Queue. The bulk of the processing time happens in the Render Settings, not the Output Modules.

What's Next?

Now that you have a solid overview of the Adobe After Effects interface, you have a choice to make. The next two chapters explore Flash and the entire Adobe CS4 Production Premium, respectively. These two chapters lay a solid foundation for the rest of the book. If you are excited about After Effects and want to continue to explore its functionality, jump to Chapter 4, "Creating Transparent Video with After Effects." Just be sure to read Chapter 2, "Flash Essentials for the After Effects User" and Chapter 3, "The Production Premium Toolset" eventually because they contain important information about exchanging data between different applications in the Creative Suite.

2 FLASH ESSENTIALS FOR THE AFTER EFFECTS USER

Flash baffles After Effects users as often as it makes them feel comfortable. It's timeline based, so in that sense it feels familiar, but its quirky way of handling tweens leaves many After Effects users puzzled. Flash is also eccentric from an After Effects point of view when it comes to rendering (publishing in Flash) and pre-composing (nesting). This chapter introduces you to Flash's interface and core animation techniques.

Creating a New Flash File

Create New

Flash File (ActionScript 3.0)

Flash File (ActionScript 2.0)

Flash File (Adobe AIR)

Flash File (Mobile)

ActionScript File

ActionScript C...munication Fil

Flash JavaScript File

Flash Project

You'll start (where else?) by launching Flash CS4 and will immediately be stymied by the myriad options for creating a new file. You want to create a new Flash animation, but of which type: Flash File (ActionScript 3.0), Flash File (ActionScript 2.0), Flash File (Adobe AIR), and so on?

Generally, you'll choose the top option, Flash File (ActionScript 3.0). Action-Script is a programming language (similar to JavaScript) that has two major versions: ActionScript 2.0 and 3.0. Since Flash is an animation and a programming tool, some users will need to consider which version of the language they'll be using.

As an animator, you probably won't be using ActionScript. But just in case one of your collaborators wants to add script later, you might as well choose the file format that supports the most recent version of the language, Action-Script 3.0.

This book focuses on the animation features of Flash. If you're interested in ActionScript, which is mostly used for adding interactivity to Flash movies (buttons, forms, games, etc.), there's a wealth of material available to help you. Be sure to read *ActionScript 3.0: Visual QuickStart Guide* (Peachpit, 2008).

The other format choices include Flash File (Adobe AIR), which is for Flash movies intended to run on the desktop as opposed to in a Web browser; Flash File (Mobile) for mobile-phone applications; ActionScript File for content that is pure programming code; and a few other, rarely-chosen formats.

Let's create a Flash file. You'll create a bumper for a TV news show, which can also be used on the station's Web site. You'll start by creating a file, adjusting its dimensions, and saving it to your hard drive.

1. At the splash screen, choose Flash File (ActionScript 3.0) in the Create New column.

● **NOTE: What about ActionScript 1.0**

There was a version of ActionScript before 2.0, but it was just called Action-Script (not Action-Script 1.0). In fact, prior to reaching a more stable state in 2.0, ActionScript went through several minor and major revisions.

▲ **TIP: More Action-Script Resources**

This book dips into ActionScript in Chapters 13 and 14. In addition, in the Chapter 13 Project Files folder, there are some video tutorials that teach Action-Script Fundamentals.

Fun with Panels

As in other Adobe programs, you can move panels by dragging them by their tabs. You can float a panel by dragging it to the middle of the screen. Or you can dock a panel by dragging it onto another panel's tab. Panels have flyout menus (in their upper-right corners) that allow you to close them. To bring a closed panel back, add it from the Window menu. If you create a panel arrangement that you like, you can save it as a new workspace. To do so, choose Window > Workspace > New Workspace.

Flash's interface appears, including the Stage (which is similar to After Effects' Composition panel), the Timeline, and some support panels. To follow along with the steps in this book, choose Window > Workspace > Classic. After you've worked with Flash for a while, you might want to try some of the other workspace options; each of which sets up the interface in a different way.

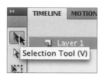

2. Choose the Selection tool (the black arrow) and then click the Stage to select it and reveal its properties. The Properties panel allows you to adjust most objects in Flash. It is context sensitive, displaying options for whatever object is currently selected. You want to change the width and height of the Stage, which is why you started by clicking the Stage.

3. Click the Edit button in the Size portion of the Properties panel. The Document properties dialog opens.

4. In the Document Properties dialog, set the Stage Dimensions to 1280 × 720. Leave the background color unchanged but set the frame rate to 30 since this is a video project intended for output to After Effects. Click OK.

5. Choose File > Save. Name the file map.fla and save it to your hard drive.

File Types

Flash's source format is the FLA (rhymes with spa) file. The FLA is similar to the AEP: It's the file you edit, but it's not the final rendered file. Like After Effects, Flash can render out in multiple formats. In other words, from a single FLA file you can output Quick-Time videos, animated GIFs, and other movie formats. You can export files in these formats via the Export command (File > Export).

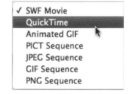

> ● **NOTE: Context Sensitive**
>
> If you don't understand what context sensitive means, click inside frame one on the Timeline and then look at the Properties panel. Then click the Text tool. As you can see, the Properties panel changes to show you options for whatever you have selected.

> ▲ **TIP: Choosing a Frame Rate**
>
> Flash only allows whole-number frame rates. The closest you can get to 29.97 frames per second is 30. Many Flash animators work at 24 frames per second, which is a well-known frame rate used in film production. Flash video files (FLV and F4V files) output from After Effects and other video-authoring programs can run at 29.97 frames per second.

● **NOTE: Two Export Options**

In addition to File > Export, you can also output rendered files by choosing File > Publish Settings from the menu. In fact, Publish Settings is Flash's main export technique. It's the option you'd choose in a typical Flash workflow, and we explain it later in this chapter. File > Export is for rendering out less-common file types.

SWF Confusion

Many programs besides Flash can output SWF files. This is confusing since people call SWFs "Flash files" or "Flash movies." Such people may say they've made "Flash movies" in programs other than Flash. For instance, After Effects can output SWFs; so can Photoshop and Illustrator, but they aren't as feature-rich (in terms of being SWF creators) as Flash. SWF has become a common output format, much like QuickTime.

Adobe has two types of applications that output SWFs: design/animation programs (such as Flash, Photoshop, Illustrator, and After Effects) and programming applications, such as Flex. Flex allows programmers to create SWFs without having to mess with timelines. Most animators dislike the Flex interface, because it's mostly a text editor for writing code.

SWF is also a common input format. Many programs, such as After Effects, allow you to import SWFs and integrate them into a larger multimedia project.

But the most common format is the SWF (pronounced swiff) file, which is exported via the Publish command (File > Publish). SWF files are the Flash files that run in Web browsers. So when you're online and you're watching a Flash movie, you're actually watching a SWF file. SWF is such a common output format that most people think of SWF files and Flash files as the same thing. So if someone asks you for a Flash file, it's important for them to specify whether they mean a SWF (the final output) or a FLA (the editable source file). As with the QuickTime movies you make in After Effects, SWFs aren't editable. If you want to make changes, you must go back to the source file—the FLA.

A FLA file is an editable animation (and programming) source-file format that can only be generated and edited in Adobe Flash. From a FLA you can output a SWF file, but you can also output SWFs from other source formats, such as AEP or AI. Although you can generate SWFs in many applications, if you start making one in Flash, you have to finish making it in Flash. This is because Flash's FLA source format is only editable in Flash. Similarly, you can generate QuickTime videos from many applications, but if your source format is AEP, you can only edit it in After Effects.

Importing Assets

You can import graphics, sound, and video into Flash. With the exception of video, assets are actually imported into FLAs, not just linked. In other words, after importing a graphic, you can delete it from your hard drive. It will still be available in the FLA file and generated SWF.

SWF files can only contain JPEG and PNG graphics and MP3 audio (and some video formats, which are discussed in a later chapter). However, you can import many other standard types, and Flash will convert them into JPEGs, PNGs, and MP3s for you.

Let's import several assets from a layered Photoshop file (Flash allows you to do this with Illustrator files, too).

1. Copy the **Chapter_02 Project Files** folder from the DVD to your hard drive.

2. Choose File > Import > Import to Library. Select the file **world.psd** from the **Chapter_02 Project Files** folder and click Import to Library.

The Flash Library

The Library is similar to the After Effects Project panel. It's a storage area for assets. As you can see from the Import options, you can also import directly to the Stage. We don't recommend this. Let's say you knew you were going to need ten JPEGs to complete your Flash project and you imported them all to the Stage. They'd wind up on top of each other. Importing them to the Stage would be like dragging every After Effects asset from the Project panel to a comp's first frame rather than dragging them into the comp as needed. A better workflow in Flash is to import all assets into the Library and then drag them to the Stage as needed.

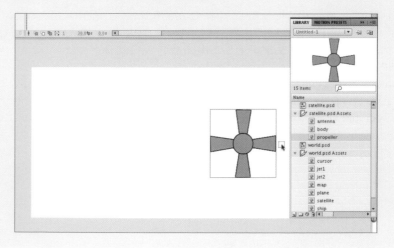

Many Flash designers like to only import JPEGs, PNGs, and MP3s so they can control the quality of these file types rather than letting Flash do it for them.

▲ TIP: Transparency Support

Although SWFs can contain JPEGs and PNGs, only the PNG type supports transparency.

● NOTE: Import a SWF into Flash

You can import SWFs into Flash, although you can't edit them. This is useful if you've generated a SWF in another application, such as After Effects or Illustrator. You can bring it into Flash and incorporate it into your project. However, if you need to make changes to it, you'll have to use whatever application you created it in.

● NOTE: **Open External Library**

The Open External Library option allows you to access assets inside another FLA. After choosing that option, select any FLA on your hard drive or network, and you'll have access to graphics, sounds, and videos inside it.

3. In the Import to Library dialog, select the plane layer, hold down the Shift key, and then select the water layer. You should have 5 layers selected.

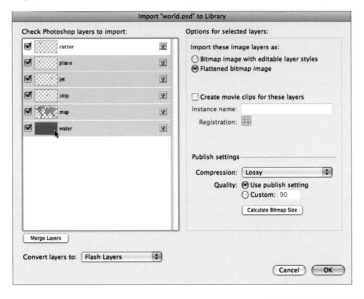

● NOTE: **What Is a Movie Clip?**

A movie clip is an animatable unit in Flash. In other words, by converting each Photoshop layer into a movie clip, you make those layers animatable. (If you don't convert them, you can still use them as static background elements.) The term movie clip is a bit of a misnomer. Movie clips are not movies (as in QuickTime movies); they are animatable objects.

4. Select the "Create movie clips for these layers" check box. Leave Instance name and Registration unchanged

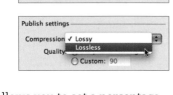

5. Under Publish settings, choose Lossless from the Compression drop-down menu.

   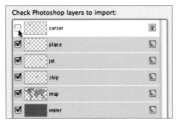

   This converts all the Photoshop layers into PNGs. If you're animating for the Web and worried about file size, you might want to experiment with the Lossy option, which allows you to set a percentage-based quality setting (100 is full quality; zero is lowest quality).

6. Deselect the layer named cursor.

   You don't want to import this layer into Flash as it is not used in the final animation. Fortunately, when you import a layered Photoshop file, Flash allows you to choose which layers you want to import. We sometimes use layered Photoshop and Illustrator files as image libraries with each image on a separate layer. We then import the whole file into Flash but only select layers containing images we want.

7. Click OK to add the files to your project's library.

Using the Library

At this point, the Stage looks exactly the same as it did before. Recall that you imported the graphics into the Library. But where is this Library?

1. To access the Library, press Command+L (Ctrl+L). Alternately, you can choose Window > Library or click the Library button.

2. In the Library panel, click the disclosure triangle to open the world.psd Assets folder.

3. Click the disclosure triangle to open the Assets subfolder.

Inside this subfolder are all the original images from the Photoshop file. The little tree icon to the left of each image's name indicates that it is a simple PNG or JPEG. The items below the images are movie clips (note the blue gear icons). There's one movie clip for each Photoshop source image (because you asked Flash to create movie clips in the Import to Library dialog).

So what's the difference between a movie clip and an image? The best way to explain this is to evoke Wonder Woman. If you're as geeky as we are, you know that Wonder Woman (unlike Superman) doesn't have the power of flight. However, she has an invisible airplane. So when you see her "flying" through the sky, it's not really Wonder Woman who is flying—it's her invisible plane. Wonder Woman is just along for the ride.

> **● NOTE: Movie Clips for Animation**
>
> To be fully accurate, you can perform some simple animations on source images. However, you can only use the full range of Flash's animation tools on movie clips, so we recommend that you use them for animations.

In Flash, images—like Wonder Woman—can't fly. That is, they can't move around the screen. They can't be animated. Instead, you have to put them inside an invisible vehicle and animate that. You move

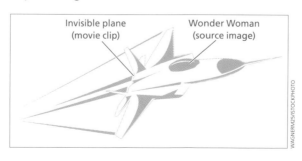

Invisible plane (movie clip)   Wonder Woman (source image)

the vehicle and the image goes along for the ride. To viewers, it looks like the image is moving, because the vehicle it's inside is invisible. Movie clips are those invisible vehicles. So all those movie clips in the Library are invisible vehicles with your Photoshop images riding inside them like passengers. When you animate, you'll use these movie clips and just leave the original source images (the ones with the tree icons) in the Library.

Adding Library Symbols to the Stage

The technical term for Library items is symbols. Adding symbols to the Stage is as simple as dragging them from the Library and dropping them where you want them to appear. A symbol on the Stage is called an "instance," because it's actually a copy of the symbol.

1. Drag the water movie clip from the Library and drop it on the Stage so that its upper-left edge lines up with the upper-left edge of the Stage.

   Notice the helpful guidelines Flash displays to help you place images. If you need help positioning the movie clip, select it and then adjust the image's X and Y coordinates in the Properties panel. Set both its X and Y coordinates to zero.

2. Drag the map movie clip to the Stage so that it covers the water.

   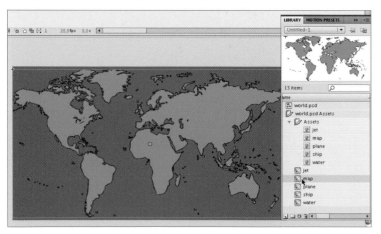

3. Drag the ship movie clip to the Stage twice, putting each instance of it in a different body of water.

4. Select one of the ships and reverse its direction by choosing Modify > Transform > Flip Horizontal.

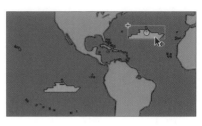

▲ **TIP: Reusing Images**

As in After Effects, you can reuse images multiple times. Drag as many instances from the Library as you want.

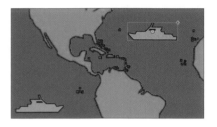

5. With the ship selected, press the Q key to switch to tool. Hold down the Shift key while dragging one of the corner handles inward to make the selected ship smaller. Press V to switch back to the Selection tool.

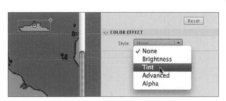

6. Select one of the smaller ships. In the Properties panel, click the disclosure triangle next to Color Effect, then choose Tint from the Style drop-down menu.

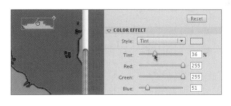

● **NOTE: Color Effects**

Color effects are fully animatable. This means that you can have an object change color over time.

7. Click the color swatch to choose a yellowish tint, and then adjust that tint with the sliders under the drop-down menu. Adjust the tint to match that in the figure shown here.

8. Add the plane movie clip to the Stage, placing it above Africa.

9. With the plane movie clip still selected, click the Add Filter button at the bottom of the Properties panel, choose Drop Shadow, and then adjust the shadow's setting to your liking in the Filters area of the Properties panel.

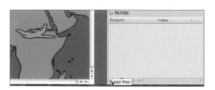

● **NOTE: Filter Settings**

Filter settings are fully animatable. This gives you controls that are similar to keyframeable effects in After Effects.

10. With the plane still selected, press Command+D (Ctrl+D) to duplicate an instance. This has the same effect as dragging another instance from the Library.

11. With the second plane selected, click the Swap button in the Properties panel. Select the jet symbol.

Note that the jet takes on all the properties (including filters and position) of the plane. Much like After Effects, you can update an item in the library to use a different source file.

12. In the Library, right-click the jet source image (not the movie clip). From the context menu, choose Properties.

13. Click the Import button and choose the file **jet2.png** from the **Chapter_02 Project Files** folder. Then click Open.

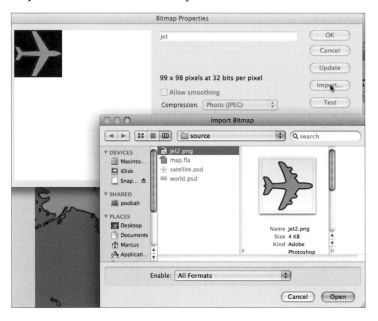

You must click OK to swap the files. Flash swaps the jet image in the Library for another image.

14. Add a few more planes and ships, resizing, flipping, and styling them as you please. Save your work by pressing Command+S (Control+S) on the keyboard.

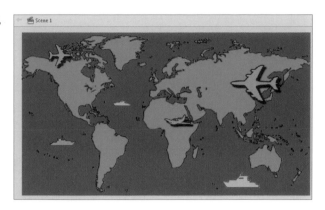

Layers

You've been placing all your movie clips on Layer 1. As with After Effects, each animated item must be on its own layer. In After Effects, you have no choice—adding footage to the Composition panel automatically creates a new layer. Flash is more like Photoshop: You have to tell it when you want a new layer. However, there's a great shortcut that allows you to quickly generate multiple layers and place each selected item on one of them.

1. Continue working in the same file or open **setup_done.fla** from the **Chapter_02 Project Files** folder. Hold down the Shift key and carefully select all the ships and planes. Don't select the map or the water. If you accidentally select something, you can Shift-click to deselect it.

2. Choose Modify > Timeline > Distribute to Layers. Flash makes a layer for each selected item.

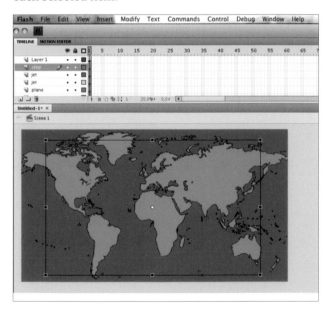

But where are all the planes and ships? They're hidden behind the water. The water and map were not in the selection set, so Flash left those items on Layer 1, and it added the new layers below that layer.

3. Drag the divider at the bottom of the Timeline panel to reveal all the layers.

4. Drag Layer 1 to the bottom of the Layer stack. Ah, there are the vehicles!

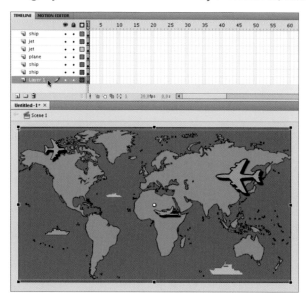

5. In the Timeline, double-click Layer 1 and rename it map.

6. Create a layer manually by clicking the New Layer button. Double-click the new layer's name and type ship. With the new layer selected, drag a ship movie clip from the Library and drop it on the Stage.

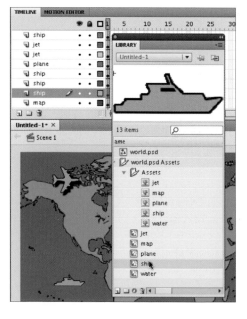

7. Click the New Folder button and name the folder vehicles.

8. Drag the plane and ship layers into the folder.

You've left the water and map on Layer 1 (which you renamed map). That's okay, because you won't be animating those items.

<aside>
● **NOTE: Folder Purpose**

Folders are for organization only. They are not equivalent to pre-comps in After Effects. In other words, you can't animate a folder. You have to animate each item inside it.
</aside>

Adding Text

Text in Flash is easy to work with but limited. You don't have access to all the fancy text-animation presets and Timeline tools that you have in After Effects. Still, if you need to add simple text to a Flash movie, it's nice to know that Flash's Text tool follows most of Adobe's typographical conventions.

1. Continue working in the same file or open **Vehicles_on_layers.fla** from the **Chapter_02 Project Files** folder. Add a new layer and drag it just above the map layer.

2. Select the Text tool and click in the Pacific Ocean. Type Pacific Ocean.

3. In the Properties panel, set the text to Static Text and adjust the Text properties until you like the look of the type. You'll want to modify font family, size, and color to improve appearance.

<aside>
▲ **TIP: Moving Layers out of Folders**

If you accidentally add the new layer inside the vehicles folder, just drag the new layer to the top of the stack to move it out of the folder. Once it's out of the stack, you can drag the vehicles folder above it to keep the new layer below the vehicles folder.
</aside>

<aside>
▲ **TIP: Static Text**

We recommend that you always use Static Text for animating.
</aside>

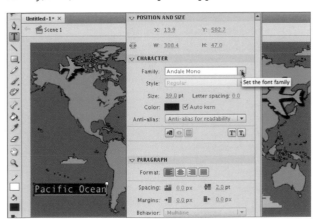

Static doesn't sound like much fun, especially when one of the other options is Dynamic Text. Truth is, these options are poorly named. Dynamic Text and Input Text are for programmers: Dynamic Text can be set via ActionScript (such as the high score in a game); Input text is for form fields. Static Text—despite its name—is animatable text. You can make it move around the screen or animate it in other ways.

5. Repeat steps 1–4, typing other location names. We labeled Russia and Australia.

Flash CS4's New Animation Method

Flash has two core animation methods: the "classic" method and the new method, which is available for the first time in Flash CS4. This new method is useful for simple animations (e.g., text flying onstage). For more complex work, switching to the classic method is often best.

Since it's a bit simpler, let's start by trying the new method.

1. Continue working in the same file or open **text_added.fla** from the **Chapter_02 Project Files** folder. Right-click a plane (making sure it's on a layer by itself).

2. From the context menu, choose Create Motion Tween.

   Flash adds a blue span to the Timeline and moves the playhead to the end of the span. On the Stage, you'll see everything vanish except for the plane. This is because the plane tweening extended the plane's "lifetime" to frame 30, whereas all the other images just exist in frame 1. Later, we'll extend all the images so that they exist as long as the plane.

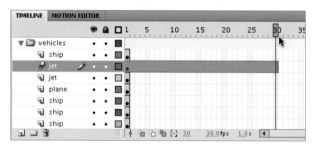

   Note that there is only one keyframe symbol for this layer (a black dot), which is at the start of the span.

3. Drag the plane to a new location on the Stage (or offstage if you want it to leave the screen—the gray area around the Stage won't be visible in the published file).

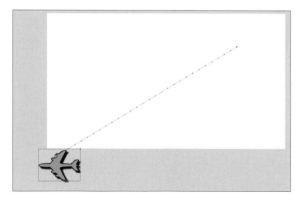

There's now a second keyframe at the end of the span. The dotted line indicates the motion path of the plane.

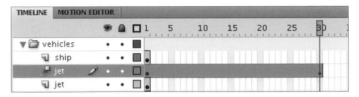

4. Point to the motion path with the Selection tool. When the cursor is right up against it, a curve appears. Click and drag to manipulate the shape of the path.

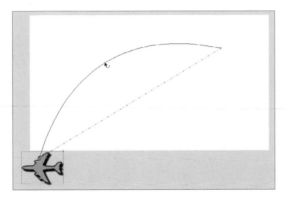

5. Switch to the Subselection tool (the white arrow), and click the head or tail, or the motion path (which looks like unfilled circles).

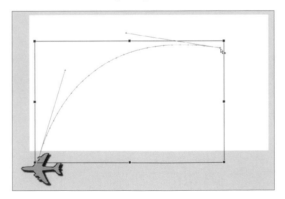

6. Flash displays Bezier control handles on the motion path. Experiment with dragging the handles to adjust the motion path.

7. Drag the playhead right and left to watch the animation.

8. Place the playhead at frame 20, and drag the plane to a new location.

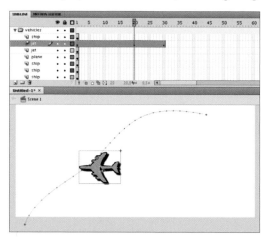

9. Move the playhead to frame 10, drag the object to yet another location. Each drag at a new point in time adds a new keyframe. The animation is not realistic because the plane isn't facing the direction it's flying.

10. To fix this, click inside the tween span in the Timeline, and then select the "Orient to path" option on the Properties panel.

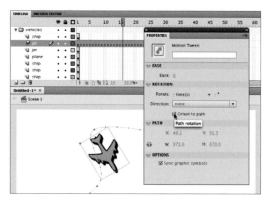

▲ TIP: Orient to a Path

For best results when orienting to a path, create the source graphic so that its "nose" faces due east (3 o'clock).

Notice that Flash places a keyframe on every frame of the tween. This is because it has to calculate frame-by-frame rotations to keep the plane facing the right direction.

11. Press the Return (Enter) key to play the animation in realtime. As the animation is playing, you can press Return (Enter) to pause it. Press Return (Enter) again to replay the animation from the beginning.

You've surely noticed at this point that the water, map, and other vehicles vanish after the first frame. By default, all layers have a one-frame duration. Don't worry, you'll solve this problem next.

44   PART I: TECHNICAL ESSENTIALS

Extending Layers in Time

When you add an asset to a new Flash layer, it only exists for one frame. However, you can extend its life so that it exists for as long as you like. Here's how.

1. Right-click frame 30 of the water/map layer.

2. From the context menu, choose Insert Frame.

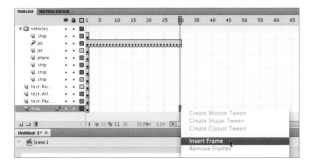

▲ TIP: Timeline Zoom

If you want to extend content to a frame much later in the Timeline, you may get tired of scrolling. You can zoom in and out of the Timeline via the options on the Timeline's submenu, which you can access in Timeline's upper-right corner. The Tiny option zooms out the farthest.

Flash extends the layer so that it lasts until frame 30. Each time you do this, a nonanimated layer will exist longer in time. Extend the text layers so that they also exist for 30 frames.

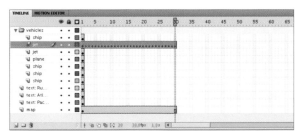

One Keyframe to Rule Them All

After Effects animators may be wondering how to access layer Transform properties. From an After Effects standpoint, it's a bit odd that you just animated the position of a layer without first accessing its Position property. If you think that's odd, prepare yourself for a real twilight-zone experience.

1. Move the playhead back to frame 1, and select a different plane. Using the Free Transform tool (Q key on the keyboard), rotate the plane so that it's facing the direction you want it to move.

2. Right-click it and select Create Motion Tween. The plane's Timeline span increases to 30 frames and the playhead moves to the end of the span.

3. Leave the playhead at the end of the span, and move the plane to a new position.

4. Press Q to switch to the Free Transform tool and resize the plane by dragging inward to make the plane smaller. Additionally, slightly rotate the plane by moving the cursor just outside the transform boundaries, and drag inward to make the plane smaller.

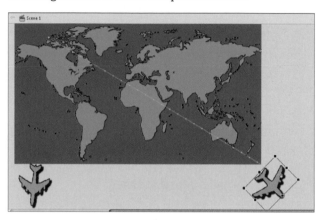

5. Press V to switch back to the Selection tool, click the plane, and in the Properties panel, choose Alpha from the Style drop-down menu (under Color Effect). If it's not already set there, drag the slider to 0%.

6. Press Return (Enter) to see the plane move, resize, rotate, and fade out.

   Notice that there is only one keyframe at the end of the Timeline. That keyframe holds information for all the animatable properties. Unlike in After Effects, there aren't separate keyframes for Position, Rotation, Scale, Opacity (Alpha), and Effects.

   This may seem too simplistic to you. When Flash is overly simple, it's usually because—historically—it was built to be a simple tool for nonprofessional animators. However, if you want finer (property-by-property) control, stay tuned.

7. If you just want to, say, get rid of the fade without deleting all the other transforms, right-click the end keyframe and choose Clear Keyframe > Color (because Alpha is a Color Effect).

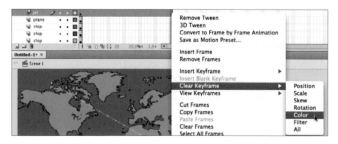

8. Press Return (Enter) again to view the animation. Remember to save your work.

Classic Animation

Now you'll look at the way all Flash animation was done prior to Flash CS4. When Adobe developers created a new workflow, they wisely left the old technique in the application to allow backwards compatibility.

1. Move the playhead to frame 1 and select another plane.

2. Right-click frame 30 in that plane's layer and select Insert Keyframe.

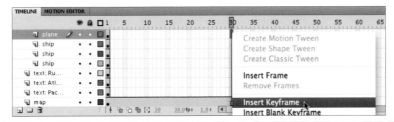

3. Right-click the plane's start keyframe (frame 1) and select Create Classic Tween.

4. Move the playhead to frame 30. Then move the plane to a new location and press Return (Enter) to play the animation.

   Flash indicates a classic tween by placing a black arrow between the tween's keyframes.

Classic tweening involves more Timeline manipulation than the newer method. We like it because it forces us to explicitly add keyframes, so we really have to think about what we're doing. On the other hand, that can get tedious. So sometimes we prefer the new (more After Effects-like) method in which you just right-click a movie clip, choose Create Motion Tween, and then adjust the movie clip on the Stage.

Timeline Editing

You're probably tired of all your tweens only lasting 30 frames. Never fear: Lengthening a tween is as simple as dragging with your mouse.

1. Continue working in the same file or open **Classic_tween_done.fla** from the **Chapter_02 Project Files** folder. To extend a tween, drag the end of its range to the right. Try this with a jet layer. (You can drag it to its left to shorten the animation, making it run faster).

Notice that when you expand or contract a tween's range, its keyframes move so that they always keep the same amount of relative space between each other. This is a great feature unless it's not what you want.

2. Shift-drag the end of a range to lengthen it without adjusting previously added keyframe positions. After doing this, your animation's range will be longer, but its keyframes will remain in place.

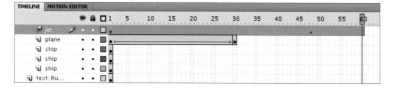

3. Move the playhead to the new end of the range and adjust the position of the movie clip on the Stage. This will add a new keyframe.

4. Extend the map layer, the text layers, and the previously animated ships and planes so that they exist as long as the layer you just extended. You can extend layers by dragging their final frames or by right-clicking the frame you want to extend to and selecting the Insert Frame option from the context menu.

Moving Tweens

You can move an entire tween in time, space, or both. To move a position tween, simply select the movie clip, select the motion path, and then drag the motion path to a new location on the Stage.

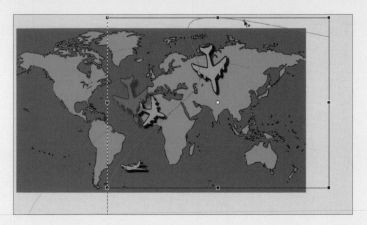

This doesn't work with classic tweens. To move a classic tween in space, you have to adjust all its keyframes, one by one.

To move an animation in time so that it starts and ends at a different point in time, drag the animation left or right in the Timeline by any frame in its span.

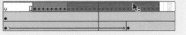

Again, this doesn't work with classic tweens. To move a classic tween in time, click its first keyframe, Shift-click its last keyframe, and then drag from the middle.

Simple Easing

As an After Effects user, you're probably familiar with "easing"—the animator's term for changing velocity over time (accelerating and decelerating). If you're like us, you rarely consider an animation complete until you've added easing. So you'll be tickled pink to discover that Flash has two easing tools: one that is quick and simple; another that is complex and feature-rich. Let's look at the simple tool first.

1. Animate the rest of the vehicles (the ones not yet animated), using whichever tweening method you want and making sure all layers extend to the same length. Or you can open **all_vehicles_tweened.fla** from the

Chapter_02 Project Files folder. Play the animation, watching one of the planes flying from point A to point B. Notice that it doesn't accelerate (ease in) or decelerate (ease out).

2. Click any frame within the tween's span.

3. In the Properties panel, scrub the Ease value (zero by default) to the left as far as it will go (-100).

● **NOTE: When Easing Isn't Easy**

Note that you can't ease a tween for which you've chosen the Orient to Path option. If you want to use both Orient to Path and easing, make sure you ease first and orient second.

4. Replay the animation, noting that the plane now accelerates. Scrub the Ease value to the right as far as it will go (100). Then replay the animation, noting that the plane now decelerates.

Just easing in is great for objects that start onstage and leave (ending in the gray area offstage); easing out is perfect for objects that start offstage and end onstage.

But a plane that moves between two points onstage should ease in at the start of its journey and ease out at the end. There's no easy way to achieve this with the simple Ease value in the Properties panel, since it forces you to choose between accelerating and decelerating.

The Motion Editor

For more complete control over animation timing and easing, use Flash CS4's new Motion Editor. Note that the Motion Editor only works with new-style tweening. If you want to ease a classic tween, you'll have to use the ease option in the Properties panel.

1. Select a plane or ship that is animating from point to point onstage.

2. Switch to the Motion Editor by clicking its tab.

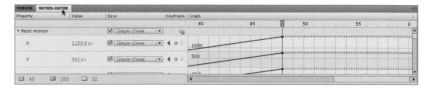

3. To view more of the Motion Editor, drag downward on the border between it and the Stage.

4. Scroll to the very bottom of the Timeline and locate Eases. Click the Add Color, Filter or Ease button.

5. From the menu, choose Stop and Start (Slow).

6. From the X and Y Ease drop-down menus (in the Basic Motion area), choose the Stop and Start (Slow) ease you just added. (It's only available because you added it in step 5.)

7. Move the split between the Motion Editor and the Stage so that you can see the whole Stage.

8. View the animation so you can see how it looks with the Stop and Start Ease.

▲ TIP: Create Your Own Ease

After experimenting with the built-in ease types, you may want to create your own ease. To do so, choose Custom from the Add Color, Filter, or Ease menu. You can then manipulate the custom ease like a Bezier curve by Option-dragging (Alt-dragging) its control handles.

Converting to a Symbol

You should have the hang of animating objects, so let's animate some of the text. Specifically, let's make the text Pacific Ocean slide in from the left.

There's only one problem: Before you can animate any item in Flash, it must a) be on its own layer; and b) be a symbol in the Library (there is an exception to this rule [called Shape Tweening], which is discussed in a later chapter). Although the text is on its own layer, it's not a symbol in the Library, which is really odd from an After Effects point of view. In After Effects, if you create anything, it automatically goes into the Project panel (e.g., if you make a solid, it's listed along with all your other footage). Not so in Flash. Imported items (such as the Photoshop images in this lesson) get inserted in the Library, but artwork and text you create in Flash doesn't. If you want to animate it, you have to manually add it to the Library. This is easy to do.

1. Continue working in the same file or open **easing_done.fla** from the **Chapter02 Project Files** folder. Switch to the Timeline then select the text Pacific Ocean.

2. Choose Modify > Convert to Symbol.

3. In the Convert to Symbol dialog, give the new symbol a name, for example, Pacific Ocean. Choose Movie Clip for the type.

   The two other types are Graphic and Button. Graphic is an older form of Movie Clip (still available from early versions of Flash that didn't yet include Movie Clip); Button is for interactivity. To work with buttons, you need to program them with ActionScript, which is explored in Chapter 13, "Creating Interactive Controls."

4. Select a Registration Point by clicking one of the small square icons. We like to click the Registration square in the upper-left corner, setting the movie clip's registration at its top left. This simplifies X and Y coordinate calculations, letting us know that if we place an image at 10 (X) and 30 (Y), its top-left corner will be at those coordinates.

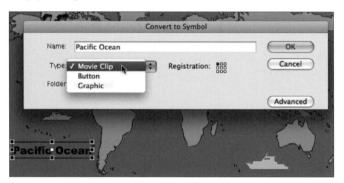

   Flash Registration Points are similar to After Effects anchor points. They place a pivot on your object that it rotates around. The Registration Point is also the origin for scaling and position changes. You can always change its location later. Click OK.

Pacific Ocean is now a movie clip symbol in the Library. You can animate it the same way you animated the boats and planes.

Creating a Symbol in the Library

You can add a symbol directly to the Library without first placing it on the Stage. For instance, say you wanted to animate the text "News of the World." You might not want that text onstage now, but you want it ready for you when you need it later. The solution is to type it directly into the Library.

1. Click the New Symbol button at the bottom of the Library.

2. In the New Symbol dialog, create a name (e.g., News of the World), select Movie Clip for the type, and click OK.

   Everything on the Stage vanishes because Flash takes you to a special "symbol editing" screen. You can return to your main animation by clicking the Back button (or the text Scene 1) in the upper-left corner of the Stage (but don't do that yet).

3. Select the Text tool and click near the crosshairs in the middle of the screen. Type News of the World.

4. In the Properties panel, adjust the text settings as desired.

5. Click the Back button in the upper-left corner of the Stage.

News of the World is now a symbol in the Library, but it's not on the Stage. You can drag it to the Stage when you're ready (remember to first add a layer for it if you want to animate it).

In step 3, you clicked with the Text tool next to the crosshairs. Those crosshairs represent the Registration Point. To adjust the Registration Point, double-click the icon next to News of the World in the Library. (If you double-click its name, Flash will think you're trying to rename it.)

This will take you back to symbol editing mode. You can drag the text to a new location so that it has a new positional relationship with its Registration Point (the crosshairs). Note that in Flash you move images around static Registration Points (in After Effects you're more likely to move anchor points).

Click the Back button when you're done editing the symbol.

Double-clicking a Symbol

If you want to edit a symbol (e.g., if you want to move it so its Registration Point is in a different place or if you want to change News of the World to News of the Universe), you have two options: You can double-click its icon in the Library, or you can double-click an instance of it on the Stage.

If you double-click a Stage instance, you're not just editing that instance—you're editing the original source symbol.

So, if you have three instances of the same symbol onstage and you double-click one of them and edit it, you'll alter all three.

▲ **TIP: Remember the Back Button**

Whether you're editing a symbol onstage or in the Library, remember to click the Back button when you're done. Users commonly forget to do this because they think they're editing their whole movie, but in fact they're actually in symbol editing mode and just editing one symbol. Look for the Back button. If you see it, you're in symbol editing mode.

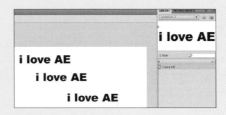

Double-clicking onstage allows you to edit a symbol without going into a special symbol editing mode. Using this technique, you can still see all the other items onstage while you're editing. Double-clicking a symbol in the Library temporarily hides all other items. It's a bit like double-clicking a layer in After Effects and opening a Layer tab. Click the Back button when you're done editing.

Nested Animation

So, why is a movie clip called a movie clip? Well, it's called that because it has the potential to be a nested animation inside your main animation (a movie inside the main movie). This makes it similar to a pre-comp in After Effects.

A simple scenario where you might want to use nested animation is a bouncing ball that travels from left to right as it bounces. A smart way to compose such an animation is to first animate a ball bouncing up and down in place. Then you animate the up-and-down-bounce moving left to right. In other words,

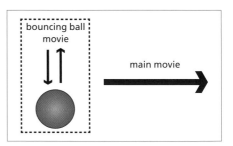

the main animation (the top level) is an item moving left to right. But that item happens to be a ball bouncing up and down.

To return to a silly analogy from earlier, imagine Wonder Woman jumping up and down inside her invisible plane. The plane is the main animation and is moving across the sky. The item it's moving is a nested animation—not just Wonder Woman but an animation of Wonder Woman jumping up and down.

Importing Layers from Photoshop

Let's explore embedded animation by animating a satellite flying over the map. The satellite will have a spinning propeller top. In that sense it's similar to the previous bouncing ball example. The spinning animation will be nested inside the flying animation.

To start, you'll import more artwork from Photoshop.

1. Continue working in the same file or open **more_text_added.fla** from the **Chapter_02 Project Files** folder. Choose File > Import > Import to Library and select **satellite.psd** from the **Chapter_02 Project Files** folder. Click Import to Library

2. In the Import to Library dialog, select all the layers, and then select the "Create movie clips for these layers" option.

3. Under Publish Settings, choose Lossless from the Compression drop-down list. Click OK.

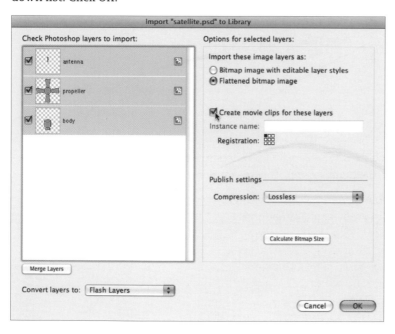

Creating a Rotating-Propeller Symbol

Double-click the satellite.psd Assets folder and locate the layers from the Photoshop file in the Library. In the following steps, make sure you use the movie clip versions, not the source images.

1. At the bottom of the Library, click the New Symbol button.

2. Name the symbol Rotating Propeller, make sure the Type is Movie Clip, and then click OK. Flash takes you to symbol editing mode.

3. Drag the movie clip symbol called propeller from the Library into the middle of the Stage, using the crosshairs as a guide.

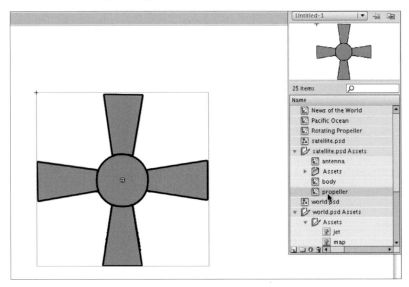

4. Right-click the propeller instance onstage and choose Create Motion Tween.

5. Click anywhere inside the tween's span.

▲ TIP: Rotation Use

Using Rotation is an easy way to animate complete revolutions. If you want to animate partial rotations, you can use Free Transform.

6. In the Properties panel, click the disclosure triangle to open Rotation and set the Rotate value to 1 time(s).

You just animated a propeller rotating but not on the main Timeline! That Timeline has a map of the world on it, and you don't see that map here.

Your rotation animation is inside a movie clip's Timeline. Movie clips are called movie clips because they have their own timelines that are independent of the main Timeline—just like pre-comps in After Effects have their own timelines that are separate from the Timeline of your final render composition.

7. Press Return (Enter) to watch the propeller spin one time around.

Nesting a Symbol Inside Another Symbol

Now we'll create a new symbol to house all the parts of the satellite. We'll nest the rotating propeller inside it. First we'll build the satellite.

1. Continue working in the same file or open **propeller_rotated.fla** from the **Chapter_02 Project Files** folder. In the Library, click the New Symbol button. Name this symbol Animated Satellite, make it a movie clip, and click OK.

   Whenever you create a new symbol and click the OK button, think about how you're being taken inside that symbol and how any animation that you do will be on its internal Timeline.

2. On the satellite's Timeline, create three layers and name them body, propeller, and antenna.

3. Select the body layer and drag the body movie clip from the Library to the Stage.

4. Select the propeller layer and drag the Rotating Propeller movie clip from the Library to the Stage. Don't drag in the stationary propeller.

5. Select the antenna layer and drag the antenna movie clip from the Library to the Stage.

6. Drag the propeller so it's sitting on top of the body.

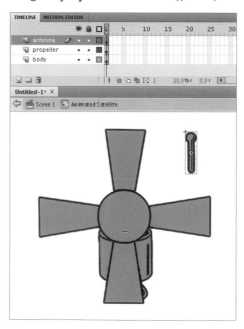

Skewing the Propeller in 3D

The propeller is now in the right position but not at the right angle. Fortunately, Flash CS4 has 3D manipulation tools that allow you to correctly adjust the propeller's angle.

1. Continue working in the same file or open **satellite_parts_in_place.fla** from the **Chapter_02 Project Files** folder. Double-click the icon next to Animated Satellite in the Library to open up the movie clip in symbol editing mode. Select the propeller onstage, and then switch to the 3D Rotation tool.

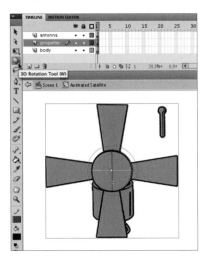

2. In the Properties panel, click on the disclosure triangle beside 3D Position and View. Set the Perspective Angle, identified by a camera icon, to 1.0.

    The Perspective Angle is similar to a camera angle. Setting it to 1.0 will make your manipulations easier.

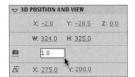

Using the 3D Rotation Tool

When you're using the 3D Rotation tool, dragging from the red line rotates the movie clip on its X axis; dragging from the green line rotates it on its Y axis; dragging from the blue circle rotates it on its Z axis; and dragging from the yellow circle rotates it freely on all axes.

If you hold down the mouse button while hovering over the 3D Rotation tool, you'll gain access to the 3D Translation tool, which allows you to move an image along the X, Y, and Z axes.

3. Rotate and reposition the propeller until it matches the following illustration. You can nudge the propeller with the arrow keys on your keyboard. See the sidebar "Using the 3D Rotation Tool" for help.

▲ **TIP: Animating 3D**

3D manipulations are fully animatable. You can keyframe them just as you would 2D manipulations.

If you switch back and forth between the 3D Rotation tool and the Selection tool (black arrow), you should be able to maneuver the propeller into place at the correct angle.

At this point, you're currently working inside a symbol called Animated Satellite. Inside that symbol, you've embedded another symbol called Rotating Propeller.

Rotating Propeller is 30 frames long, but it's embedded inside another symbol (Animated Satellite) that is only 1 frame long. This *Alice in Wonderland* situation is possible because each symbol's Timeline is independent.

The Rotating Propeller and the static "movie" of the satellite body and antenna will play at the same time, fooling the viewer into thinking that the satellite has a rotating propeller on it.

▲ **TIP: Adding Verbs**

You might find it useful, as we do, to add verbs to the names of movie clips that are animations. For example, Bouncing Ball, Running Water, and Rotating Propeller.

Independent Timelines

To visualize a symbol 30 frames long inside a symbol that is one frame long, imagine a photographer taking a still photo of a television. The still photo is similar to a one-frame-long Timeline.

The Photographer then cuts a rectangular hole in the photo where the TV's screen was and places a computer monitor behind the photo, so that videos show through the hole as if they were on the TV screen. The videos are similar to the 30-frame-long animation. They are nested inside the 1-frame-long TV image. Even though the videos and the TV seem to create a single image to the viewer, they are actually two independent images that just happen to be composited together.

4. Switch back to the Selection tool, and drag the antenna into place on top of the propeller.

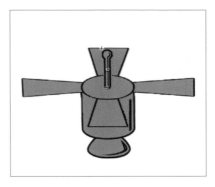

If you press Return (Enter) now, you won't see any animation because the only animation inside Animated Satellite is the propeller, and that is nested inside another movie clip (Rotating Propeller). When you press Return (Enter), you only see top-level animation. At the end of this exercise we'll show you a way to preview nested animation, too.

Animating the Satellite on the Main Timeline.

Now that we've put our satellite together, it's finally time to make it fly over the world.

1. Continue working in the same file or open **propeller_skew_done.fla** from the **Chapter_02 Project Files** folder. Click the Back button to return to the main Timeline (the world map).

   In Flash, the main Timeline is also called Scene 1.

2. Add a layer and name it satellite. Drag the layer to the top of the stack if necessary.

3. With the satellite layer selected, drag an instance of the Animated Satellite movie clip from the Library to the Stage.

4. Right-click the instance and select Create Motion Tween.

5. Animate the satellite so that it arcs over the world (starting offstage and ending offstage). Make the animation's span last for at least 200 frames. Remember, you can extend a tween further in time after animating it. The keyframes will move to new positions, keeping relative distances from each other intact.

6. Extend the other layers. You can extend many layers at once by clicking the frame you want to extend to in the top layer and then Shift clicking the same frame in the bottom layer. Then Control-click (right-click) any frame in the selected range and choose Insert Frame from the context menu.

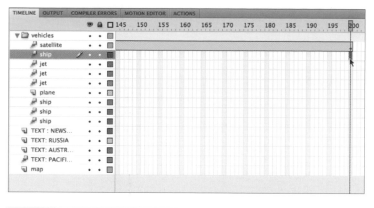

▲ TIP: Stop
the Looping

In general, you
should use Movie Clip
symbols as opposed
to Graphic Symbols.
But if you want to
create an embed-
ded animation that
doesn't loop, it's
easier to do this
inside a Graphic than
a Movie Clip. Just
follow all the same
steps you would if
you were creating
an animated Movie
Clip, but set the type
to Graphic. After you
drag an instance of
the animated Graphic
to the Stage, you can
tell it not to loop in
the Properties panel.
Movie Clips don't
have this option.

7. Press Return (Enter) to view the animation.

You'll see the satellite move, but you won't see its propeller spin. Again, this is because pressing Return (Enter) only shows you top-level anima-tions. The spinning propeller is nested, so you can't see it this way.

8. Press Command+Return (Ctrl+Enter) to see a preview of the final animation.

Now you'll see everything—the top-level animation and any nested anima-tions. In Flash, Command+Return (Ctrl+Enter) is the shortcut for Control > Test Movie. Since it gives us a more accurate view of the final result than just pressing Return (Enter), we tend to use it most of the time to preview mov-ies. Test to make sure movies open in their own window. When you're done watching them, you can close them and return to working in Flash.

You probably noticed some looping. The Rotating Propeller looped and the main Timeline (Scene 1) looped. In Flash, all movie clips (and Scene 1) loop by default. This is very useful when you want to create bouncing balls and propellers. You only have to animate one bounce or one spin—the looping will happen automatically. If you don't want your main Timeline to loop, you can stop it from doing so when you publish your movie (see "Publishing" next in this chapter).

Publishing

When you're finished animating and ready to generate a SWF file, your first (and last) stop is Publish Settings.

1. Continue working with the same file or open **satellite_animated.fla** from the **Chapter_02 Project Files** folder. If necessary, press Command+S (Ctrl+S) to save your final changes.

2. Choose File > Publish Settings.

3. In the Publish Settings dialog, select the file types you want to "render." In Flash, rendering is called publishing.

    By default, Flash outputs .swf and .html file formats. These are the two file types you'll need if you want to deploy your movie on the Web. After you've published the Flash movie and the HTML file, you'll need to move both files onto a Web server.

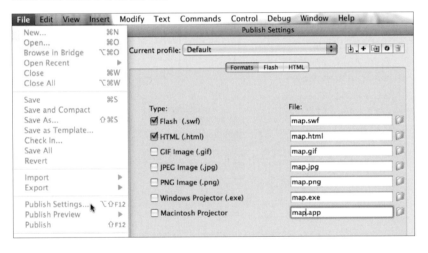

    If you're not deploying your Flash movie online—for example, if you're bringing it into After Effects or PowerPoint—you can deselect HTML. For those purposes, you'll only need a SWF file. In Chapter 9, we'll go into greater detail about prepping SWF files for import into After Effects.

4. By default, your published files are named the same as your FLA source file but with unique extensions such as .swf and .html. You can override default names by typing new ones in the File fields. Also, the published files are placed in the same folder as your FLA files. You can override this by clicking the folder icons to the right of the File fields and selecting different locations.

The Scoop on HTML

Web pages are HTML files. HTML is a simple language that describes the content of a Web page—the text on it and any images or Flash movies it's to display. On the Web, Flash movies are embedded inside HTML pages, so to put Flash files online, you need both an HTML file and a Flash file.

We're using a convenient figure of speech when we say that Flash movies are embedded inside HTML files. In fact, there's nothing in HTML files except for text. Some of the text is display text—articles that actually appear on the Web page; some of it is code that explains what the text should look like, where it should appear on the page, and what other items should be displayed, such as graphics and Flash movies. A code might specify the equivalent of "Display a Flash movie called map.swf in the upper-left corner of this page." Web browsers, such was Firefox and Internet Explorer, read the codes and then find the files mentioned in them. So it's more accurate to say that the HTML file contains an instruction about which Flash file to display than it is to say that a Flash file is embedded inside an HTML file.

Sometimes, people claim that their entire Web site is Flash. This is a convenient way of speaking, but it's not really true. Their Flash "site" is still embedded in an HTML file. But since there's nothing in the HTML except for the Flash movie, some Web developers don't bother mentioning the HTML file—it's basically an empty envelope that just contains their Flash movie.

In most cases, HTML files do contain additional content, for example, text and graphics that display next to or near the Flash movie. So most Web developers will create HTML files in programs like Adobe Dreamweaver or they will code them by hand, because Flash doesn't let you add extra content to HTML files. (Of course, you can always let Flash generate a simple HTML file and then add items to it in Dreamweaver or some other program.)

Flash is only capable of creating "empty envelope" HTML files—those that only contain your Flash movie. If you want to add more content to the generated HTML file, you'll need to do it outside of Flash (e.g., in Dreamweaver). But since you need at least a bare bones HTML file to deploy a Flash movie online, it's a good thing that Flash can create one for you.

▲ **TIP: Avoid Looping**

If you don't want your main movie to loop when it's online, click the HTML tab (which is only available if you've selected HTML as one of the published formats) and deselect the Loop option.

5. Click the Publish button to publish (render) the output files. Then click OK to close the Publish Settings dialog.

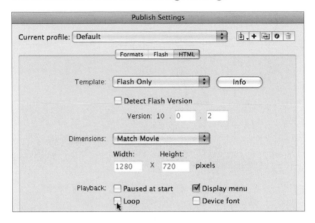

Flash Forward

Congratulations! You've now explored all the core animation features of Flash. But—as they never tire of saying on infomercials—there's more! Flash also ships with Illustrator-like drawing tools. You'll explore those in Chapter 6, "Raster vs. Vector." It also allows you to use some advanced animation techniques, such as Shape Tweening and Inverse Kinetics. You'll delve into those in Chapter 8, "Advanced Animation Tools in After Effects and Flash." In addition, Flash can import video and give it interactive controls. We'll show you how to do that in Chapter 13, "Creating Interactive Controls." In the meantime, happy tweening!

What's Next?

Now that you've explored the basics of After Effects and Flash, it's time to take a look at how those applications fit into Adobe's big picture. Sure, you can use these programs on their own, but you'll only realize their true power if you use them as part of a suite. Adobe's philosophy is that a hammer is a hammer, a screwdriver is a screwdriver, Flash is Flash, After Effects is After Effects, and Photoshop is Photoshop. But to build a house. . .er. . .to create an animated movie, you need an entire tool chest.

3 THE PRODUCTION PREMIUM TOOLSET

Although this book focuses closely on the interaction between Flash and After Effects, it's difficult to ignore the bigger picture. The interaction of all the applications within the Creative Suite is one of the most compelling reasons to utilize the entire suite. It is difficult to create motion graphics without the graphic component (which leads to the need for Photoshop and Illustrator). Likewise, you might want to utilize video in your Flash or After Effects work, which means Adobe OnLocation and Adobe Premiere Pro will be useful. Want to polish your audio or add a little music? Then don't miss Adobe Soundbooth.

▲ **TIP: Great Tips on AE**

Be sure to check out the After Effects Region of Interest blog. Visit blogs.adobe.com/toddkopriva

This chapter explains the Adobe Creative Suite 4 Production Premium and identifies ways in which the components influence a Flash or After Effects production workflow. Flash and After Effects can be purchased independently, but the aggressive pricing of the bundle makes it increasingly more likely that you will have a bigger toolbox at your disposal.

Integrated Software

Creative Suite Production Premium offers a complete solution for post-production tasks. The tools will frequently intersect as you complete tasks like audio mixing, video compression, or motion graphics. Fortunately, Adobe has tied all the tools together with great technologies like Adobe Dynamic Link and XMP metadata to make the entire post-production process easier. Creative Suite Production Premium allows you to output your final project to multiple formats for viewing on air, online, and on device. Let's explore the support role each component plays when working with After Effects or Flash.

Adobe® After Effects® CS4

After Effects is a robust motion graphics tool that offers precise control over nearly every property of visual content. It offers a responsive 2D and 3D compositing and animation environment that easily imports graphics created with other Adobe software. The greatest benefit of After Effects is its seamless ability to combine elements in 2D and 3D space. This allows for great design options when creating animation or preparing elements to use in another application.

After Effects can easily exchange material with Flash using the XFL export option. Additionally, it can import SWF, FLV, and F4V files for use within After Effects projects. The use of Dynamic Link simplifies the process of working with audio and video files from Premiere Pro or Soundbooth to even further streamline the post-production process.

Adobe® Flash® CS4 Professional

Flash Professional is a new member of Creative Suite Production Premium. Flash was originally sold by Macromedia, but when the two companies merged, Adobe integrated it into its product line. The latest version of Flash has evolved with a distinct emphasis on integration.

Flash has a long history of being the tool of choice for developing rich interactive content. On its own, it offers sophisticated tools for animation, video delivery, and interactive design. When combined with the other components in Creative Suite Production Premium, its power truly shows.

The latest version of Flash also sports powerful animation tools including inverse kinematics (the Bones tool). This robust animation style uses a series of linked objects to create relationship-based animation. Additionally, a single shape can also be distorted or animated using the Bones tool. Flash now has an easier-to-use animation model for creating animations in its Timeline for use in multimedia projects or for export to After Effects.

Adobe® Photoshop® CS4 Extended

Photoshop is the leading choice for editing raster graphics such as photos and scanned artwork. The current version of Photoshop significantly improves upon the nondestructive editing capacities, allowing for even greater control. Flash and After Effects rely heavily on Photoshop for raster images. Both applications can also import layered Photoshop files, which can greatly accelerate animation and interactivity tasks.

Creative Suite Production Premium includes the additional capacities of Photoshop Extended. This allows for easier integration of video files and also provides advanced options like Vanishing Point Exchange (to create 3D objects from photos) and 3D Object Layers when working with After Effects.

Adobe® Illustrator® CS4

As Photoshop is to raster graphics, Illustrator is to vector graphics. Vector graphics can be infinitely scaled and often have very small file sizes. The use of vector graphics is very popular in After Effects and Flash.

For After Effects, vector files offer the flexibility of scaling to any size without pixelization. They can be used as design elements or vector masks as well. After Effects can also import layered Illustrator files, which makes animation tasks easier.

> ● **NOTE: FreeHand No More**
>
> With the merger of Adobe and Macromedia, FreeHand has been discontinued. Fortunately, Illustrator can open and use FreeHand files.

Flash users can draw on the benefits of Illustrator. For example, vector objects can speed up the loading of SWF files. Vector objects are also commonly used in the design of user interfaces to accommodate scaling in the browser window. Be sure to check out Chapter 6, "Raster vs. Vector."

Adobe® Premiere Pro® CS4

The presence of video in Flash or After Effects projects is commonplace. The use of Premiere Pro enables a user to capture, organize, edit, and output video more efficiently than any other tool in Creative Suite Production Premium. Premiere Pro shares many similarities to After Effects and Flash, so a user familiar with either application should find Premiere Pro an easy application to use.

Premiere Pro allows you to professionally polish your video footage. By creating a sequence, you can assemble shots in the correct order, trim away unwanted portions, seamlessly blend audio, adjust color and volume, and add transitions. Premiere Pro is an efficient and powerful, yet easy-to-use solution.

Adobe® Soundbooth™ CS4

Soundbooth is a recent addition to Creative Suite Production Premium and represents a significant evolution in approaching audio tasks. The software is designed to simplify essential audio tasks like mixing audio tracks, sweetening sound, and creating music or sound beds.

Soundbooth even allows you to mix multiple audio tracks together to create complex sound beds. You can save these mixes using the new Adobe Sound Document (ASND) format. An ASND file can also be brought into Flash or After Effects, which keeps your timelines clean without sacrificing your ability to make adjustments.

Many users bypass Soundbooth and miss out on significant features. Some mistake its ease of use for a lack of functionality, whereas others avoid it due to past experiences with the complexity of other audio tools. Both categories of users should take a closer look, because Soundbooth offers a truly useful toolset that works well for After Effects and Flash. You'll explore two uses at the end of this chapter and learn about transcription in Chapter 14.

▲ **TIP: Get More from Soundbooth**

Be sure to visit the extensive Adobe TV online learning center at tv.adobe.com for more on Soundbooth. You should also check out the official blog at blogs.adobe.com/insidesound.

Adobe® OnLocation™ CS4

OnLocation is a direct-to-disk recording and monitoring solution. By using OnLocation during the pre-production and production stages of a project, you can accelerate the pace of post-production. During the planning of a video project, OnLocation allows you to create interactive shot lists or shooting plans that you can check off as you acquire shots. You can even use this organization to improve logging and note taking during the video shoot.

While you are shooting, OnLocation offers you several valuable features. It offers powerful calibration tools including waveform and vectorscopes you can use to set up your camera accurately. You can also compare multiple shots for continuity in lighting and exposure. The shots you record can be written directly to a hard drive, which means the footage is organized and ready for Flash or After Effects quickly.

Adobe® Encore CS4

What began as a powerful tool to create DVDs has evolved into a multiformat authoring tool. Encore is a suite of tools that allows video and photos to be authored for deployment as a DVD, Blu-ray disc, and SWF file.

After Effects and Flash users may have a need for these output tools. Encore accepts video files as well as photos, music, and sound. Flash users can convert their animation using After Effects (which we discuss in depth in Chapter 11, "Converting Flash to Broadcast Standards with After Effects").

Adobe® Bridge CS4

Adobe Bridge is a command center for the entire Creative Suite. The most useful function of Bridge is its ability to visually manage media, which includes moving, copying, and renaming files. Bridge can also facilitate tasks that involve multiple applications within the Creative Suite (like creating contact sheets or Web sites for client review). You'll also use Bridge in Chapter 5 to browse text animation presets.

Bridge allows for the organization of files for Web deployment. A rich set of tagging tools allows for the addition of metadata. By adding information about files, they are easy to find online.

Adobe® Device Central

Device Central is designed to simplify the production of content for mobile phones and consumer electronic devices. At its core is an extensive and frequently updated database that profiles many devices. From here, several options exist.

The primary use of Device Central is as a launching pad. Because it knows what size and type of files work best on each device, it can create template projects for Flash or After Effects.

▲ TIP: Into Mobile Development?

For more on Device Central (including profiles for the latest phones) visit www. adobe.com/support/ devicecentral.

After a project is built, you can test it on a virtual device (even simulating different viewing conditions and connection speeds). Device Central works closely with Adobe Bridge and makes it easy for multimedia designers to create, test, and deploy their work to consumer electronic devices and phones.

Adobe® Media Encoder

Adobe Media Encoder is a powerful application that offers a wealth of output options. Audio files can be transcoded between AIFF and WAV for authoring tasks or optimized for Web deployment as MP3 files. Video can be optimized for use in Flash as an FLV or F4V file, or compressed to higher data rates for use in DVD or Blu-ray projects.

While you can output to many of the supported formats within individual components of Creative Suite, Adobe Media Encoder is much faster to use. In fact, other components in Creative Suite often give certain tasks over to Adobe Media Encoder, which then compresses the files. Because of its dedicated focus as well as its ability to process multiple files in a batch, you can process video much more efficiently. You'll explore Adobe Media Encoder in depth in Chapter 12, "Professional Encoding of Flash Video."

Exploring Workflow

The principal reason to work within Creative Site Production Premium is the efficiency it can add to your workflow. With the release of Creative Suite 4, Adobe has made it even easier to move media between applications and complete advanced tasks that use more than one software program. You'll explore several instances of a Creative Suite workflow throughout this book, but let's start by taking a look at some of the most useful tasks.

Capturing Video with Premiere Pro

To use video in an After Effects or Flash project, you first need to capture the material. This is where Premiere Pro comes into play. The exact method you use will vary depending on the recording format chosen and the hardware attached to your machine. Fortunately, Premiere Pro is very flexible and supports numerous cameras and third-party options that allow it to work with footage from nearly any camera.

Working with DV/HDV tape

The two most common tape formats in use are DV and HDV, both of which Premiere Pro handles with ease. You can capture both audio and video by connecting a camera or deck with a FireWire cable. You can control the device and capture audio and video over one cable. Here are the steps for capturing video. If you have the required equipment, follow along; otherwise, use this as reference material.

1. If it's already running, quit Premiere Pro. With the camera or deck powered off, connect the device with a FireWire cable.

2. Connect the analog outputs from the camera or deck to a television set or broadcast monitor so you can accurately view the image and preview audio. If you're working with HD, you can use the HDMI connection.

3. Turn on the deck or camera. Make sure the camera or deck is set to VTR or Play mode. If you're using an HDV camera, make sure it is in HDV or DV mode to match the footage. Load your tape.

● **NOTE: Feeling Left Out?**

If you own Flash and After Effects, but not Adobe Creative Suite 4 Production Premium, you have two options. You can download the 30-day trials to complete some of our exercises. If you like what you find, you qualify for a deep discount when upgrading from two applications in the suite.

▲ **TIP: In/Out Traffic Jam**

If you are capturing video using the FireWire port on your computer, you may experience problems writing to FireWire-based drives as you try to push material through the ports in both directions (in and out). Consider installing a third-party FireWire card to add additional ports to the machine.

4. Launch Premiere Pro. At the Welcome screen, click New Project.

5. Enter a name for the project and click Browse to specify a location. From the Capture Format menu choose QuickTime for DV material or HDV for HDV footage. Enter a sequence name in the Name field. Click OK. The New Sequence window opens.

● **NOTE: HDV Means Limited Previews**

When using an HDV device, be sure to hook up the camera to an external video monitor. If you're working in Windows, you can preview HDV footage in the capture window, but you cannot see it during capture. On the Mac platform, you can never see the HDV footage in the preview window, and you must rely on the external monitor when browsing footage to capture.

6. Select the DV or HDV preset in the Sequence Presets panel that matches your footage format. Click OK. A new project opens.

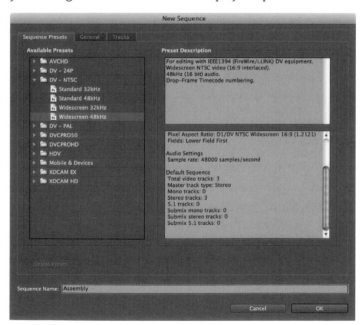

● NOTE: **Using Third-Party Capture Cards**

The process of digitizing analog video at Standard Definition sizes is very similar to loading HD video. Be sure to load the drivers and sequence presets from the device manufacturer.

7. Choose File > Capture. Choose a capture format and click OK. In the Capture panel inspect the settings in the Settings panel to make sure the device is properly detected and that the sequence is set correctly to match your footage.

8. Do one of the following to complete the capture:

   • If the capture device does not offer device control, cue up footage using the device's analog control buttons. Click Play to roll the footage, and then click the Record button in the Capture panel.

   • If the capture device offers device control, you can use the controls in the Capture panel to cue the footage and control the capture.

Batch capturing clips

If you're working with footage shot on tape, it's likely that you have multiple clips to load. By logging and capturing clips in a batch method, you can be more efficient. This is the best way to load material because it allows you to do other tasks as the footage is captured. It also has numerous benefits throughout the design process, and footage is easier to track and manage since it is divided into smaller (more useful) clips. The footage takes less time to transfer, is less of a burden on computer performance, and is easier to back up.

To perform a batch capture, you must first log clips. This is the process of setting In and Out points to define a region on the tape, and then assigning a unique and descriptive name to make the material easier to sort. If your camera or deck supports device control, you can load clips by letting the computer control the device.

1. Look in the Capture panel to make sure your camera or deck is online and available to use (Window > Capture).

2. Insert a tape into the device. Premiere Pro prompts you to name the tape. It is essential that you give each tape a unique name or number so the footage is associated with the tape it came from. This will make it easier to recapture footage in the future if you need to restore a project or replace footage due to data loss.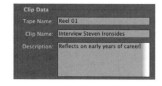

3. Use the controls in the Capture panel to shuttle through your tape. Move to the first frame you want to use and click the Set In button. Move to the end of the first shot and click the Set Out button.

4. In the Setup area, be sure to specify the media type you are using from the Capture pop-up menu.

5. Click the Log Clip button in the Timecode area of the Logging panel. This logs the clip using the In and Out points.

6. Enter a name for the clip when prompted and click OK.

7. Repeat steps 3–6 for each additional clip you want to load.

8. When you're ready to capture, select all the offline clips you want to capture. Choose File > Batch Capture.

   In the Batch Capture dialog you can choose to add handles (additional frames outside the In and Out points) or to override the logged capture settings with new specs.

9. Make sure the deck is powered on. Insert the requested tape and click OK. If additional tapes are needed, insert them when Premiere Pro prompts you.

10. To stop a batch capture, press the Esc key. When the capture finishes, choose File > Save.

Using tapeless sources

A popular trend in video cameras is the move to using tapeless recording. Premiere Pro supports most of the options on the market including Panasonic P2 camcorders, Sony XDCAM HD and XDCAM EX camcorders, Sony CF-based HDV camcorders, AVCHD cameras, and the Digital Cinema cameras from Red.

There are two major benefits to importing tapeless sources. The first is sheer speed. It takes much longer to load footage from tape (usually 1.5 to 2 times the actual runtime to allow for shuttling and playback). Tapeless sources can transfer much faster than realtime. The second benefit is that the tapeless formats are more likely to have extensive metadata already attached. This information about the shot will come in automatically with the file on import.

1. In Premiere Pro, open the Media Browser panel (if it's not visible, choose Window > Media Browser). If necessary, drag the edge to make the Browser larger.

2. Browse to the folder or disk containing the media files. The Media Browser will show a thumbnail of the footage if the format supports it and the name of each shot.

▲ **TIP: Capturing Video into an After Effects Project**

If you want to capture video for After Effects choose File > Import > Capture In Adobe Premiere Pro. Premiere Pro will launch and switch to a mode ready to capture video. When you finish, the clips will be added to your After Effects project.

▲ **TIP: Designate a Driver**

If you're working with tapeless sources, be sure to download the appropriate drivers from the manufacturer's Web site. Otherwise, you may have difficulty mounting disks and transferring footage.

● NOTE: **Master the Project Manager**

Once you start capturing media, you'll likely end up with more than you need. When you start to edit, you can reduce a Premiere Pro project to only include the footage used. This is useful for media management as well as efficiency purposes. Be sure to look up the Project Manager in the Adobe Premiere Pro Help file to ensure the proper steps for reducing, collecting, and moving project assets.

3. To preview a shot, double-click it. Premiere Pro allows you to play the clip in the Source Monitor without importing it into the Project panel.

4. When you're ready to import, choose File > Import From Browser. Premiere Pro imports the selected footage as single clips.

Importing Clips from an OnLocation Project

Premiere Pro can easily import clips captured with OnLocation. If you are using a different machine to edit than the one you used when shooting, you'll need to copy the media to a removable drive or to the new computer.

1. In the Media Browser panel, select the folder with the clips from OnLocation. Then select the clips that you want to import into your Premiere Pro project.

2. Choose File > Import From Browser. Premiere Pro adds the selected clips into the Project panel.

Using Dynamic Link to Exchange Files

Adobe introduced its Dynamic Link technology to allow the tightest integration between its core video applications. Nothing could be easier than moving assets between After Effects, Premiere Pro, Soundbooth, or Encore.

Dynamic Link removes the need for intermediate rendering. This means you can place an After Effects project into a Premiere Pro sequence without needing to render until final output. Additionally, footage can be edited in Premiere Pro and easily exchanged to After Effects for compositing and motion graphics tasks. You can choose to bring over a series of clips as individual clips or to use an entire Premiere Pro sequence as a single video track in After Effects.

Assembling your sequence in Premiere Pro

One reason to use Premiere Pro is the ease of editing multiple video clips together. This process is fast due to Premiere Pro's ability to edit and trim with real time performance.

1. From the book's DVD, copy the **Chapter_03 Project Files** folder to your computer.

2. If it's not already running, launch Premiere Pro CS4. At the Welcome screen, click the Open Project button. Navigate to the **Chapter_03 Project Files** folder and open the file **01_Premiere_Pro_Editing**. A project with footage and a completed sequence for reference opens.

3. Double-click the Completed Edit sequence in the Project panel to load it and click Play. This is a simple sequence of events that shows a woman pumping gas into her car. The action shown in the footage is an event most of you can relate to. Study the edit and take any notes necessary. You will be editing a similar sequence on your own.

> ● **NOTE: Missing Previews?**
>
> If you move a project, it is possible for the preview files to become missing. If this happens, just click Skip and you can invoke a new Preview by pressing Return).

4. Click the New Item button at the bottom of the Project panel and choose Sequence.

5. In the New Sequence dialog choose DV-NTSC Widescreen 48 kHz. Name the Sequence Gas Pump and click OK.

6. Double-click the new sequence to load it.

7. Click the disclosure triangle next to the Gas Pump footage folder in the Project panel. Double-click the shot Gas Cap.mov to load it.

8. In the Source window, move the Current Time Indicator to approximately 0;00;02;20 and press the I key to mark an In point.

9. Move the Current Time Indicator (or playhead) for the clip to approximately 0;00;07;25 and press the O key to mark an Out point.

10. Click the Overlay button or press the period key to create an Overlay edit and add the shot to the Timeline.

11. Repeat the preceding steps for the remaining shots. Do not worry about perfection, merely practice editing to create a logical flow of events. Use the Completed Edit sequence as a point of reference for your work.

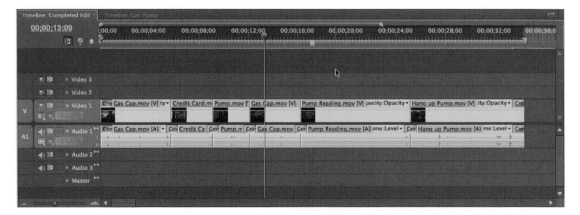

12. Place the Current Time Indicator at the first edit point and choose Sequence > Apply Audio Transition.

13. Repeat step 12 for each audio edit to smooth the changes in audio between each edit.

14. Place the Current Time Indicator at the start of the sequence and choose Sequence > Apply Video Transition. The default Cross Dissolve is applied, creating  a fade up into the video. Add a Cross Dissolve to the end of the sequence. Press the Return (Enter) key to preview your work. Choose File > Save and capture your work.

Moving footage to After Effects

After you've edited video in Premiere Pro, it is easy to move the clips into After Effects. To do this, simply copy the video in Premiere Pro, and then paste it into After Effects.

After Effects converts all the assets into layers and copies the source footage into its Project panel. Unlike Premiere Pro, which allows multiple objects into one track, After Effects will convert each item to its own layer. Additionally, any effects or transitions will attempt to be transferred as well.

1. In Premiere Pro, make sure your edited sequence is loaded.

2. Click in the Timeline to select the sequence.

3. Choose Edit > Select All. Then choose Edit > Copy.

4. Launch Adobe After Effects CS4. At the Welcome screen, choose New Composition.

5. In the Composition Settings dialog, choose NTSC DV Widescreen from the Preset drop-down menu. Enter a duration of 0;00;40;00. Name the composition Gas Pump and click OK.

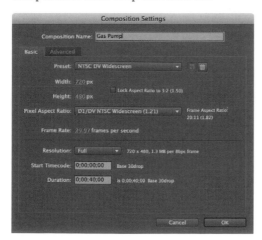

6. Select the composition and choose Edit > Paste. Notice that the dissolves and transitions did not come across, but the clips, their edit points, and arrangement did.

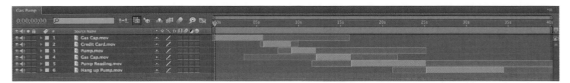

When you copy an asset in Premiere Pro and paste into an After Effects composition, keyframes, effects, and other properties are converted as shown in the table.

▲ TIP: Audio in After Effects

After Effects is rarely used for its audio abilities. Typically, the audio track is exported from Premiere Pro or Soundbooth and resynced with the final composition.

Adobe Premiere Pro Asset	Converted to in After Effects	Notes
Audio track	Audio layers	Surround sound or tracks greater than 16 bit aren't supported. Mono and stereo tracks are imported as one or two layers.
Bars and tone	Not converted	
Blending modes	Converted	
Clip marker	Layer marker	
Color mattes	Solid-color layers	
Crop filter	Mask layer	
Frame Hold	Time Remap property	Bezier, Auto Bezier, Continuous Bezier, or Hold is retained.
Motion or Opacity values and keyframes	Transform property values and keyframes	Bezier, Auto Bezier, Continuous Bezier, or Hold is retained.
Sequence marker	Markers on a new solid-color layer	To copy sequence markers, you import the entire Premiere Pro project as a composition or copy the sequence.
Speed property	Time Stretch property	Speed and time stretch have an inverse relationship. For example, fifty percent speed in Premiere Pro becomes a two hundred percent stretch in After Effects.
Time Remapping effect	Time Remap property	After Effects doesn't display unsupported effects in the Effect Controls panel.
Volume and Channel Volume audio filters	Stereo mixer effect	Other audio filters are ignored.

7. Select the first clip in the Timeline.

8. Choose Effect > Color Correction > Auto Levels to automatically adjust exposure levels in the clips.

9. Choose Effect > Color Correction > Tritone to tint the footage.

10. In the Effect Controls panel, click the brown swatch next to Midtones to apply a new tint color.

● NOTE: **Adjustment Layers and XFL**

If you apply an adjustment layer to your After Effects composition, it will flatten the layers upon export to XFL. This means a little more work in After Effects but preserves future edits.

11. Choose a rich, blue value and click OK.

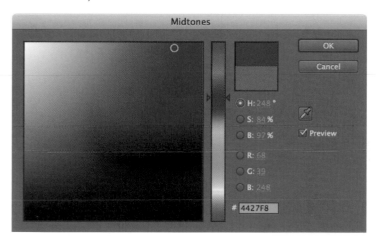

12. Choose Effect > Color Correction > Exposure to boost the shot.

13. In the Effect Control panel, set Exposure to 2.

14. In the Preview panel, click the RAM Preview button to see the effects.

15. Select the first clip in the Timeline and press the E key to see all added effects. Click the Auto Levels effect, and then while holding the Shift key click the Exposure effect. All three effects are selected. Choose Edit > Copy to copy the effects.

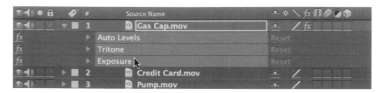

16. In the Timeline click the second clip, and then Shift-click the last clip.

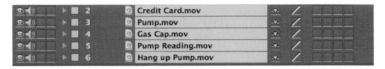

17. Choose Edit > Paste to apply the effects to the other layers.

18. Choose File > Save. Name the project 02_After Effects and store it in the **Chapter_03 Project Files** folder on your hard drive.

XFL Format Exchange

A new feature in Creative Suite 4 is the ability to send an After Effects composition to Flash via an XFL file. This allows you to send layers intact over to Flash where you can add interactivity. When you export a composition from After Effects, all layers and keyframes are preserved.

The XFL file is essentially a bundle that contains all the pieces in a neat file. When you import the XFL file into Flash, it unpacks the assets and adds them to the project file according to the instructions in the XFL file.

1. If it's not open, reload the After Effects file you created in the previous section. If you skipped steps, you can open the file **02_After Effects Completed.aep** from the **Chapter_03 Project Files** folder.

2. Choose File > Export > Adobe Flash Professional (XFL).

3. The Adobe Flash Professional (XFL) Settings window appears and prompts you to choose options for the conversion. Choose Rasterize to FLV to convert the video layers to Flash Video files.

4. Click the Format Options button to access advanced choices. Because the video you have been using in After Effects has non-square pixels, it will need to be converted to display properly in Flash.

5. In the FLV|F4V window click the Preset list and choose FLV - Widescreen Source, Web Medium (Flash 8 and Higher). Click OK to capture the Format Options.

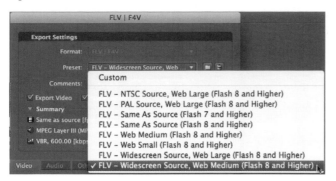

6. Click OK to close the Adobe Flash Professional (XFL) Settings window. The Export window opens and asks you to specify a location. Target the **Chapter_03 Project Files** folder and click Save. After Effects converts the files.

7. Launch Adobe Flash CS4 Professional. At the Welcome screen click the Open button. Navigate to the **Chapter_03 Project Files** folder, select **Gas Pump.xfl**, and click Open. Examine the layered Flash file that was created.

▲ **TIP:** Watch XFL in Action

For a video tutorial about exporting XFL files from After Effects, see "Exporting from After Effects to Flash via XFL" at www.adobe.com/go/lrvid4098_xp.

Adding Music or Sound with Soundbooth

Adobe Soundbooth is designed to make music creation simple. Soundbooth gives you access to several musical scores as well as sound effects. Let's add music to a Premiere Pro project, and then save the sound file for later use.

Previewing scores

The first step to scoring music with Soundbooth is to preview scores. Most of the scores are not loaded by default, but they are easy to access with an Internet connection.

1. If it's not running already, launch Adobe Soundbooth CS4.

2. Let's add more scores to Soundbooth. Choose Window > Resource Central. If your computer is connected to the Internet, you'll see new content load. Drag the edges of the window to make it as large as needed.

3. Click the Scores tab to see the free scores for download. Items in the Score Bundles are for sale, and the sounds in the Sound Effects tab are free to use.

4. The Ambient category is loaded by default. Click the Preview button for Middle East to preview the score. When you're done previewing, click Stop.

5. Let's try another category of music. Click the category drop-down menu (currently labeled Ambient) and choose Environment.

6. Click the Preview button for Downtown. This sound bed would work well for an urban sound.

7. Click the category drop-down menu and choose Electronic 2.

8. Click the Preview button for River of Unreality.

9. Let's give this track a try. Click the download button to save the file. A Save window appears asking you to specify a location.

● NOTE: Don't Switch When Downloading

When downloading items in Resource Central, do not switch categories or tabs. It interferes with the download's progress.

10. Choose the desktop and click Save. Wait until the file finishes downloading to proceed.

11. Click the Scores tab to switch to the Scores panel (not within Resource Central, but at the top of the window).

12. At the bottom of the Scores panel, click the Import Scores to Score Library button.

13. A file navigation window appears. Navigate to the desktop and choose the file called River of Unreality.zip.

14. The file is expanded and copied into the Score Library. You can safely remove the .zip file.

Using scores

After a score is selected, you can add it to a movie file, an After Effects composition, or a Premiere Pro sequence. Soundbooth makes it easy to adjust the length of a score to get a customized sound that fits the duration of your video.

1. In the Scores panel, select the score River of Unreality.

2. Click the Add Score to Multitrack button. The score moves into the Editor window. You can now add a Premiere Pro sequence.

3. Choose File > Adobe Dynamic Link > Import Premiere Pro Sequence. A new window opens asking you to specify a location for the Premiere Pro project.

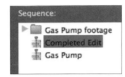

4. Navigate to the **Chapter_03 Project Files** folder on the desktop. The navigation window is a nonstandard window, so you will need to pay attention to details. Select the Premiere Pro project **01_Premiere_Pro_ Editing.prproj**.

5. Select the sequence Completed Edit and click OK. The Premiere Pro sequence is added to the Multitrack editor.

6. The music is too long, so click the score track, and then move the pointer over the end of the audio track until it turns into a red cursor.

7. Click and drag to shorten the audio track to match the video's length.

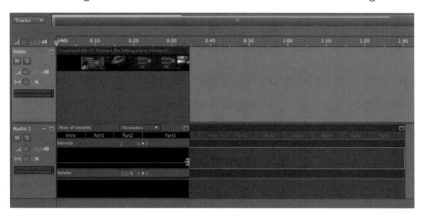

8. Choose Window > Video to see the video you are scoring to. Click Play to preview the music and video. Not bad, but you can make a few adjustments to improve it.

Mixing scores

A score can be customized using basic presets to set the intensity or adjusted over time using keyframes. This flexibility greatly improves the usefulness of each score because it provides many options.

1. In the Multitrack editor click the Maximize Clip button. The clip is now easier to see because it fills the entire editor.

2. At the top of the Editor window, click the Parameters drop-down menu and choose Show All to see all keyframeable properties for the track.

3. In the upper-left corner of the editor, lower the track volume to -10 dB. This lower volume is needed to avoid any distortion as the ambient sounds and music combine to create a louder volume.

4. Click to add five keyframes in the Intensity area of the editor. Add a frame at the start and then four additional frames spread evenly apart.

5. Experiment with dragging the sliders up and down to change Intensity.

6. Try dragging sliders left and right to better synchronize with the action or scene changes. Use the following figure as a guide.

7. Position the Current Time Indicator near 00;00;15;00.

8. Click Add/Remove Keyframe near the middle of the editor for Background 1 and Background 2.

9. Add a keyframe at the end of the track for Background 1 and Background 2.

10. Raise the ending keyframes to 100% to get an increase in Background instrumentation.

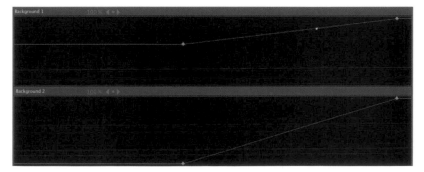

● **NOTE:** **Where to Now?**

The ASND file can be added to any of the projects you built for this lesson. You can import it into Premiere Pro, After Effects, or Flash. Feel free to experiment.

11. Use Keyframes to create a fade in the volume for the last three seconds of music.

12. Click the Go to Previous button to move the Current Time Indicator to the beginning.

13. Click the Play button to preview the track. Choose File > Save and save your work to the **Chapter_03 Project Files** folder. Name the file and save it using the ASND format.

What's Next

Now that you understand the essentials of After Effects and Flash as well as how they fit into the bigger toolbox of the Production Premium Creative Suite, you're ready to explore the practical application of these tools. The next chapter focuses on the important task of preparing video files with alpha channels to integrate into a Flash project. You'll learn the essential techniques needed to shoot and ingest the footage as well as how to prepare it for use with Flash projects.

4 CREATING TRANSPARENT VIDEO WITH AFTER EFFECTS

Transparency plays a key role in the success of animation and interactivity. By embedding transparency into graphic elements, you can composite together different elements created at different times, allowing for true flexibility.

The alpha channel is the technology behind transparency in computer graphics. It first evolved in the late 1970s at the New York Institute of Technology and then continued to be refined at Lucasfilm and at Pixar. When you employ alpha channels embedded into footage layers, transparency data can travel seamlessly between After Effects and Flash.

The original footage is used to generate a matte file, which can be stored with the layer for export as an alpha channel or can be used to composite over a different background layer in After Effects or Flash.

You can create alpha channels in several ways. One common technique you can use for video footage is chroma key technology. By shooting elements against a blue or green screen, you can easily remove the background. This technology is hardly new, making its first appearance at RKO Radio Pictures in the 1930s. The popularity of chroma key technology has grown immensely, bringing the technology and tools within reach of most content creators.

Shooting Chroma Key Right

Successful use of chroma (or color) key requires properly acquired footage. While software tools are fairly forgiving of poorly shot footage, the most professional results start with well-executed acquisition. With this in mind, let's explore effective techniques for creating footage.

Acquisition Format

Video cameras have become significantly more affordable in recent years. Consumer-grade, high-definition video cameras can be found at prices below $1,000 US. Unfortunately, these cameras may not be the best for keying. The footage of many consumer-grade cameras is heavily compressed to save on the costs associated with the storage of footage.

A bigger image does not necessarily mean better chroma keying. Do your best to avoid shooting on formats like DV or HDV because these apply heavy compression to the footage when they write to tape. Similarly, options that use SD cards or DVDs often compress the footage heavily to fit on affordable storage media.

This is not to say you can't "make do" with the camera technology you have, you just may need to "work harder" to get acceptable results. For professional projects, many multimedia producers and motion graphic artists utilize higher-quality cameras (that generally start at $5,000 US and increase significantly).

> ▲ **TIP:** Rent vs. Buy
>
> In most major cities you can always find video production companies that have equipment and studios. If you only occasionally need footage, renting (or hiring) may be a better option.

The Footage You'll Be Keying

The footage used in this chapter was shot using a Panasonic HPX-500 camera. The material was acquired in high definition with a display frame size of 1280 × 720 and a frame rate of 29.97 frames per second. The material was shot using DVCPRO-HD, a codec that uses 100 megabits a second to express the acquired images. The footage was also shot using a progressive frame mode.

▲ TIP: Choosing
an HD Format

When shooting HD,
the 720P format is
the most common
for progressive
video. Most cameras
shooting 1080 do so
with an interlaced
approach. If you're
shooting 1080, be
sure to choose a
camera that supports
progressive acquisi-
tion. Every camera
shooting 720 will
offer progressive
frame rates; some
cameras shooting
1080 will do the
same.

Progressive vs. interlaced

Video footage has traditionally been shot using interlaced fields. Historically, interlaced video allowed for smoother image quality on CRT-based devices (such as traditional television sets). The technology was first implemented in the 1930s as cathode ray tubes became brighter (and subsequently flickered more).

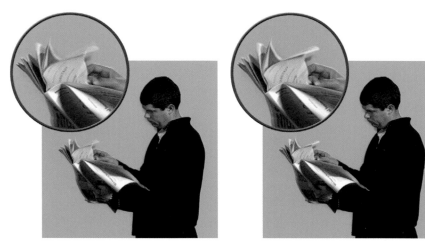

The image on the left shows the "tearing" that is visible with interlaced footage when viewed on progressive displays. The image on the right is a cleaner plate and shows the benefits of shooting progressive when keying.

For better appearance on these tube-based devices, the image was split into fields. When this interlaced process is used, half the image loads onto the CRT display from the top-left corner to the bottom-right corner. The process then repeats for the second half of the image. This approach is ideal for CRT displays but produces jagged looking footage on other display types (especially computer displays).

Fortunately, video technology has evolved. Cameras are now readily available to shoot video using progressive formats. This means the camera records full frames instead of interlaced fields. Choosing a progressive format is highly desirable because it produces a clearer image that will work better for chroma keying tasks and will play back smoother on modern displays.

Tape vs. tapeless

The use of tape has been the traditional approach and a cheap way to archive footage for cameras. It does have its drawbacks, though, because it requires hardware for playback and loading of the footage into a computer. It also must compress the footage further to store the acquired information. Another drawback is that loading tape is a real-time process; it takes at least one hour to load an hour of source material.

With Cameras, Auto Is a Bad Word

When shooting chroma key footage, make sure all the Auto settings on your camera—auto exposure, auto-white balance, and auto-focus—are turned off. If any of these settings are on, the footage you are trying to key will constantly change as your model moves.

Even if you've hired a professional videographer, don't assume that these options have been turned off. Double-check to make sure that the videographer has turned off these settings or you will waste time trying to fix the footage.

While accessing the camera settings, turn off sharpening as well. Most consumer (and even prosumer) cameras have a sharpening filter that is turned on by default. This has the effect of increasing contrast in the edges but will destroy subtle edge detail.

These limitations have been largely responsible for the increasing popularity of "tapeless" cameras. Manufacturers have approached tapeless acquisition in different ways. Some use hard drives built into the cameras, whereas others favor removable storage. These solutions can speed up the process of loading material into the computer. Additionally, some offer storage of HD video with less compression than their tape-based counterparts. Generally speaking, tapeless solutions are preferable for a modern HD workflow.

Frame rate

The frame rate of video indicates the number of still images shown every second to create the illusion of motion. This phenomenon is referred to as persistence of vision and means that the human eye can connect a series of still images into smooth motion due to the chemical transmission of nerve responses.

The frame rates used to create smooth motion often vary. Video frame rates tend to rely on frame rates between 24 and 60 frames per second for common uses. Film has traditionally been shot at 24 frames per second, whereas cartoon cel animation is most often drawn at only 12 frames per second. In Flash animation you may even encounter frame rates as low as 8 frames per second.

What does this all mean? Quite simply, computers are not televisions (there we've said it). Video cameras shoot video with the intention of playback on video devices like television sets. These higher frames rates are desirable but will often need to be simplified for use in Web deployment. This process can be easily accomplished in the conversion from After Effects to Flash.

> ● NOTE: **Avoid HDV**
>
> When HDV burst onto the scene, it was very popular. It appeared that HD was finally going to be accessible to more modest budgets. But HDV creates many postproduction issues, including keying. HDV uses 4:2:0 chroma subsampling (just like DVDs), which means that tasks like chroma keying and color correction are made much more difficult because of the lack of color information in the video. (Most professional formats are 4:2:2.)

Frame size

Video is often acquired using non-square pixels, meaning that pixel width is not the same as pixel height. There are numerous reasons for this discrepancy ranging from the need for flexibility in supporting multiple frame sizes within the same camera to limitations in digital formats. It is important to realize that you will often need to reshape video when preparing it for use in Flash; if you don't, your images may appear heavily distorted when viewed on computer displays. You'll learn more about this later.

Backdrop Choices

You'll need to make many choices when shooting chroma key. The backdrop you use will greatly impact the quality of the key you perform. Here are some considerations when selecting a backdrop.

- **Size.** Be sure the backdrop is large enough to accommodate all the action. If full-length body shots are needed, especially for walking scenes, a studio approach is generally the solution. If tighter shots can be used, portable backdrops are a much more affordable choice.

- **Fabric.** Many fabric choices are available. The most popular backdrops use polyester fabric stretched by a metal frame, which offers an easy-to-light surface that avoids wrinkles and shadows. These backdrops can be easily folded and transported. Muslin backdrops are also used but may require more attention to lighting to avoid wrinkles and bad keys.

- **Chroma key systems.** Much of the material shot for this chapter uses a Reflecmedia Chroma Key system. This approach relies on an LED disc attached to the camera lens that reflects light on a special fabric containing millions of glass beads that reflect the lower-powered light and create an  even-colored surface. Systems like this are costly but are popular because of their ease of use and portability.

- **Color.** Use a backdrop color that is the opposite of the foreground color. Blue or green is usually chosen because human skin contains very little of those colors. But if you're shooting a product that has lots of blue and green in it, you might be better off using a red screen.

  If you're shooting DV or heavily compressed HD, definitely choose a green backdrop. These video formats show less noise in the green channel, which makes for a better key. Otherwise, the choice of blue or green is really based on the subject matter you are shooting. In fact, other colors are sometimes used (such as red) for special situations.

Lighting Essentials

Effective keying relies on good lighting. It is essential to minimize variation in colors for the backdrop, meaning that you must evenly light the background to avoid hot spots. Additionally, you'll want well-lit subjects that don't cast shadows on the backdrop. This might sound a bit challenging, so here are a few tips on doing it right:

- **Spill is bad.** Your backdrop *must* be evenly lit. You'll also want to place the foreground person or object far enough away from the backdrop (with their own lighting) to avoid spill. When subjects stand too close to the backdrop, the color can spill into lighter areas of their hair or clothing, which causes keying problems. Additionally, if the foreground and background are too close, you'll get shadows on the backdrop.

- **Get rid of hot spots.** Avoid variation in brightness for the backdrop so you can get a better chroma key. To do this, look for hot spots. Simply turn down the exposure of your camera and look through the viewfinder. Your hot spots will be quite visible. Adjust your lighting by softening it, and then set your exposure back to a normal level.

- **Light with softboxes or fluorescent lights.** The use of these specialty light types will better enable you to get an evenly lit backdrop. The goal is to spread an even amount of light across the surface of the backdrop.

- **Match the foreground to the background.** If possible, you should know what your keyed footage will be composited with so you can adjust lighting. The most believable keys try to match the lighting of the replacement background in the final composite. Make sure that the light is shining from the same direction (and with the same color and intensity) as the light shining on the background plate you plan to use.

Shooting Essentials

The last step to shooting great chroma key is the actual shooting (yes, good keying takes work). Our book can't teach you to be a top videographer in a few paragraphs, but we can offer some important advice that will make your keying easier:

- **Keep your subject and your camera as far away from the screen as possible.** It is better to increase the shooting distance, even if it means nongreen edges appear in the shot. You can always crop out these edges in After Effects.

- **Avoid fast movement.** After Effects is quite good at handling motion blur, but you'll see better results if you can avoid it. Motion blur is typically where keys become "obvious."

- **Use shallow depth of field.** If your camera supports it, lower your aperture. You want to blur the background as much as possible so that wrinkles, seams, and hot spots blend away. Adjusting your camera's aperture setting allows elements farther away to fall out of focus.

- **Use a garbage matte.** You don't need to key everything in the frame. In After Effects you use the Pen tool or a mask to crop out portions of the background. So, it is necessary to only key the most active areas, which can hide issues. It also means that the green screen needn't fill the entire frame when you're shooting.

▲ **TIP: Making Easy Mattes**

Looking to create a custom mask that animates with your footage? Be sure to look at the Auto-trace command (Layer > Auto-trace).

▲ **TIP: A Better Key**

Be sure to check out the KeyerforDV animation preset. You can download it from http://community.adobe.com/help/search.html?q=keyerfordv

About DV

The affordability of DV-based cameras means they are readily available. Unfortunately, the DV format heavily compresses the video image. As a result, color artifacts are introduced, which can ruin the color even in video that has been carefully lit. Quite simply, avoid DV if at all possible.

If you must shoot DV, consider preprocessing the footage in After Effects before attempting the key.

1. Place an adjustment layer above your footage by choosing Layer > New Adjustment Layer.

2. Choose Filter > Blur > Gaussian Blur. Set the blur to a value of 2–5 pixels and change the adjustment layer's blend mode to Color.

3. Select the footage and adjustment layer, and then choose Layer > Pre-Compose. Move all attributes into the new composition.

4. Proceed with your keying plug-in.

Keying in After Effects

The best way to create transparent video for use in Flash projects is with Adobe After Effects. There are two reasons for this: First, After Effects offers advanced tools for masking, keying, and compositing. Second, you can easily access technology for converting video layers into Flash Video files with embedded alpha channels. Let's explore the process with three sample compositions.

Using Keylight

Included with After Effects is a powerful chroma key plug-in called Keylight. The technology used in Keylight uses a core algorithm written by the Computer Film Company. This technology has been used on numerous feature films including *Harry Potter*, *Mission Impossible*, and *Sweeney Todd*. Keylight has won the Academy Award for Technical Excellence and is a one-stop-shop for keying, despill, and color correction.

When you apply Keylight to a footage layer, you choose a color to key out. The effect then performs two tasks. First, it erases all the pixels that match the color. Second, it removes that color spill from other pixels. So if you select green, it will remove the backdrop and greatly reduce any green reflections on the foreground. Keylight is relatively easy to use (once you understand its options). It is also quite adept at properly keying reflections, semitransparent areas, and hair.

Getting started

The Keylight plug-in can be a bit intimidating because it has nearly 60 parameters. The good news is that there are only a few main controls and the rest are just used for fine-tuning. Let's start with some basic material that needs to be keyed.

1. Copy the **Chapter_04 Project Files** folder from the DVD to a local hard drive. Open the file **Chapter_04.aep** from the **Chapter_04 Project Files** folder. This project file contains all the elements you will use for this chapter.

2. In the Project panel, double-click the composition **01_Keying_Start** to load it. Four clips are loaded into a Timeline. This composition uses non-square pixels, which will not work well in Flash. So, you'll need to modify the composition's settings.

3. Choose Composition > Composition Settings. From the Preset list choose HDV/HDTV 720 29.97 to switch to a square Pixel Aspect Ratio. Click OK. After Effects changes the composition size and automatically adjusts the clips to display properly.

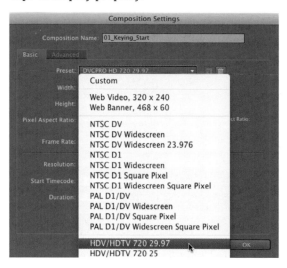

4. Choose Edit > Select All to select the four clips.

5. Choose Effect > Keying > Keylight to apply the Keylight plug-in. Nothing appears to happen.

6. At the top of the Effect Controls panel click the drop-down menu and choose the topmost layer called 01_Keying_Start • Cell_Phone2.mov.

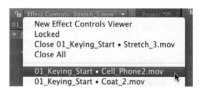

7. Move the Current Time Indicator to the start of the composition by pressing the Home key. You are now ready to start the keying process.

Pulling an initial key

Keying is often a multistep process. You will find yourself finessing and refining to get the best results. However, the most dramatic change starts with a single click. When using Keylight, you'll first choose the Screen Colour you'd like to remove (yes, the plug-in is British). The Screen Colour is the color you want removed from the background that Keylight will also despill from the rest of the scene.

1. Click the eyedropper next to Screen Colour to activate the selection eyedropper. Click just over the shoulder of the subject. You want to click close to the person to remove the green areas closest to the subject.

At first glance, the key looks "perfect." But it's not. Close examination will reveal that the image has extra transparency and some spill that needs to be corrected.

2. Click the drop-down menu next to View and switch to Screen Matte. This lets you see the grayscale matte that Keylight uses to create transparency.

The matte indicates transparent areas with black, opaque areas with white, and partially transparent areas with gray. Close examination of the matte indicates that the background has not been completely removed and that the shirt is showing undesirable amounts of transparency.

 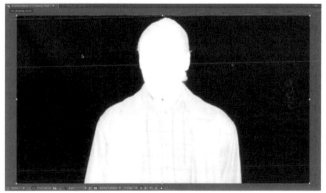

3. Increase the Screen Gain parameter until the background is a clean black plate. For this first shot, a value of 110.0 works well. Some users alternately use the Clip Black slider discussed in the next section for similar results.

4. Change the Screen Pre-blur to a value of 1.0 to slightly soften the edges of the generated matte. Avoid using a high value or halos will occur.

Cleaning up the matte

For a believable key, it's best to have some gray pixels around the edge of the subject (so hairs and other semitransparent elements can blend into the background). However, the background should be solid black, and the foreground should be solid white. Currently, the background is in good shape, but the foreground could use some work.

1. Click the disclosure triangle next to Screen Matte to reveal several controls that you can use to fix matte problems.

   Use one or more of the following sliders to refine the mask:

   • **Clip Black.** Makes the blacks in the matte darker.

   • **Clip White.** Makes the white areas in the matte whiter. Be careful with the Clip Black and Clip White controls so you don't overdo it and ruin the edges of your foreground.

   • **Clip Rollback.** Allows you to undo clipping and bring the edges back.

   • **Screen Shrink/Grow.** Contracts or expands the matte.

   • **Screen Softness.** Softens the generated matte.

   • **Screen Despot White.** Removes white specks that are inside a generally black background.

   • **Screen Despot Black.** Removes black specks that are inside a generally white foreground.

▲ **TIP: Gently Scrub Your Keys**

When adjusting properties in Keylight, you need a gentle hand. Go even slightly too far and you'll produce poor results. When using sliders, try holding down the Command (Ctrl) key to scrub any property value in tiny, subtle increments.

2. Lower Clip White to 85.0 to remove most of the "holes" in the matte.

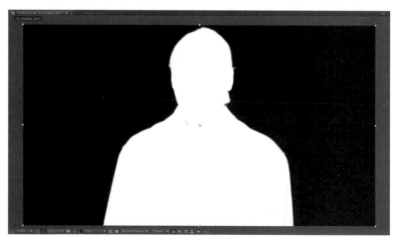

3. Adjust the Clip Rollback to 5.0 to restore edge detail and set the Screen Softness to 1.0 to remove fringe at the edges.

4. Adjust Screen Despot Black to 5.0. You may need to resize the Effect Controls panel to see the full name. Click in the area between the Effect Controls panel and the Composition panel, and then drag to resize.

5. Click the View drop-down menu and choose Final Result to see your keyed footage.

▲ TIP: Toggle Views

As you make adjustments to your key, you should toggle back and forth between Screen Matte view and Final Result view. This makes it easier to check your progress. Your end goal, as you view the Screen Matte, should be to have an all black background and an all white foreground with a little bit of gray around its edges. Wispy elements, like hair, should be gray.

Correcting color

After you've keyed the background, you'll usually need to adjust the foreground colors so they properly match the colors of your new background. Fortunately, Keylight offers two sets of controls to fix these issues.

Foreground Colour Correction. Affects the majority of the person or object left behind after Keylight has removed the background.

Edge Colour Correction. Modifies a thin band of pixels running around the person or object. This is where the majority of color spill occurs from the background reflected on the subject and is a critical area to tweak when you are trying to make a believable composite.

1. From the Project panel, drag the file Rooftop.tif to the bottommost position in your active composition. You'll use this outdoor scene to adjust the colors of the footage to match.

2. Reselect the top layer and in the Effect Controls panel, click the disclosure triangle next to Foreground Colour Correction. Select the Enable Colour Correction check box. Increase the Saturation slider to 115 to boost the color in the foreground.

3. Adjust the Contrast and Brightness to match the foreground subject to the background plate. For this image, try a Contrast setting of 4.0 and a Brightness setting of –5.0.

4. Click the disclosure triangle next to the Colour Balance Wheel. This allows you to adjust the white balance of the image and tint the foreground to better match the color temperature of the background.

5. Slowly drag the x of the wheel to the left. Experiment with different positions until the color matches well.

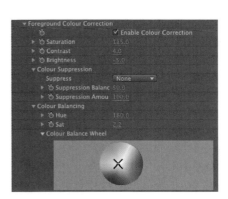

▲ **TIP: Controlling Edges**

To adjust how thick of a band Keylight treats as an edge, examine the Edge Colour Correction view. You can then adjust the Edge Grow parameter.

The Edge Hardness and Edge Softness parameters are also useful. Edge Hardness controls how much the edge color correction merges into main foreground color correction, whereas Edge Softness blurs the edges.

6. Click the disclosure triangle next to Edge Colour Correction. Select the Enable Edge Colour Correction check box. Set Edge Grow to 10.0, Saturation to 80.0, and Brightness to -10.0 to reduce the richness of color at the edges (the results will be subtle). Set Edge Colour Suppression to Suppress Green.

7. Open the Colour Balancing area and set Saturation to -2.0 to further remove color from the edges.

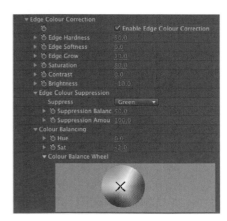

Adjusting edge crop

Sometimes your image will need a slight crop or reposition due to its edges. It's essential that you carefully examine the edges of the image when keying to look for undesired transparency or black fringe. The footage layer you are working with has both.

Let's start with the stray transparency at the bottom of the frame. You need to nudge the layer down slightly to hide the soft bottom edge.

1. Select the layer Cell_Phone2.mov in the Timeline.

2. Press P to access the Position property. Set the Y value to 400.0 to reposition the footage in the Composition panel. For best results, type the number into the entry field. A decimal point value often results from dragging, which can lead to subpixel resampling and image softness.

The bottom edge is fixed, and the composition of the shot looks good. Close examination reveals a black edge along the top of the frame.

3. In the Effect Controls panel, scroll to the bottom to see all the controls.

4. Click the disclosure triangle next to Source Crops. Change the X Method and Y Method to Repeat the Edge Color. This removes most of the fringe.

5. Change the Top crop to 99.0. The edge is fairly clean, but a small color shift exists because the top corner of the matte has a little hot spot left.

6. Scroll up in the Effect Controls panel and enter a value of 3.0 for the Clip Black property to clean up the matte further and to produce a great edge with a smooth transition.

Your key is now complete. Three more shots are in the current Timeline with which you can practice. Each offers slightly different challenges including wispy hair and color spill. Use the techniques you've learned so far and practice keying these additional shots. When you are ready, continue with the lesson.

Using Masks

Sometimes you'll need to combine masks to improve the quality of your keys in After Effects. This might be because the chroma key background is not big enough to fill the frame or because you have color spill or reflections. Let's try keying a shot that needs a little extra work.

Adding a garbage matte

Sometimes areas of footage just need to be cropped before you even start the keying process. This is generally referred to as using a garbage matte and allows for areas to be masked.

1. In the Project panel, double-click the composition **02_Masking_Start** to load it. This composition contains one HD clip and is set to use square pixels. Notice that the background does not fill the entire screen.

2. Select the layer Camera_Man.mov in the Timeline.

3. Double-click the Rectangle tool in the toolbar to add a rectangular mask to the footage. A new rectangular mask is added to the footage layer, and the Timeline expands to show Mask 1.

4. With layer 1 selected, press Command+T (Ctrl+T) to transform the mask. Control handles appear on the mask to control its size.

▲ **TIP: Auto-Trace a Matte**

An alternative to drawing mattes by hand is the Auto-Trace command. You can select the footage layers and choose Layer > Auto-Trace to create a usable mask.

5. Drag the left and right edges in toward the center of the window to crop the black area from the video frame.

6. Press Return (Enter) to apply the transformation. The footage now has the nonkeyable areas masked off with a garbage matte.

7. Perform the initial key by choosing Effect > Keying > Keylight. Using the techniques you learned earlier in this chapter, perform an initial key and clean up the matte using the Screen Matte settings. Be sure to crop a few pixels off the top of the frame as well. Also, set both X and Y Methods of Source Crop to Repeat.

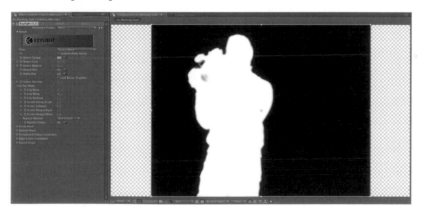

▲ TIP: Getting
the Best Key

When using Keylight, be sure your layers are set to Best Quality. You'll also want to set the Composition panel to 100% magnification and full quality. This is the only way to accurately judge the results of your keying.

Limiting the key with a mask

Keylight will sometimes remove more from the footage than you want. In this particular shot, you'll notice that the lens of the camera is reflecting green (which lenses naturally do even when they are not placed near a green screen). This is causing the camera to show partial transparency. Fortunately, a mask can also be used here to limit Keylight's reach.

1. Make sure layer 1 is selected and that Keylight's controls have View set to Final Result. Closely examine the camera lens to see the unwanted transparency.

2. Click and hold on the Rectangle tool in the toolbar to reveal the other shapes available.

3. Choose the Ellipse tool. Double-click the Ellipse tool to add an elliptical mask to the footage layer. The two masks combine to create a hybrid shape, which is not desired and can be easily fixed.

4. In the Timeline, make sure Mask 2 is selected, and then change its mode to None so the mask does not hide any parts of the footage.

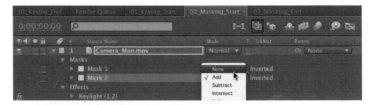

5. Press Command+T (Ctrl+T) to transform the mask.

6. Adjust the corners and position of the mask so it covers the front of the camera lens.

7. Press Return (Enter) to apply the transformation. The mask can now be transformed over time with keyframes to follow the moving footage.

8. Click the triangle next to Mask 2 to reveal its keyframeable properties. Click the stopwatch next to Mask Path to enable keyframes for the shape and position of the mask.

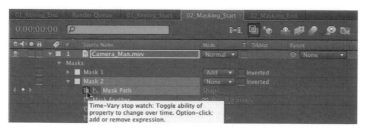

9. Move the Current Time Indicator forward to 1:00. The mask no longer covers the front of the camera. Press Command+T (Ctrl+T) to move and size the mask to cover the front of the lens.

10. Press Return (Enter) to store the transformation; a new keyframe is added.

11. Move the Current Time Indicator to 2:00 and repeat the mask move and sizing.

12. Repeat the mask movement and positioning every second in the Timeline. You should now have a keyframe for the Mask Path at each second in the Timeline. Now check to see if more keyframes are needed.

13. Press the Home key to return to the start of the composition and press the spacebar to watch the footage play slowly. Watch closely to see where the mask needs additional keyframes to ensure the lens reflection is covered.

14. The following points may need additional keyframes added to refine the mask. These times are approximations and may vary slightly depending on the initial shapes you created.

    - 00;00;01;15
    - 00;00;02;15
    - 00;00;04;20
    - 00;00;05;10
    - 00;00;06;10
    - 00;00;06;20
    - 00;00;07;15
    - 00;00;09;15

15. In the Effect Controls panel, click the disclosure triangle next to Keylight's Inside Mask property. Set the Inside Mask drop-down menu to Mask 2. Adjust the Inside Mask Softness to a value of 1.0

16. Check the effect by clicking the RAM Preview button in the Preview panel. Make sure the Resolution is set to Full Quality to properly judge the accuracy of the key and mask.

Exporting with transparency to Flash

Now that the footage layer is properly keyed, it is ready to export to Flash. While Flash supports three different codecs for video (Spark, On2, and H.264), only On2 VP6 supports the use of an alpha channel. Fortunately, After Effects makes this an easy export.

The video you want to export has lots of empty space, so you can nest this to create a smaller frame size.

1. In the Project panel, select the composition **02_Masking_End**. Drag the composition onto the Create a New Composition button at the bottom of the Project panel. This creates a new composition that nests the original inside of it and also matches the size and duration of the original.

2. Double-click the new composition called 02_Masking_End 2 to open it.

3. Choose Composition > Composition Settings to modify the file.

4. In the Composition Settings dialog, rename the composition Camera Man with Alpha. From the Preset list choose Custom. You will make a smaller-sized composition to size the video for Web use. Enter a Width of 250 pixels and a Height of 340 pixels. Be sure the Pixel Aspect Ratio is set to Square Pixels.

5. Click OK to change the composition settings. When you reduce the frame size the resulting video file will load faster.

6. Select layer 1 in the Timeline. Press P for position.

7. Hold down the Shift key and press S for scale. Change the Scale to 50% for both the width and height.

8. Drag the position slider to position the video within the new comp. A value of 217.0 and 175.0 should work well.

9. In the Preview panel, click the RAM Preview button to review your animation. Watch the animation through to make sure the video is not cropped at any point.

10. Choose Composition > Add to Render Queue. The Render Queue controls how animations are processed and written to disk. Click the Best Settings text next to Render Settings to customize Output.

11. Because the output of Flash Video is intended for Web use, you can specify a lower frame rate. Select Use this frame rate and set its value to 15.

12. To ensure that the entire animation renders, set the Time Span to Length of Comp. Click OK to store the Render Settings.

13. In the Render Queue click the Lossless Output Module text label to open the Output Module Settings window. Change Format to FLV. You now need to specify options for the format. Click the Format Options button.

14. From the Preset list choose FLV – Same as Source (Flash 8 and Higher) to match the output size to the composition size. Deselect the Export Audio check box because there is no audio for this composition. Choose the On2 VP6 codec.

15. In the Basic Video Settings area, select the Encode Alpha Channel check box to include transparency with the exported file.

16. In the Advanced Settings area click the Quality list and choose Best for the highest quality (yet slowest) encode.

17. Lower the data rate to 1000 kbps in the bitrate settings section. and then click OK to store the Format Options. Click OK to store the Output Module Settings.

18. Click the filename next to Output To and specify the **Chapter_04 Project Files** folder that you copied at the start of the lesson.

19. In the Render Queue click Render to create the file. The resulting file is now ready to use in a Flash project. The transparency is embedded into the file.

▲ TIP: Background Check

When keying, it can be difficult to judge the quality of a key. One technique is to put a brightly colored solid behind the keyed footage (Layer > New > Solid). Make the solid color a different color from the original screen color. For example, if the original image was shot against a green screen, try laying it over a red solid. Be sure to check the key by moving the CTI to check the key at a few points in time.

Using Transparent Video in Flash

Once your Flash video file is rendered, you can import it into Flash. The import process is quite simple as it is treated like any other footage item. You'll learn more about Flash video options in Chapter 12, "Professional Encoding of Flash Video."

1. Launch Flash Professional. In the Welcome screen, click the Flash File (ActionScript 3.0).

2. In the Properties panel, click the Edit button. Set the document to 400 px × 400 px at 30 fps and click OK.

3. With the Rectangle Tool, draw a rectangle to fill the canvas.

4. Click the Fill Color and choose the Black to Blue gradient.

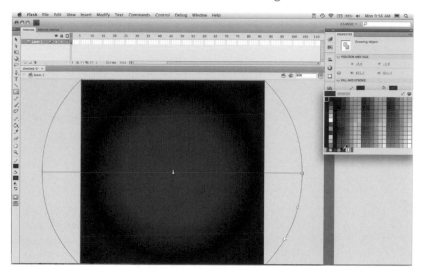

5. Add a new layer in the Timeline and name it cameraman.

6. Choose File > Import to Stage.

7. Navigate to the FLV file you just rendered and click Import. The Import Video window opens.

8. Choose Embed FLV in SWF and play in timeline. Click Continue.

9. A second window appears, the default options are okay for this example. Click Continue then click Finish.

10. Position the video on the Stage using the Selection tool.

11. Select the bottom layer in the Timeline. Move the playhead to frame 300.

12. Right-click in the Timeline and choose Insert Frame to extend the background layer.

13. Choose File > Publish Preview > Default to test the file. Close Flash (there is no need to save your test file).

Additional Practice

If you'd like some additional keying practice, we've included one more task. You can open the file **03_Composite_Start** to use the techniques you've learned so far as well as to experiment with new techniques. Gain confidence by exploring the footage and composition. You can compare your progress with the composition **03_Composite_End**.

- Size the composition using a smaller size (640 × 360).
- Use square pixels for output to Flash.
- Perform a clean key of the TV_Shot.mov layer.
- Composite the Screen_Content.mov layer below the television. Use Position and Scale properties to resize and accurately place the layer in the right position.
- Use the Fast Blur effect to defocus the Screen_Content.mov layer.
- Export the composition as a layered file for Flash by choosing File > Export > Adobe Flash Professional (XFL).
- Import the XFL file into Flash Professional and explore the layered file.

What's Next?

In this lesson you learned how to prepare footage for use with Flash. Because After Effects and Flash have slightly different end deliverables, this preparation takes a little extra knowledge on your part but is still relatively easy to implement. Next, you'll explore another way that After Effects can assist Flash, and that is with powerful text animation tools. Because After Effects supports a true 3D environment, you can create stunning text animation. If you design with the Web in mind, After Effects can even export to a vector format for easy import into Flash. Let's explore the great integration between Flash and After Effects, this time with great type as the goal.

5 DYNAMIC TEXT WITH AFTER EFFECTS

Why use After Effects instead of Flash for text animation? After Effects has a rich pedigree in text animation, including feature film title sequences and broadcast commercials. If you want to animate text, After Effects is the best tool in existence. We recommend if you want to animate text for a Flash project, animate it in After Effects and then export it as a SWF or XFL file for import into Flash. It might seem like a few extra steps, but the results are worth it.

After Effect's text engine is so good that if you can imagine a text effect, you can create it (with the exception of extruded, 3D text effects). The only downside of this much power is complexity. The methods for working with text in After Effects aren't immediately intuitive. But never fear; you'll learn how to wrangle the text engine in this chapter. And, in the end, if you find text animation too complicated or time-consuming, you can skip the sweat and tears by applying one of the many text animation presets that ship with After Effects.

The Project

In this chapter, you'll work on one big project: an animated bumper to a news magazine feature story about the decline of literacy. The project will show text in a book. One by one, individual words will jump off the page and come together to form the phrase "the death of reading." At the end, all the leftover words will disappear, leaving just the phrase.

The Setup

To start the project, you'll import a layered document from Photoshop and convert a Photoshop text layer to an After Effects text layer.

1. From the book's DVD, copy the **Chapter_05 Project Files** folder to your hard drive.

2. Start a new After Effects project, and save it in the copied folder as reading.aep.

3. Choose File > Import > File and select **book.psd** in the **Chapter_05 Project Files** folder. In the Import File dialog, select Composition – Cropped Layers from the Import As drop-down menu.

This ensures that each layer from the Photoshop file has the same width and height in After Effects that it did in Photoshop. (If you import as a Composition without cropped layers, After Effects sizes each layer to the width and height of the Photoshop file. If you import as Footage, After Effects flattens all the layers into a single layer.)

4. The next dialog lets you specify how to handle Photoshop layer styles and 3D layers. We're working with neither here so click Open.

5. Double-click the book comp in the Project panel. In the Composition panel, you see some text in a book. The book is the bottom layer. Above it is the text on its own layer.

6. In the Timeline, select the text layer, and then choose Layer > Convert to Editable Text. This turns the Photoshop text layer into an After Effects text layer, allowing you to apply After Effects text animators to it.

7. Select the Rectangle tool and draw a rectangular mask around the word "reading" in the first paragraph. You may need to zoom in your comp window to make it easier to make an accurate mask. Hold down the spacebar and drag in the comp window to pan around the zoomed in comp.

The goal is to hide the word "reading" while revealing all the other text. By default, masks do the opposite—they show whatever is inside the mask and hide everything else. This default is easy to override.

8. On the Timeline, set Mask 1's Apply Mode to subtract.

9. Repeat steps 7 and 8, masking the word "death" in the final paragraph, "of" in the second paragraph (after the word "mixture"), and "the" in the third paragraph (right before the word "dream").

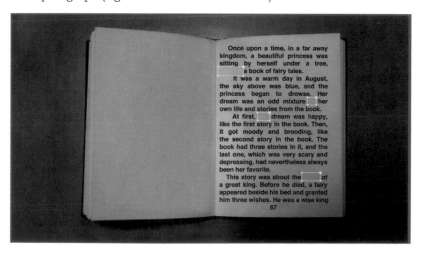

▲ TIP: Invert or Subtract?

You might be tempted to select the Inverted check box instead of setting the mode to Subtract. Normally, this would work. Invert means that the mask should show everything that it's hiding and hide everything that it's showing. However, in this case we're going to add multiple masks to the same layer. Setting the option to Subtract makes each mask hide content instead of reveal it. If we set multiple masks to invert, the inversions would conflict with each other.

10. Lock the original text layer. You're about to create more text layers by clicking with the Type tool, and you don't want to accidentally edit the original text. Click the lock icon next to the text layer's name.

11. Select the Horizontal Type tool.

12. In the Character panel (Window > Character), set the Font Family to Helvetica Bold, the Font Size to 20, and the Fill Color to Black. Select Center justification. (This will allow text to scale from its center, rather than from its corner.) In the Paragraph panel, choose the Center text option.

13. Click with the Type tool anywhere in the Composition panel, and type the word "the."

14. Switch to the Selection tool and move the word "the" into place (over the mask that's hiding the original word "the"). You may have better luck nudging the word into place with the arrow keys than with your mouse.

15. Repeat steps 13 and 14, creating layers for the words "death," "of," and "reading," and nudging them into place.

● **NOTE: Compare Your Work**

You can compare your work to 05_setup_complete.aep if needed.

Text Animation with Animation Groups

Now you'll animate the words "the," "death," "of," and "reading" so they stand out. You'll make them scale up and then down again, like this:

death, **death**, death.

In addition to general scaling, you'll make each letter scale up, one by one:

death, d**e**ath, de**a**th, dea**t**h, deat**h**.

As each letter gets bigger, you'll also make it jump up, so it's higher than the other letters:

death, d**e**ath, de**a**th, dea**t**h, deat**h**.

Finally, you'll make the word's tracking expand and contract while it turns red:

death, d e a t h, death (in red).

Note that you're applying four distinct animations to each word:

- The whole word will scale larger and then back to its original size.
- Each letter will get larger, jump upward, and then shrink and move back down.
- The whole word will track out and then track back again.
- The whole word will gradually turn from black to red.

You might think of the second animation as two distinct animations, getting bigger/smaller and jumping up/down. But as you'll see, it's useful to think of it as one animation, because the same letters jump and resize. Group animations this way: If multiple animators are altering the same characters at the same time, think of them as a single animation.

Animation One: Scaling the Whole Word

After Effects can scale text in a couple of different ways: It can scale each character individually or it can scale the entire text layer as a whole. Let's start with the latter and then explore the former.

1. Continue with the same project or open **05_setup_complete** from the **Stages** folder in the **Chapter_05 Project Files** folder.

2. In the book comp, move the Current Time Indicator to about half a second into the comp (15 frames or 0;00;00;15).

3. Select the "the" layer in the Timeline and press S to reveal the Scale property. Click the stopwatch to enable animation and set a keyframe.

4. Move the Current Time Indicator forward half a second (0;00;01;00) and scale the layer up to 200%.

5. Move the Current Time Indicator forward another half second (0;00;01;15), select the start keyframe, copy it to the clipboard by pressing Command+C (Ctrl+C), and paste it by pressing Command+V (Ctrl+V) so that the layer animates from 100% to 200% and then back to 100%.

> ▲ **TIP: Jumping in Time**
>
> A useful way to jump forward in time is to click the Current Time Display. The Go to Time window opens. Type +15 to move forward 15 frames and click OK.

6. Select all three keyframes by clicking the word Scale in the Timeline. Enable Easy Ease by pressing the F9 key (or by choosing Animation > Keyframe Assistant > Easy Ease).

In general, animations look better with easing. But to save space, you won't be continually reminded to ease in this lesson. For the rest of this chapter, this step will be omitted, but you can take it as a given that after you complete keyframing your layers, you should select all the keyframes and apply Easy Ease.

Animation Two: Scaling and Positioning Each Letter

As you can tell from the previous section, you have access to all the usual properties on text layers: Anchor Point, Position, Scale, Rotation, and Opacity. You also have access to properties special to type, such as Font Size and Tracking, but you have to indicate to After Effects that you want to add these properties to the Timeline.

1. Click the disclosure triangle to close the "the" layer, hiding the Scale property, and then click the disclosure triangle again to reveal its default properties.

2. From the Animate menu (unique to type layers), select Scale.

This tells After Effects you'd like to animate the Scale property. After Effects adds it to the Timeline. But there's already a Scale property in the Timeline. In fact, you just animated it. The truth is, the Scale option on the Animate menu is not well named. It would be best if it was called Font Size. It's the animatible version of setting the font size in the Character panel, and it allows you to affect a word's individual characters. On the other hand, the regular Scale property—the one in the Transform group—affects the entire layer.

3. In the Timeline, locate the Scale property inside the group called Animator 1 and unlink its width and height dimensions by clicking the chain icon. This is because you want to scale height without also scaling the width.

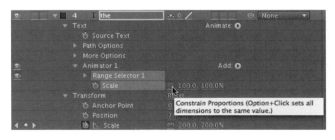

4. Scrub the height dimension up to 300% . All the letters get taller. You just want the "t" to get taller (at first, anyway).

5. Click the disclosure triangle next to Range Selector 1. Range Selectors are After Effects' version of highlighting. In word processors, such as Microsoft Word, you can highlight individual characters in a word to specify which letters you'd like to affect. Range Selectors allow you to do the same thing in After Effects.

6. Adjust the End property until just the letter "t" is affected by the scaling. (Set End to about 30%.) If you wanted to select just the letter "h," you would have had to adjust both the Start and End properties of the range. With the "t" you don't have to adjust the Start property, because "t" happens to already be at the start of the word.

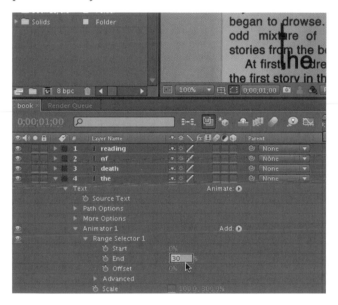

At this point, think about what you want to do: You want to select each letter, one by one. So after the "t" is done animating, you want to move the Start of the range to the right before the "h" and the End of the range to the right after the "h." Then you want to move the Start to the right before the "e" and the End to the right after the "e."

You could accomplish this by keyframing the Start and End properties, moving them over time. But there's an easier way. The solution is the Offset property, which moves the Start and End properties at the same time, keeping the distance between them consistent.

The Offset Property Clarified

If you're confused by the behavior of the Offset property—it moves the Start and End properties at the same time, keeping the distance between them consistent—imagine holding a *Torah*-like scroll, one handle in your left hand and the other in your right with a portion of the scroll showing between the two handles.

The part that's showing (the part that you can read that isn't rolled up on either side) is the range (or selection). If you want to select a different part, you can twirl the handle in your left hand (the Start property) to hide some of the currently showing text; you can twirl the handle in your right hand (the End property) to show some of the subsequent text; or you can twirl both handles at once, shifting to a whole new section of the *Torah*. That last move is like adjusting the Offset property.

▲ **TIP: The Keys to Success**

A quick way to jump through keyframes are the J and K keys. Press J to move back one keyframe and K to move forward one keyframe.

7. Move the Current Time Indicator to the start of the "the" animation (to the point where the whole word first starts scaling up at 0;00;00;15).

8. Turn on the stopwatch for the Offset property.

9. Scrub Offset to the left so that no characters are selected and the Start and End of the range are before the "t." An Offset of -34% will do the trick.

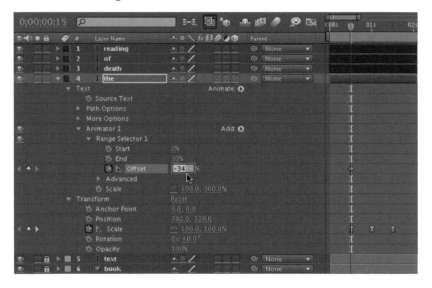

10. Move the Current Time Indicator forward to the end of the "the" animation (a second later at 0;00;01;15).

11. Scrub Offset to the right so the Start and End are just after the "e."

The animation should look like this: **the, the, the, the, the.**

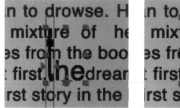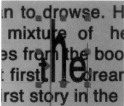

Now you want each tall letter to jump upward. You've already defined and animated a range, so you don't want to start a whole new animation. Instead, you just want to add another property (Position) to the same range.

12. Click the Add button (next to Animator 1) in the Timeline, and select Property > Position.

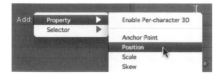

As with the Scale property, text layers have two different Position properties. There's the well-known one in the Transform group. It affects the entire layer. The new one you're adding affects ranges of characters.

13. Move the Current Time Indicator to a place where you can see one of the characters taller than the others—it doesn't matter whether you're looking at the "t," "h," or "e."

14. Adjust the Y dimension of Position (in the Animator 1 group) so that you see the letter move up, positioned above the other letters (a Y value of -27 works well).

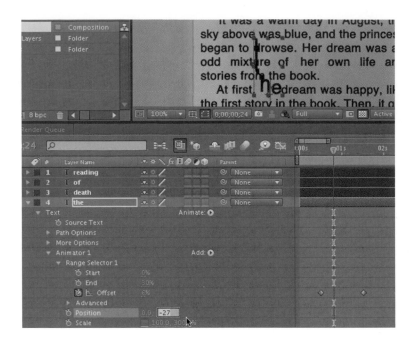

That's it. You don't have to animate the letter moving down again, and you also don't have to animate the other two letters jumping up and down. They're already animated. The Offset animation you created in step 8 takes care of everything.

Note that both Scale and Position are in the Animator 1 group (you added Position to this group). All properties in an Animator group are affected by the range in that group. If you added another property—say Rotation—to the Animator 1 group and spun it to 45 degrees, the "t" would get taller, jump up, and rotate to 45 degrees, next the "h" would do the same, and then the "e" would do it.

If you want some other animation to affect the word, but not the same range, you need to add another Animator group. You'll get to that shortly. Meanwhile, Animator 1 is not a very descriptive name for what's going on with the letters, so let's change it.

15. Select the Animator 1 group in the Timeline, and press the Return (Enter) key. Rename the group Jump and Scale Group and press Return (Enter) again to finalize the name.

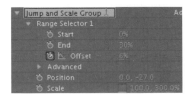

Animation Three: Tracking

You want the entire word (not the "t" then the "h" then the "e") to track out and then back, so you can't add the Tracking property to the Jump and Scale Group. If you did, it would be affected by the range in that group, which targets each letter via the Offset property animation. So you need to add another Animator group—one that will have its own range.

1. Deselect the Jump and Scale Group (otherwise, when you add the Tracking property, it will go into that group). You can deselect by clicking a blank area of the Timeline, but it's best to press Shift+Command+A (Shift+Ctrl+A), which is the keyboard shortcut for Edit > Deselect All.

2. From the Animate pop-up menu, choose Tracking. After Effects creates a new Animator group—Animator 1—with its own Range Selector and the Tracking property inside.

3. Rename the new group by selecting its name, pressing Return (Enter), typing Tracking Group, and pressing Return (Enter) again.

4. Move the Current Time Indicator to the start of the "the" animation and turn on the stopwatch for Tracking Amount.

5. Move to 1 second into the Timeline (0;00;01;00) and scrub Tracking Amount so that the letters fan out (Tracking Amount = 30%).

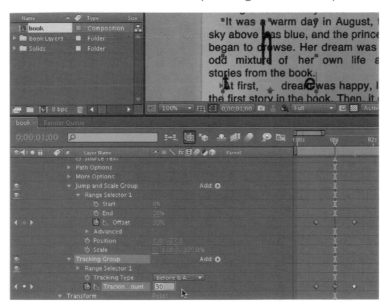

6. Move to the end of the animation (half a second later) and scrub Tracking Amount back to zero.

You don't have to adjust the Range Selection, because by default the range is the whole word.

Text-like Shapes

There's one good reason to animate text in Flash: Although text is vector based in both applications, only Flash allows you to edit the underlying shapes of characters. (Though you can achieve a similar effect in After Effects by auto-tracing text characters and then animating the resulting mask. See more below.) If you want, you can shape tween a letter A into an airplane or a B into a buffalo, but to do this, you first have to break apart the letters. Once you break them apart, Flash no longer recognizes them as text, so broken-apart text can't be edited as text. Make sure you get the spelling right before you break text apart.

To treat characters as shapes in Flash:

1. Select the text.

2. Choose Modify > Break Apart to break a word into individual characters. But you still won't be able to edit each character as a shape.

3. Choose Modify > Break Apart a second time. If the text is only one character long, you only have to choose Break Apart once.

4. Edit the shapes with one of Flash's many vector tools (see Chapter 6).

Actually, there *is* a way to edit text-like shapes in After Effects, but it's a little more roundabout:

1. Select a text layer and choose Layer > Create Shapes from Text..

After Effects creates a new Shape layer with shape versions of the characters in the original text.

This technique works well to create shapes that can be individually distorted and animated for warping effects.

Animation Four: Color

You'll add a final Animator group to change the color from black to red. Since you're affecting the whole word, you could just add this animation to the Tracking Group, because the range in that group is the whole word. But for organizational purposes, let's create a new group for the color animation.

1. Press Shift+Command+A (Shift+Ctrl+A) to deselect the Tracking Group (or any selected property inside the group).

2. From the Animate menu, select Fill Color > RGB.

3. Select the new Animator 1 group and change its name to Color Group.

4. Turn on the stopwatch for the Fill Color property.

5. Animate the property so that the Fill Color starts as black (at the beginning of the "the" animation) and ends as red (at the end of the "the" animation). To change color, click the color swatch to open the Adobe Color Picker.

Save an Animation Preset

Completing the four animations was cool, but wouldn't it be a drag if you had to repeat all those steps for the other words? Fortunately, you don't. You can save your animation as a text animation preset and apply it to the other layers.

1. Click the disclosure triangle to close the "the" layer, select it, and press UU (the U key twice in rapid succession). This exposes all the properties you've adjusted or keyframed.

2. Select the Jump and Scale Group, hold down the Shift key, and select the Tracking Group and the Color Group. With the Shift key still held down, select the Scale property in the Transform group.

3. On the menu, select Animation > Save Animation Preset.

▲ **TIP: Recent Presets**

If you want to reuse a recently applied or created animation preset, choose Animation > Recent Animation Presets

4. In the Save Animation Preset dialog, name the preset JumpScaleTrack-Color.ffx and save it in Documents (My Documents on Windows)/Adobe/After Effects/User Presets.

5. In the Effects & Presets panel (Window > Effects and Presets), click the disclosure triangle to open Animation Presets > User Presets to expose the preset you just saved.

6. Move the Current Time Indicator to the end of the "the" animation.

7. Drag the preset from the Effects & Presets panel and drop it on the death layer.

8. Repeat step 7, dragging the preset to the "of" and "reading" layers. But before dragging the preset, move the Current Time Indicator forward so that each animation begins after the previous one ends. Presets are applied so that they start wherever the Current Time Indicator is located.

9. Invoke a RAM Preview and watch the comp, seeing each word animate.

Scaling and Positioning Text

Your text animation is almost complete. To finish it, let's bring the red words over to the left page.

1. Continue working with your file or open the file **05_preset_complete.aep** from the Stages folder in **Chapter_13 Project Files** folder.

2. Move the Current Time Indicator to 0;00;05;00.

3. Let's synchronize animation across several layers. Select layer 1 reading then Shift+click to select layer 4 the.

The four isolated words are selected in the Timeline window. Let's take advantage of the vector-based text and scale it much larger.

4. Press P to show just the Positon property for each of the selected layers.

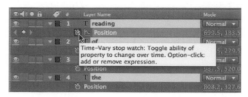

5. Click on the first stopwatch in layer 1.

   Because all of the layers are selected, all four stopwatches are enabled.

6. Now, let's a scale animation. Hold down the Shift key and press S to add the Scale property.

7. Add a Scale keyframe to layers 1–4 for 100%.

   Now that the starting point for each of the four words is set, you can animate the text flying to the left page.

8. Move the Current Time Indicator to 0;00;08;00.

9. Enter a Scale value of 500% for layers 1–4.

10. Select just the word the and drag it to the left page.

11. Repeat the scale and reposition for layers 2–4.

Use the figure for guidance. Don't worry about precise alignment, you'll fix that next.

Aligning Text

To improve the finished layout, we can use the Align panel. You'll find that After Effects shares a very similar text engine to other Adobe applications and offers precise alignment controls.

1. Click on layer 1 to select it.
2. Hold down the Shift key and click on layer 4 to select layers 1–4.
3. Choose Window > Align to show the Align panel.
4. Click the Align Left button.

   The selected text boxes are now aligned along their left edges. Now let's distribute the text evenly from top to bottom

5. Click the Vertical Center Distribution button in the Align panel.

   The text on layers 2 and 3 is evenly distributed between the top and bottom layers (1 and 4 respectively).

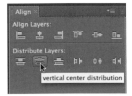

6. Invoke a RAM preview and watch your animation.

   It's looking pretty good. The text scales very large without pixelization because it is vector-based. Let's complete the animation by animating the leftover text on the right page

7. Choose File > Save to store your work so far.

Text Animation Presets

For the final text animation, you'll make all the remaining words on the right page rain down until they're off the screen.

1. Keep working with your current file or open the file **05_alignment_complete.aep** from the **Stages** folder in the Chapter_05 Project Files folder.

2. Move the Current Time Indicator to the final animation (0;00;05;00).

3. Unlock and select the layer called text (the layer that contains the bulk of the text).

4. Choose Animation > Browse Presets. After Effects launches Adobe Bridge.

5. In Bridge, double-click the **Text** folder. Then, double-click the **Animate Out** folder.

6. View animation presets by clicking their thumbnails.

● **NOTE:** Animation Presets in the Effects & Presets Panel

You'll find the same Animation Presets in the Effects & Presets panel. To apply an animation preset from the Effects & Presets panel, drag it from the panel to a layer in the Time-line or Composition panel. If you don't like the result, press Command+Z (Ctrl+Z) to undo and try another animation preset.

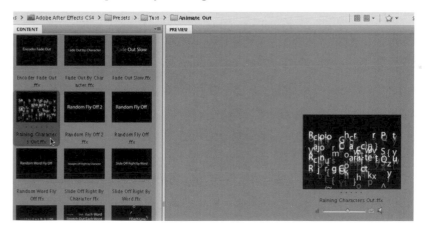

7. To apply a preset to the selected layer (starting at the position of the Current Time Indicator), double-click a thumbnail. Do this now with the Raining Character preset (part of the Animate Out category). Double-click it to apply it to the text layer.

8. Invoke a RAM preview to see your animation.

9. Choose File >Save to capture your work.

Exporting Text for Flash

Most of After Effects animation presets and text animation commands can be exported as vector-based SWF files (notably the Blur effect cannot). Text characters are added to the SWF as vectors once and then referenced on all subsequent frames, unless you choose Fill Over Stroke from the Fill And Stroke options menu; in that case, the characters are added as vectors on every frame.

If you have blending modes, motion blur, or certain pixel-based effects like drop shadows, these cannot be represented as vectors in the SWF file and are rasterized.

1. Select the composition containing just the text you want to export.

2. Choose File > Export > Adobe Flash Player (SWF). Enter a filename (making sure to include the .swf extension) and location. Click Save.

3. Specify options as appropriate.

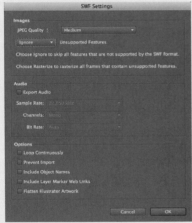

You can choose to ignore unsupported features so the SWF file includes only the After Effects features that can be converted into native SWF elements as vectors.

Alternatively, you can choose to rasterize frames that contain unsupported features and add them to the SWF file as JPEG-compressed bitmap images.

The following is a list of supported/unsupported features for the SWF format export:

- After Effects text layers are exported to SWF format as vector graphics.

- The following layer types and layer switches aren't supported: track mattes, 3D layers, 3D cameras, 3D lights, adjustment layers, shape layers, Preserve Transparency, Collapse Transformations, and motion blur.

- The Fill Over Stroke character option and the Blur animator property aren't supported, and only Normal blending mode is supported.

- Nested compositions aren't supported and are rasterized.

- All Path Text options are supported, except the following: Composite On Original, Fill Over Stroke, and Difference mode.

(continued on next page)

Exporting Text for Flash *(continued)*

4. Click OK.

After Effects generates a SWF and a report HTML file. The report also links to the SWF file so you can preview the output using the Flash Player plug-in.

5. Open the .htm file in a Web browser to view the SWF file and see which items in the composition are unsupported.

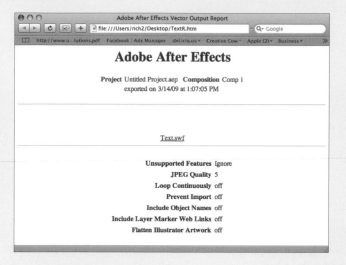

6. Click the hyperlink in the report to view the animation.

7. When finished, import the SWF into your Flash project or library as needed.

The animation presets are expertly animated, but in theory, you could create them on your own. They don't use any special tricks, just regular features of After Effects. To see how a preset was created (and to alter it if you want), select the layer you applied it to, and press UU (the U key pressed twice in rapid succession). After Effects reveals all animated and adjusted properties.

Final Touches

To pull everything together, you'll add a few finishing touches to your animation.

1. Continue in the same project or open **05_all_animations_complete.aep** from the **Stages** folder in the **Chapter_05 Project Files** folder.

2. Select layers 1–5 by Shift-clicking. Let's now place these layers into a nested composition so we can apply an effect to them all at once.

3. Choose Layer > Pre-compose. The Pre-Compose window opens.

4. Name the Pre-composition Text Animation. Click OK to create the pre-composition.

5. Select the pre-composed layer (the top layer), and then choose Effect > Distort > Corner Pin.

6. If necessary, zoom out so that you can see the whole comp and some space around it. Drag the four corner-pin controls so that the layer is skewed, making the text sit more realistically on the page.

● NOTE: What, No Controls?

If you don't see the controls, click the words Corner Pin in the Effect Controls panel. An effect's name must be selected for you to see its controls in the Composition panel.

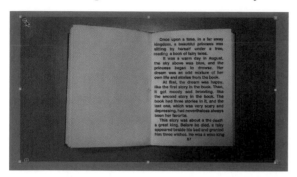

7. Choose Effect > Noise & Grain > Fractal Noise. In the Effect Controls panel, lower Opacity to 40%. This should give the text a more worn appearance, matching the age of the background layer.

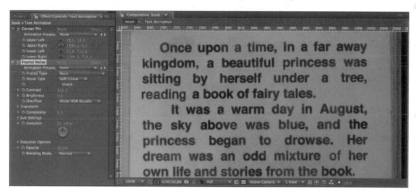

▲ TIP: Text on a Path

There's so much you can do with text in After Effects, we didn't have room for everything in the book. We had to leave out one of our favorite tricks: putting text on a path. Never fear! We cover it in a video demo in this chapter's Project Files folder. Watch it and explore the creative possibilities!

8. Preview the comp (or watch **05_COMPLETE.m4v**).

What's Next?

Congratulations! Shakespeare was a master of words, but he couldn't have held a candle to you. You're a master of characters! (Well, maybe Shakespeare was good with characters, too, but those were different sorts of characters.)

The coolest thing about After Effects text is that it's vector based, even after you animate it. What does vector based mean? Turn to the next chapter.

6 RASTER VS. VECTOR

People think of graphics as images: a company logo, a smiling child, a beautiful sunrise, and so on. Computers identify graphics as data stored in a file. That data can be stored in two main formats: raster (sometimes called bitmap or pixel-based) and vector.

Common raster formats include PSD, JPEG, PNG, MOV, GIF, and TIFF. Common vector formats are AI, EPS, SVG, and SWF. Confusing things a bit is that these formats sometimes "blend" and support both. For example, EPS and SWF are usually vector-based but can contain a mixture of raster and vector graphics.

Adobe Photoshop is often used to create and edit raster graphics, although it has some vector capabilities; Adobe Illustrator is often used to create vector graphics, although it has some raster capabilities. In addition, After Effects and Flash ship with simple vector drawing tools. Currently, neither ships with raster drawing tools, but both let you import raster graphics created in other applications.

Does this seem a little confusing? Why all the mixing? Well, most graphic projects usually contain both raster and vector images. This is due to a combination of stylistic and technical factors, all of which you'll explore in this chapter.

Raster Images

In a raster file, the computer stores a grid containing the color of each pixel. If you could peer inside the file and see it as a computer recognizes it, it would look something like the magnified area on the right in this image.

In other words, you'd see a mosaic—one in which the "stones" are really tiny.

The great thing about raster graphics is their high level of fidelity. They record exact information about the color of each pixel. This makes them perfect for storing photographs and highly detailed drawings or paintings. But raster graphics also pose a couple of problems: file size and scaling.

File Size

Raster graphics tend to be large. A 100 × 100 pixel graphic doesn't take up much space on your screen. It's about the size of a postage stamp (depending on your screen resolution). But it contains 10,000 pixels (100 times 100 equals 10,000). While that may not seem like much, it can start to add up.

A raster file stores the exact color of each of those pixels—that's 10,000 pieces of information. If you're working on a full-screen image for video and the image is 1280 × 720, it contains 921,600 pixels! That will take up a lot of space on your hard drive, and if it winds up in a Flash file on the Web, it will take a while for the viewer to download it when they want to see it.

Video files are made up of multiple raster images, shown one after the other. In America and some other countries, videos flip through 30 images every second. So, that's 30 times 921,600 pixels every second, or 27,648,000 pixels per second! No wonder uncompressed video files are so large. With compression (through the use of a video codec), this number is reduced quite a bit, but at the cost of losing some quality.

Scaling

Raster files don't scale up well, meaning that if you make them larger, they look pixelated or blurry. To understand why, think again of raster files as mosaics with very small stones. The stones are so small—pixel size—that unless you're standing close to them, you don't perceive them as stones. You perceive them as continuous streaks of color. But if you magnify the image, you magnify each stone. The stones become clearly visible, making the image look pixelated.

▲ **TIP: Animating Raster Images**

If you're animating a raster image, you want to think of its end position. If you want it to start small and get bigger (maybe to simulate zooming in on a detail), start with a really large image, scale it down for the first keyframe, and then scale it back up to its original size for the final keyframe.

The image on the left is the original. The image on the right has been blown up 200% and starts to show pixelation.

As a general rule, you can sometimes get away with doubling the size of a raster image. When each pixel is doubled, people generally still perceive the colors as continuous, although the image might lose a little sharpness. But once you scale it beyond doubling, pixelation becomes painfully obvious.

Vector Images

Vector graphics don't pose size and scaling problems. When a computer stores an image in vector format, it doesn't identify it as a grid of pixels. Instead, it stores it as a series of lines, curves, and fills.

▲ TIP: Animating Vector Images

With a vector image, start with any size and scale up as much as you want. If you're using After Effects, however, you'll need to click the continuously rasterize switch or the vector file will be pixelated.

If you could peer inside a vector graphic and see it as the computer recognizes it, you'd see something like this:

- Blue triangle in the upper-left corner.
- Below that a red rectangle.
- To the right of that a green circle.

Such graphics are often called "resolution independent," because you can scale them up or down without any loss of quality. If you scale them up 1,000 percent, the blue triangle (and all the other shapes) just gets bigger. You can take a postage-stamp-sized vector and scale it up to the size of a billboard without any loss of quality.

Also, because vectors don't store data about every pixel, they generally take up much less space than raster images. Imagine a 100 × 100 image of a black square over a white background. In a raster image, that's 10,000 pieces of data; each piece details whether a particular pixel is black or white. In the vector version, there are only three pieces of information: the color of the background, the relative location of the square, and the square's color.

But vector files can get large, too. Imagine trying to create an authentic vector reproduction of the Mona Lisa—one that would look just like a photo of the original painting. You'd have to make tiny shapes for every brush stroke. The shapes would be so small they'd be close to pixel size. If you get to the point where a vector file has as much (or more) information than there are pixels in the image, it will be as large (or larger) than a raster version.

The bottom line is that you should use raster images for photos and complex, nuanced drawings; use vectors for line art, technical illustrations, logos, text, and so on.

Raster and Vector Animation in After Effects

Enough theory! Let's play with rasters and vectors in After Effects and Flash.

1. From the book's DVD, copy the **Chapter_06 Project Files** folder to your hard drive. Then open the file **01_egg.aep** in After Effects. Open the composition called Start. This is a news graphic about the price of eggs. You'll zoom in on a fried egg while some text flies in from the right. The text is already animated, so you'll work on the zoom.

2. With the Current Time Indicator at the start of the Timeline, select the egg layer and reveal its scale property by pressing S. turn on the stopwatch for the egg's Scale property.

3. Move the Current Time Indicator to 5 seconds.

4. Scale the egg layer up to 1,000 percent and then preview the composition.

The egg looks fuzzy at 1,000 percent. This is After Effects' way of interpreting the pixelation you get when you scale up a raster image. The program does its best to smooth the colors, but the result looks pretty rough.

● **NOTE: Scaled for Emphasis**

The egg layers have already been scaled to help emphasize the pixelation.

5. Select the egg layer in the Timeline.

6. Select the composition vector eggs in the Project panel.

   This composition contains egg artwork created using vector shape layers in After Effects. The original vector egg art is the same size as the raster version, but since it's vector it should look crisp when scaled to 1,000 percent.

7. Hold down the Option (Alt) key, drag the composition vector eggs from the Project panel, and drop it onto the egg layer in the Timeline.

   Option-dragging (Alt-dragging) footage from the Project panel to a selected layer on the Timeline replaces that layer with the footage from the Project panel. But you must select the layer before Option-dragging (Alt-dragging).

8. Invoke a RAM Preview to preview the composition.

The egg still looks fuzzy, but why? It's vector so it should look crisp at any scale. The problem is that After Effects rasterizes vector images. Rasterizing is the process of turning a vector graphic into a raster graphic. In other words, After Effects "scans" the vector and rerecords it as pixel-by-pixel data. Let's fix this.

9. Reveal the Switches panel if necessary by clicking the Toggle Switches/Modes button until you see the Switches icons in the Timeline.

● **NOTE: Continually Rasterize Off**

You may want to temporarily deselect Continually Rasterize while you're working so that previews will be quicker.

10. Select the Continually Rasterize switch for the egg layer. This forces After Effects to rerasterize the graphic on every frame. The upside of this is that the graphic remains crisp as it scales. The downside is that rasterizing demands computing processing power,

adding to render time. Still, smooth scaling is one of the chief advantages of vector files, so it's often worth accepting the increase in render time.

11. Preview the composition and note the crispy eggs. Too bad there's no bacon!

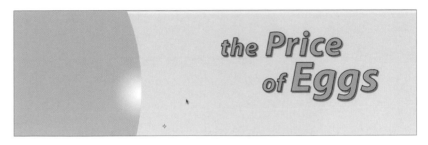

Raster Animation in Flash

Now you'll look at a similar animation in Flash. Flash can also work with raster and vector graphics. In the following example, you'll use raster eggs. You'll keep them looking crisp by working with a large file. This will significantly add to the file size. It's a worthwhile trade-off, because you get a photo-realistic look.

1. Open **02_egg.fla** in Flash and move the playhead to the start of the Timeline..

2. Select the egg layer in the Timeline. Then drag the egg movie clip from the Library to the Stage.

3. Using the Free Transform tool (Q), scale the egg image down to its starting size. Zoom out if you can't see the transform handles.

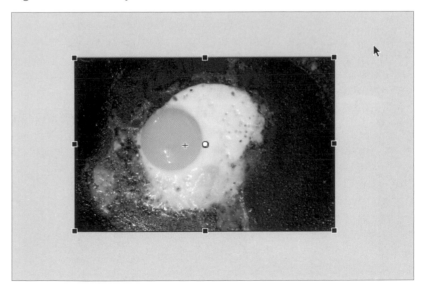

4. Right-click the image and choose Create Motion Tween.

5. In the final frame, free transform the egg to a larger size.

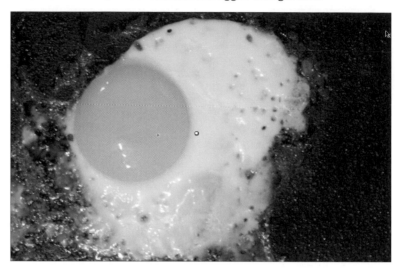

6. Make the egg layer persist for as long as the text layer: In the Timeline, drag the egg layer's final frame to frame 60. Then right-click frame 95 on the egg layer and choose Insert Frame. Since you're just scaling it back up toward its original size, it doesn't pixelate.

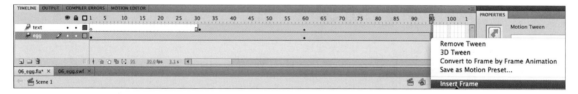

7. Preview the movie. As you do, you may notice some odd flickering as the image scales. Flash sometimes has trouble animating raster images cleanly. One solution (that often helps but doesn't completely solve the problem) is to turn on bitmap smoothing.

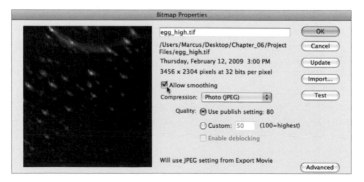

8. In the Library, right-click the original image (**egg_high.tif**) in the sources folder, and select the Properties option.

9. In the Bitmap Properties dialog, select the Allow smoothing option. Then preview the movie again.

Vector Drawing Tools in Flash

Now that you've had more time to think about it, you might regret using a raster egg. Sure, it's yummy looking, but it makes the SWF file too large.

You want it to load quickly, so it's best to use a vector egg instead. You could create it in Adobe Illustrator, but an egg isn't the most complex image in the world. Flash has perfectly acceptable built-in vector drawing capabilities. Since you'll be animating the egg in Flash, you might as well draw it in Flash.

Working with the Pencil Tool

The Pencil tool has three modes: Straighten, Smooth, and Ink. Each has its uses, and you should become familiar with each mode's strengths.

- **Straighten.** If you draw while using Straighten mode, Flash attempts to straighten all your lines. For instance, you can draw a rough triangle and Flash will straighten it into a perfect triangle.

- **Smooth.** Smooth mode takes some of the shakiness out of hand-drawn lines, making them more streamlined.

- **Ink.** Ink mode doesn't make any changes to your lines, so it's the choice you'll want to make if you want Flash to be completely faithful to whatever you do with the Pencil tool.

Let's give drawing a try and create an egg.

1. Open **03_vector_egg.fla** from the **Chapter_06 Project Files** folder.

2. At the bottom of the Library, click the New Symbol button. Name the symbol egg and make it a Movie Clip.

   Let's start with the white part of the egg: You'll draw an outline and then fill it with white.

3. Select the Pencil tool from the toolbar, then set the Pencil mode to Smooth.

> ▲ **TIP: Brush vs. Pencil**
>
> You can use the Brush tool in place of the Pencil tool. The most noticeable difference between the two tools is that the Pencil tool draws using the stroke color, whereas the Brush tool draws using the fill color.

▲ TIP: A Better
Brush

Here, we're using the
Pencil tool, because
it's simple and serves
our purpose. How-
ever, you should take
the time to check out
Flash's Brush tool,
especially if you own
a pressure-sensitive
table. The Brush
tool's most stunning
feature is only avail-
able to Flash users
who have pressure-
sensitive tablets. If
you select the Brush
tool and draw with
it using a tablet, the
stroke's width varies
as you put more or
less pressure on your
tablet.

4. Select a stroke color for the Pencil tool by clicking the stroke color chip. It doesn't matter what color, because you're going to delete the stroke shortly.

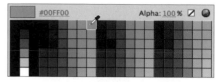

5. Make sure the Object Drawing icon (at the bottom of the Tools panel) is toggled off. Then draw a large, blobby shape for the egg white. Make sure it's a closed shape—the beginning and end of the line should meet.

Object Drawing

When you select any of Flash's drawing tools (the Pen tool, the Pencil tool, the Brush tool, and the shape tools), an innocent-looking icon appears at the bottom of the Tools panel. This is the Object Drawing icon. When it's selected, the drawing tools behave differently than when it's not selected.

In Flash, fills and strokes are separate objects. For instance, you can draw a circle, select the fill, and drag it away from the stroke. (If you want to select both the fill and the stroke, just marquee-select them.) We've come to enjoy having separate control over fills and strokes, but people coming from Illustrator (or pretty much any other drawing program) are understandably baffled. They often ask: Hey, I dragged my fill, so why did my stroke stay behind?

To make fills and strokes behave as single objects (so if you drag the fill, the stroke moves with it—and vice versa), enable Object Drawing before creating a shape.

Object Drawing is less profound than it seems. You can group any fill and stroke together, even if they were created with Object Drawing turned off, by marquee-selecting them and then choos-

ing Modify > Group. So all Object Drawing mode really does is automatically group the fill and stroke immediately after you draw them. This means that if you create a shape with Object Drawing mode enabled and then change your mind and want separate control over the fill and stroke, you can just select the shape and choose Modify > Ungroup.

6. Select the Paint Bucket tool. From the Fill swatches, choose white.

7. Click inside the blobby outline to fill it with white. If it doesn't fill, select the Close large gaps option from the Gap Size property.

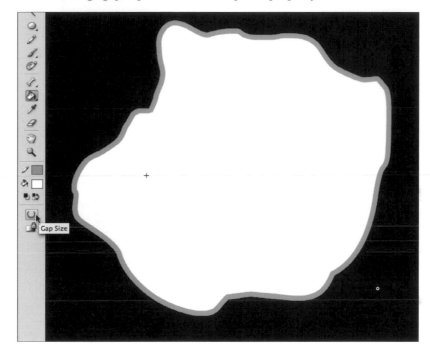

▲ **TIP: Reshaping with the Selection Tool**

If you deselect the shape in step 7 (if it was selected), switch to the Selection tool (the black arrow), and point to the stroke, you'll see a small curve appear next to the cursor. At this point you can drag to reshape the stroke. You can use the Selection tool this way to reshape vector drawings in Flash.

▲ **TIP: Reshaping with the Subselection Tool**

You can also reshape vector drawings with the Subselection Tool (the white arrow), which allows you to manipulate individual vector control points, as you can in Illustrator, Photoshop, and After Effects.

Sometimes Flash won't fill an area, even if it looks closed. Adjusting Gap Size can usually fix this problem.

8. Switch to the Selection Tool or press V. Then double-click the stroke to select it and press the Backspace (Delete) key to delete it.

9. Select the egg-white shape and repeatedly click the Smooth button on the Tools panel until you like the look. If necessary, edit the shape even more with the Selection tool or Subselection tool as explained in the corresponding Tips.

● **NOTE: Smooth Option**

The Smooth option is available for any vector shape in Flash.

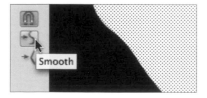

Adding a Filter

To make the egg white look a bit more realistic, you'll add a bevel filter to it. However, notice that if you select it, no filter options are available in the Project panel. This is because you can only add filters to instances of symbols. The egg white is not an instance of a symbol; it's just a vector shape.

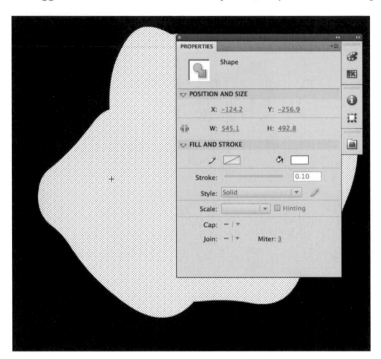

But you started the egg-white drawing by creating a new symbol in the Library! If it's in the Library, surely it's a symbol.

To deal with this confusion, let's once again think about Wonder Woman and her invisible plane (see Chapter 2, "Flash Essentials for the After Effects User"): Let's say there's some sort of "effect" you want to apply to the plane, maybe putting a decal on it that says "Wonder Woman's Amazing Invisible Airplane." The key point here is that you can't add the decal to the plane while you're *inside* the plane with Wonder Woman. You can only do it from the outside.

The outside of our egg symbol is Scene 1. But you're not looking at Scene 1 right now. You're looking at the egg symbol. You are effectively inside the egg symbol. You can only add a filter to it from the outside, just as you can only add a decal to Wonder Woman's plane from the outside. You could return to Scene 1, drag an instance of egg from the Library to the Stage, and then add a filter to that instance (from outside it).

The problem with doing that is that the filter will then be added to the yolk, too. You haven't drawn the yolk yet, but if you add it inside the egg symbol and then from the outside add a bevel to the symbol, you'll be adding a bevel to the entire symbol, white and yolk. But you just want to add the bevel to the white.

This is similar to what happens in After Effects if you add a blur effect to a pre-comp. You'll blur the entire pre-comp. If the pre-comp has three layers internally and you just want to blur the top one, you must do that from inside the pre-comp.

So you need to bevel just the white from inside the egg symbol. Keep in mind that from within the symbol the white is just a vector shape, and you can't add a bevel filter to a shape. The solution is to turn the white into its own symbol. The white will then be a nested symbol inside the egg symbol.

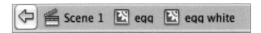

1. Select the white shape and choose Modify > Convert to Symbol. Name the symbol egg white and make it a Movie Clip. Click OK.

2. In the Properties panel, click the Add Filter button and select Bevel. Set the Bevel properties as follows: Blur X: 15 px; Blur Y: 15 px; Strength 90%; Quality: high; Shadow: light gray; Highlight: white; Angle: 45 degrees; Distance: 8 px; Knockout: deselected; Type: Inner.

Flash Filters

One of the coolest subtle features of Flash is filters. Sure, they're the same sort of effects you see everywhere—bevels, drop shadows, blurs, and so on—but the extra coolness comes from the fact that you can apply Flash filters to vector shapes and those shapes will remain vectors. This is because the filters are built into the Flash Player engine. Filters are never "baked in" to graphics. They get reapplied on the fly every time your movie plays. The upshot is that you get raster-like filters with vector-like footprints (e.g., small file size).

▲ TIP: Finding the Oval Tool

If you can't see the Oval Tool on the Tools panel, it may be hidden. It shares real-estate space with the Rectangle tool and the other Shape tools. Hold down your mouse button while hovering over whatever Shape tool you see (by default, it's the Rectangle tool), and you'll see options for choosing other Shape tools appear, including the Oval tool.

▲ TIP: Free Transform

To resize the oval, press Q to switch to the Free Transform tool. When you're finished resizing, press V to switch back to the Selection tool.

▲ TIP: Don't Click the Color Chip

When adding a gradient fill in the Color panel, click the paint bucket icon to indicate that you want to add a fill, not a stroke. Make sure you click the icon, not the color-selector chip to its right.

3. Name the layer with the egg-white shape on it "white." Create a new layer for the yolk.

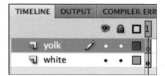

4. Select the Oval tool, set the stroke color to none, and set the fill color to yellow.

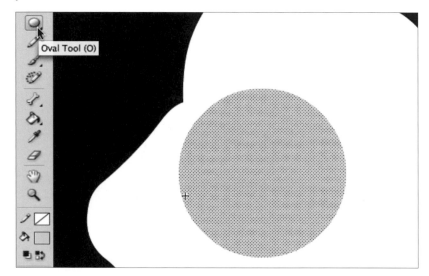

5. While holding down the Shift key (which constrains the oval to a perfect circle), drag to draw the yolk. If necessary, move the yolk into place with the Selection tool.

6. With the yolk selected, choose Window > Color. In the Color panel, select the Fill. Change the Fill type to Radial.

7. Double-click the gradient's start color chip and choose white. Then double-click the gradient's end color chip and choose yellow.

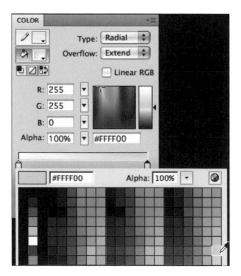

8. Select the Gradient Transform tool. With the yolk selected, drag the center of the gradient to the yolk's upper-left side. Switch back to the Selection tool.

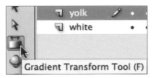

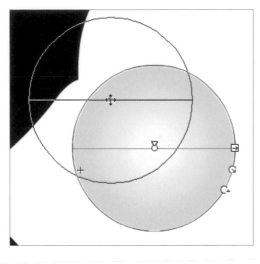

● NOTE: **Finding the Gradient Transform Tool**

The Gradient Transform tool is grouped with the Free Transform tool. You may need to hold your mouse button down, while hovering over the Free Transform tool to gain access to the Gradient Transform tool.

9. Return to Scene 1, drag an instance of the egg symbol to the egg layer, and tween it so it starts small and grows bigger over time. Select the egg, right-click it, and choose Create Motion Tween. Use the Free Transform tool to scale down the egg in its start keyframe. Scale it up on its end keyframe.

Shape Interactions in Flash

If you're used to drawing shapes in other programs, you may be surprised at how Flash shapes interact with each other when they overlap. To test this feature (which seems like a bug to some people), follow these steps:

1. Start a new Flash (ActionScript 3.0) file.

2. Select the Oval tool, and make sure you're not drawing in Object Drawing mode. For the stroke, choose none. For the fill, choose red.

3. Draw a circle somewhere on the Stage.

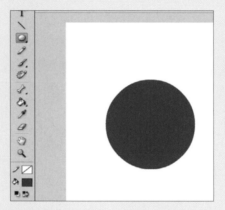

4. Using all the same settings, draw another circle overlapping the first one.

5. Switch to the Selection tool, and deselect the second circle by clicking the Stage background. Now select the first circle and drag it to a new position.

As you can see, the two circles are fused together. They are not grouped. They can't be ungrouped. They are inseparable parts of the same shape.

This only works because the circles were the same color. The stroke was turned off to avoid introducing another color into the mix.

6. Select the Oval tool again, and draw a third circle somewhere else on the Stage, not overlapping the first two. Keeping the Oval tool selected and the stroke color set to none, change the fill color to green.

7. Draw a forth circle overlapping the third one—the one you just drew.

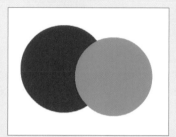

8. With the Selection tool, deselect the green circle by clicking the Stage. Then reselect the green circle and drag it away from its companion.

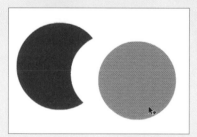

As you can see, it cut into the other circle, turning it into a waning moon. When shapes overlap, they fuse together if they're the same color; if they're different colors, the second shape cuts into the first shape. Rather than seeing this as a problem, we urge you to get creative with it. You can use this feature to quickly create complex vector shapes from simple ones.

However, if you dislike the feature, just choose Modify > Group after creating a shape. The fusing/cutting feature won't work on grouped shapes (which means it also won't work if you're using Object Drawing mode, because that mode automatically groups shapes). Fusing/cutting also doesn't work with shapes that have been converted to Library symbols or shapes that are on different layers from each other.

Vector Drawing in After Effects

Flash and After Effects share many similar vector-drawing tools: tools that create basic shapes and a Pen tool. After Effects has an additional trick up its sleeve: RotoBezier. If you enable the RotoBezier option, After Effects' Pen tool loses some of its trickiness, becoming a more user-friendly tool for novice vector artists.

1. From the **Chapter_06 Project Files** folder, open the file **04_vector_egg.aep** in After Effects. Double-click the egg comp in the Project panel. It's empty.

2. Select the Pen tool and click the Tool Creates Shape icon.

3. Set the Fill color to white and the Stroke width to 0 px. Select the RotoBezier option.

Is RotoBezier Right for You?

RotoBezier allows you to use the Pen tool in an intuitive way that is unlike a traditional Bezier Pen tool, which many people find difficult to use.

If you'd like to learn how to use the Pen in the more traditional way, your best bet is to read a good book about Adobe Illustrator, such as *Adobe Illustrator CS4 Classroom in a Book* (Peachpit, 2008). Even if you're not an Illustrator user, you will learn everything you need to know about vector-graphic drawing from such a book, because Adobe's vector tools, which were developed originally for Illustrator, work the same way in other Adobe programs. In other words, aside from nontraditional features like RotoBezier, the Pen works the same way in Illustrator, Photoshop, After Effects, and Flash.

4. With the Pen tool—even when it's set to RotoBezier mode—you don't click and drag. Just click to lay down a point, move to another spot on the screen, click again, move to a third spot, click again, and so on. On your third click, the lines will automatically turn to curves. Your goal is to make a blobby, egg-like shape, so you don't have to be too careful where you click. To complete the blob, click the initial point a second time, closing the shape.

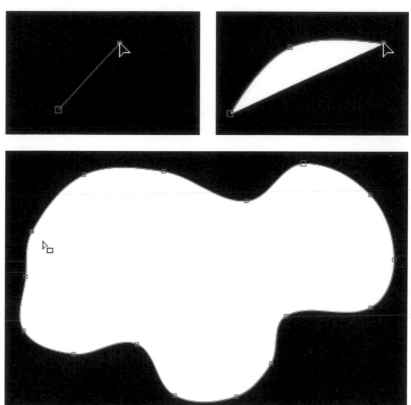

5. If you want to edit the blob, switch to the Selection tool. Click the edge of the blob if necessary to gain access to the vector control points, and drag the points around to move them.

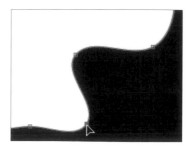

6. With the blob selected, choose Effect > Perspective > Bevel Alpha. Set Edge Thickness to 26.

7. Choose Effect > Blur and Sharpen > Fast Blur and set Blurriness to 20.

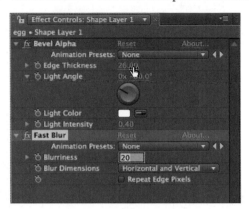

▲ TIP: Zoom To See

You may need to zoom out in order to see the Ramp controls in the Composition panel.

▲ TIP: Another Way To Add A Gradient

Instead of using the Ramp Effect, you can select the yolk in the Composition panel, and then click the Fill option on the Tools panel. The Fill Options dialog will appear, allowing you to choose a linear or radial gradient. You can then adjust the gradient colors by clicking the fill-color chip on the Tools panel. Move the center of the gradient by switching to the Selection tool and dragging in the Composition panel.

8. Deselect the white layer by choosing Edit > Deselect All. If you skip this step, some of the following steps, which are meant to apply to the yolk, will accidentally be applied to the white instead.

9. Select the Ellipse tool, set the Fill color to yellow and the Stroke width to 0 px. Make sure the Tool Creates Shape icon is selected.

10. Hold down the Shift key to constrain the ellipse to a perfect circle, and drag to create the yolk. Position the yolk so it's in place on top of the white.

11. With the yolk selected, choose Effect > Generate > Ramp. Set the Start Color to white, the End Color to yellow, and the Ramp Shape to Radial Ramp. Adjust the Start of Ramp until you can see the white highlight inside the yolk. Do the same for the End of Ramp.

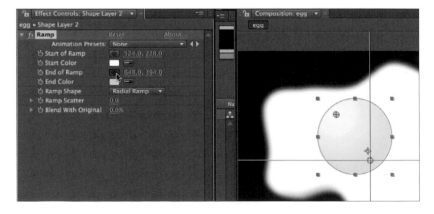

12. Switch to the Final composition and drag your egg comp inside it, so that it's nested inside Final as the bottom layer.

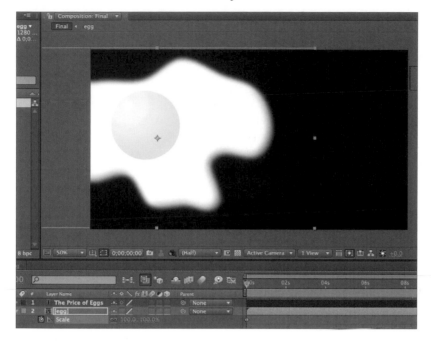

▲ **TIP:** Don't Remember How To Scale?

See page 137 in this chapter for a recap on scaling.

13. Animate the egg pre-comp so that it starts small and ends up large.

14. Turn on the Continually Rasterize switch for the egg layer. Then preview the composition.

Primitive Shapes

Both Flash and After Effects ship with tools that allow you to easily draw common shapes. Flash has a Rectangle tool, an Oval tool, and a polygon/star maker called the Polystar tool. After Effects has a Rectangle tool, a Rounded Rectangle tool, an Ellipse tool, a Polygon tool, and a Star tool. Here are some tips that will help you use these tools effectively.

In both applications:

- Holding down the Shift key while using a shape tool constrains the proportions of the tool, causing Rectangle tools to draw perfect squares and Oval/Ellipse tools to draw perfect circles.
- Holding down the Option (Alt) key in Flash and the Command (Ctrl) key in After Effects draws shapes out from their centers rather than from their corners.

In After Effects:

- Holding down the spacebar while drawing allows you to move a shape while you're drawing it.
- To adjust the corners of a rounded-corner rectangle, click the disclosure triangle to open the shape layer in the Timeline, and then choose Contents > Rectangle [number] > Rectangle Path [number] > Roundness. In general, you'll find many options for editing (or animating) After Effects' shapes in their Timeline properties.
- To adjust the number of sides of a polygon or spikes on a star, click the disclosure triangle to open the shape layer, and then choose Contents Polystar [number] > Polystar Path [number] > Points.
- If you draw a new shape while an old shape layer is selected, the new shape will be part of the old layer. If you want a new shape to appear as its own layer, deselect any selected shape layers before drawing.

In Flash:

- Flash has two versions of its Oval and Rectangle tools: the normal ones and the "primitive ones." Confusingly, the primitive ones give you *more* options on the Properties panel after you've drawn the shape. For instance, after using the Oval Primitive tool, you can adjust the Start Angle or End Angle slider to open the oval, like a Pac-Man. The Inner Radius slider places a hole in the middle of the oval, making it look like a donut. The slider at the bottom of the Rectangle properties allows you to round its corners. (Similarly, After Effects shapes are either Bezier or Parametric, which are like Flash primitives.)

Primitive Shapes *(continued)*

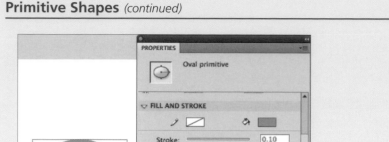

- While you're drawing a rectangle (primitive or normal), repeatedly pressing the up arrow key will round its corners; repeatedly pressing the down arrow key will unround them.

- Selecting the Polystar tool and then clicking the Options button on the Properties panel will open a Tool Settings dialog that lets you choose between a polygon and a star and the number of sides/points.

Exporting from After Effects as an XFL File

You can create a SWF file in After Effects and then import that SWF into Flash. The limitation of this technique is that SWFs are a rendered format, which means they're not editable. So if you realize you need to make a change to a SWF file after importing your SWF into Flash, you'll have to go back to your original AEP file, make the change, and then export another SWF.

Also, keep in mind that many After Effects' features do not export well into the SWF format, including After Effects' shape layers. The only way to export them is to rasterize them, which will lead to an unfortunate increase in file size.

Perhaps a better workflow is to export an XFL file from After Effects. XFLs can be imported into Flash as FLA files—that's right: editable FLAs! Flash will make a valiant effort to recreate your After Effects Timeline as a Flash Timeline, and you can then edit it in Flash.

1. Open **05_vector_egg_complete.aep** from the **Chapter_06 Project Files** folder, and make sure you're working in the Final comp.

2. Choose File > Export > Adobe Flash Professional (XFL). In the Adobe Flash Professional (XFL) Settings dialog, click OK.

   Some After Effects' effects won't translate easily to Flash. If you don't choose the Ignore option, After Effects will render these features as FLV videos.

3. In the Export As Adobe Flash Professional (XFL) dialog, name the file eggs.xfl and save it on your desktop. It may take a while for the export to complete, but that's okay, you wanted to check your email anyway.

4. After the export is complete, switch to Flash and choose File > Open. Select the eggs.xfl file on your desktop to open it in Flash.

5. Preview the movie by pressing Command+ Return (Ctrl+ Enter).

▲ **TIP: Reset To Defaults**

If you're having trouble getting the XFL export to work, click the Reset to Defaults button in the Adobe Flash Professional (XFL) Settings dialog. Also, make sure the Rasterize to option is selected.

Limitations of XFL

At the time of this writing, here is the official word on XFL from Adobe After Effects CS4 Community Help, which you can view by choosing Help > After Effects Help:

"After Effects relies on the Adobe Media Encoder to create FLV files. The Adobe Media Encoder can't create FLV files with pixel dimensions greater than 1920 × 1080.

When you export a composition to the XFL format from a 32-bpc project, the rendering of colors with values under 0 and over 1 does not produce results that preserve the appearance of the composition in After Effects. You should only work in an 8-bpc or 16-bpc project when creating a composition that you intend to export to Flash Professional in XFL format.

Audio is not exported to the XFL file."

Importing a SWF into After Effects

Let's end this chapter with something really simple: importing a SWF into After Effects.

1. Open **06_import_swf.aep** from the **Chapter_06 Project Files** folder, and make sure you're working in the Final comp.

2. Choose File > Import > File. Select the file **06_vector_egg.swf** in the **Sources** folder in the **Chapter_06 Project Files** folder and import it.

3. If necessary, move the Current Time Indicator to the beginning of the Timeline. Then drag **06_vector_egg.swf** from the Project panel into the comp.

The file **06_vector_egg.swf** had a black background in Flash, but it came into After Effects with a transparent background. The red you see is the background color of the comp Final.

Adobe refers to this as a feature, not a bug. It allows you to easily composite Flash elements on top of other graphics. If you want a black rectangle to appear behind the egg, you'll have to actually put a rectangle behind it (in After Effects or Flash).

4. If you scale up the SWF layer, it may become pixelated, even though it's a vector, so enable the Continually Rasterize switch.

What's Next?

If you found this chapter overly technical and short of artistic merit (or if you just don't like eggs), you're in for a treat. In the next chapter you'll learn how to give After Effects footage that ever-popular cartoon look. If you meet any eggs in that chapter, they'll probably be wearing top hats and they'll be googly-eyed!

7 "TOONING" FOOTAGE WITH THE CREATIVE SUITE

There are many reasons to process video footage to look more like animation. Some simply want to stylize their footage for artistic effect. Others want to simplify the footage so it will compress to a smaller size for use in a Flash project. Additionally, video shapes can be converted into vector outlines for even more options. In this chapter, you'll explore three very different techniques. Shooting approaches as well as post-production techniques will be discussed. Which method you choose will vary depending on your source footage and the desired output.

The Cartoon Effect in After Effects

The Cartoon effect is a new addition to After Effects CS4. It allows for easy conversion of video footage to a more cel animation-like appearance. The Cartoon effect works by simplifying the image to reduce the amount of detail in the frame; smoothing the shading and colors of an image does this. The effect also offers the ability to detect edges within the frame and add strokes.

The overall result of the Cartoon effect is that it decreases contrast in areas with low contrast while increasing contrast in areas with high contrast. When used correctly, the resulting footage takes on the look of a sketch or cartoon. You can choose this effect to simplify footage for Flash compression, for stylistic reasons, or to hide quality issues in poor footage.

The image on the right has been processed with the Cartoon effect in After Effects. The circles show enlarged details of the footage. Footage treated in this manner is still raster-based, but will compress further due to its simplified appearance.

The Details

Many motion graphic artists have their own workflow for creating cartoon-style effects, but the new Cartoon effect has some great advantages. Because the Cartoon effect utilizes temporal coherence, you will see less "jumping" between frames of video. The Cartoon effect tries to keep similar results across multiple frames, which produces a much smoother animation. The effect also supports work in 8-, 16-, or 32-bits per channel (the higher bit rates produce less banding in the color).

The Cartoon effect processes footage in three stages:

1. The image is smoothed using a gentle blurring. This softening is controlled using the Detail Radius and Detail Threshold properties.

2. The effect detects the edges of the footage and applies a stroke. This process is similar to the Find Edges effect. To control the stroke, use the Edge and Advanced property groups. You can adjust how edges are determined as well as how the strokes are drawn on the footage.

Shooting Advice

The Cartoon effect looks for areas with contrast, so you should avoid flat lighting. Your footage should also have proper exposure. Both underexposed and overexposed footage lack proper contrast. The simple solution is to shoot with proper exposure, but a few dramatic shadows also go a long way toward making footage look good.

3. The image is posterized. The effect reduces the amount of variations in the luminance and color of the image. To control this process, modify properties in the Fill group.

The Effect in Action

Let's explore the effect by putting it into action. In this lesson, you'll use some footage shot in challenging lighting conditions. The goal is to stylize the footage with the Cartoon effect as well as convert it to a Flash Video file for use in Adobe Flash.

1. Copy the **Chapter_07 Project Files** folder from the DVD to a local hard drive.

2. Open the file **Chapter_07.aep** from the **Chapter_07 Project Files** folder. This project file contains all the elements you will use in this chapter.

3. Click the After Effects composition **01_Toon_Start** to open the starting composition. This comp contains four shots that can be stylized with the Cartoon effect.

Pre-processing footage with color correction

Recall in the sidebar "Shooting Advice" that we discussed the importance of proper exposure. If the white and black points of your footage are not properly set, the Cartoon filter produces subpar results. Fortunately, this is an easy fix with the Levels effect.

1. Select all the video tracks in the composition 01_Toon_Start. Click track 1 in the Timeline. Then hold down the Shift key and click track 4.

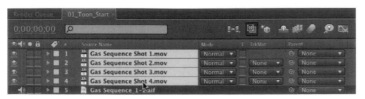

2. Choose Effect > Color Correction > Levels. The Levels effect is applied to each shot. Press E to reveal the applied effects for each layer.

3. Select just the first track named Gas Sequence Shot 1.mov. In the Effect Controls panel, choose the Levels effect.

4. Adjust the Input White and Input Black sliders to modify the white and black portions of the image. For this footage we suggest leaving the Input Black slider set to 0.0 and adjusting the Input White slider to 223.0. This makes the whites brighter in the image.

● NOTE: Seeing the Whole Histogram

You may want to resize the Effect Controls panel to see the entire histogram for the Levels effect.

5. Adjust the middle Gamma slider to make the shot brighter. For this footage set the Gamma to 1.41.

6. Using similar parameters, adjust the remaining shots so the Black, White, and Gamma points produce proper exposure and contrast. Click each layer one at a time in the Timeline and adjust the Levels effect properties so the blacks and whites pop and the midtones look evenly exposed.

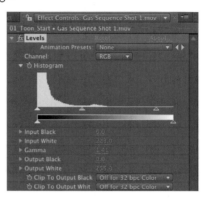

Creating the fill

To get the most out of the Cartoon effect, it is best to adjust the fill and stroke for the effect independently. This allows for precise focus and better control of the effect's properties.

1. Select all the footage layers in the Timeline and choose Effect > Stylize > Cartoon.

2. Click the first footage layer named Gas Sequence Shot 1.mov to adjust its properties in the Effect Controls panel during the next few steps.

3. Move the Current Time Indicator to 0;00;00;20.

4. In the Effect Controls panel, set the Render property to Fill Only to precisely control the color aspects of the footage.

5. Adjust the Detail Radius slider to smooth the footage. Higher values will remove more details from the image before the operation tries to find edges. Decreasing the Detail Radius results in a clear image, whereas increasing the Detail Radius makes the image blurrier. For this footage layer try a value of 20.0.

6. The Detail Threshold property controls how the Cartoon effect selectively blurs an image. The Detail Threshold value determines which areas contain features to preserve and which to blur. A higher Detail Threshold value causes a more simplistic cartoon-like result with fewer details preserved. For this footage layer try a value of 15.0.

7. The footage is posterized according to the settings of the next two sliders in the Cartoon effect. Higher Shading Smoothness values produce a gentler posterization of the image (which is generally more attractive). Adjust the number of steps to increase the amount of shading used. Do not use a high value unless the footage is very complex. For this footage leave the Shading Steps set to 8.0 and adjust Shading Smoothness to 80.0.

8. Adjust the remaining three shots as desired using similar values.

Creating the stroke

Now that the fill is looking good, you can move on to the stroke. The Cartoon effect detects the edges of the image before drawing the stroke. Depending on how dark the footage is, you may need to use the Levels effect to tweak the exposure.

1. Click on the Cartoon effect applied to the first footage layer named Gas Sequence Shot 1.mov to adjust its properties in the Effect Controls panel.

2. Move the Current Time Indicator to 0;00;03;20.

3. Choose Edges from the Render property pop-up menu in the Effect Controls panel. You can now use the Edge properties to adjust what is considered an edge and how the stroke applied to an edge is drawn.

The effect is detecting too many edges, creating a busy stroke.

▲ **TIP: Keyframing the Cartoon Effect**

Like all effects, the properties of the Cartoon effect can be adjusted over time. This works well if you have a lot of changes in the footage (such as a zoom from a tight shot to a wide shot). If there is little change in the footage, avoid keyframing properties because they will create a more jerky conversion between frames.

4. Decrease the Threshold to 1.20 to cause fewer areas to be defined as an edge. Set the Width property to 5.0 to create a thicker stroke. By using a thicker stroke, you can also clean up areas with too much detail. Set the Softness value to 70.0 to create a softer transition between the edge's stroke and the surrounding colors.

5. Click the disclosure triangle next to the Advanced properties at the bottom of the Effect Controls panel to gain greater control over edges and performance.

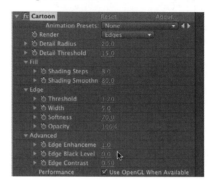

6. Use the Edge Enhancement slider to sharpen the edges of the stroke. Using a negative value spreads the stroke wider, whereas a positive value tightens it. For this footage use a value of -25.0.

7. You can use the Edge Black Level adjustment to modify how much black is used in the stroke. Use only small values to change the footage gently. For this footage try a value of 0.3 for a slight boost.

8. The Edge Contrast property can add more gray to the image, which can be used to increase the impact of the stroke. For this footage try a value of 0.45.

9. Choose Fill & Edges from the Render property pop-up menu in the Effect Controls panel to see the composite effect.

10. Adjust the Cartoon effect for the other three footage layers to taste using similar values.

Preview and Create an FLV File

Now that the footage is processed, you can watch your work, and then export it for use in Flash. The goal here is to check the animation, and then save it for use outside of After Effects.

1. In the Preview panel set Resolution to Full and click the RAM Preview button to load the composition preview. If you don't have enough RAM to preview the entire animation, that's okay. You can always preview portions using the work area settings.

2. When either the RAM preview completes or you run out of available RAM, the preview will start to play. You can press the spacebar at any time to start the RAM preview earlier. If you're satisfied with the animation, choose Composition > Add to Render Queue. The composition is queued with the default settings applied.

3. In the Render Queue panel click Best Settings to open the Render Settings window.

▲ **TIP: The GPU Accelerator**

The Cartoon effect is greatly impacted by the speed of your Graphics Processing Unit (aka your video card). Many high-end pro machines come with 256 or 512 MB graphics cards: These really do make a difference. The more Video RAM you have, the more responsive the effect is to work with (and the faster it renders). To access OpenGL acceleration, adjust the performance properties in the Advanced section of the effect.

It's very important to see the animation at full quality to accurately judge the effect.

4. Because the output of Flash Video is intended for Web use, you can specify a lower frame rate than the original footage. Select Use this frame rate and set its value to 15.

5. To ensure that the entire animation renders, set the Time Span to Length of Comp. Click OK to store the Render Settings.

6. In the Render Queue panel click Lossless to open the Output Module Settings panel. Change Format to FLV. Click OK.

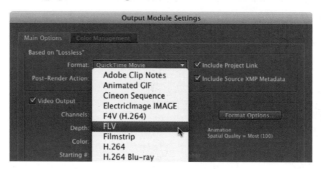

7. The video used in this project was shot using a DVCPRO-HD camera with non-square pixels. Therefore, the pixels must be converted to a square aspect ratio for Web use. Select the Stretch check box.

8. The original footage is normally interpreted as 1280 × 720. To shrink it for the Web, reduce it by 50%. Deselect the Lock Aspect Ratio check box and stretch the image to 640 × 360 using a Stretch Quality of High.

9. Select the Audio Output check box to include the sound of the gas station.

10. While digital video generally uses a Sample Rate of 48.00 kHz, this can cause audio issues with Flash. Set the Sample Rate to 44.100 kHz using the first drop-down menu.

11. Change the channels from Stereo to Mono to reduce the size of the final file. Then click OK to store the Output Module settings.

12. Click the filename next to Output To and specify the **Chapter_07 Project Files** folder that you copied at the start of the lesson. Save your project by choosing File > Save.

13. Click the Render button if you'd like to process the file for use in Flash.

● NOTE: Reduction in File Size

When converted to a Flash Video file, the file size of the footage was reduced from 212 MB to 2.8 MB—a tremendous savings.

Live Trace with Creative Suite

A hallmark of the Creative Suite is the ability for multiple applications to work together. You can use this next technique to vectorize footage, which can be done for stylistic reasons but also allows for dramatic resizing of frames since the footage is truly vector-based. To complete this technique, you'll use Adobe Illustrator's Live Trace feature and Bridge (in addition to After Effects and Flash). All four applications are included in the Production Premium and Master Collection versions of Adobe Creative Suite 4.

Process the Footage with After Effects

Before converting your footage to vectors, you'll need to preprocess it with After Effects. The goal here is to get the best-looking footage. After Effects offers several options under Color Correction (Effect > Color Correction) for improving footage. Consider the following to enhance your clips:

- Use **Levels** to adjust midtones of an image.
- Use **Color Balance** if your image has a color cast.
- Use the **Shadow/Highlight** adjustment for footage with problems in the brightest and darkest areas.
- Use the **Color Stabilizer** effect if your video is flickering with different color levels.

▲ TIP: Capturing Video for After Effects

Do you want to load video from a camera into an After Effects project? Once you've launched After Effects and saved your project, you can jump to Adobe Premiere Pro to capture video by choosing File > Import > Capture in Adobe Premiere Pro. After capturing the video, it will load into your After Effects project.

Shooting Advice

To create the cartoon look with Live Trace, you'll need to shoot video properly. For best results make sure you have a clearly recognizable subject, a high level of contrast between the subject and background, and even lighting without a lot of shadows.

Let's prepare a clip with After Effects.

1. Click the After Effects composition **02_Live_Trace_Start** to open the starting composition. Select the one layer.

2. Choose Effect > Color Correction > Auto Levels to quickly adjust the image.

3. Set Temporal Smoothing to 1.00 to smooth out adjustments over time. Increase the black clip to 4.00% to increase contrast in the dark areas of the image.

4. Soften the image to make a better image when you are converting to vectors. Choose Effect > Blur & Sharpen > Bilateral Blur. Set the Radius to 20.0 to increase the amount of blurring. Lower the Threshold to 5.0 to blur the less detailed areas the most.

5. Select the Colorize check box to restore the original color from the image.

Convert to Still Image Sequence

After your footage is prepped, you'll need to use the Render Queue panel to create a folder full of sequential images. The Render Queue can process effects as well as convert file formats.

1. Choose Composition > Add to Render Queue then click the Output Module Settings panel and change the format to TIFF sequence. Close the Output Module Settings panel.

2. Click the Output To area in the Render Queue.

3. Create a new folder on your desktop and name it Live_Trace images. Click Save to target the folder.

4. Click Render to create the sequential images.

▲ TIP: Remember to Resize

In Chapter 4 you learned how to use the Resize option inside the Output Module. You can easily convert between square and non-square pixels. The footage in 02_Live_Trace_Start has already been converted into square pixels.

Process with Adobe Illustrator (Live Trace)

Adobe Illustrator offers powerful tools for creating and modifying vector objects. Live Trace is especially adept at making vector files from raster images. The interface is a little daunting at first but is easy to master.

1. Launch Adobe Illustrator CS4 and choose File > Open.

2. Navigate to the first frame you rendered from After Effects. The file should be in a folder on your desktop and be named 02_Live_Trace_Start_00000.tif. Click Open.

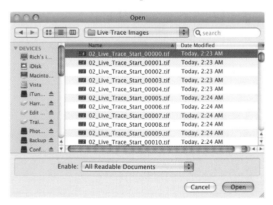

3. Click with the Selection tool (V) to make your photo the only active object. For best results make sure you're viewing the image at 100% magnification for the following steps.

4. With your photo active, choose Object > Live Trace > Tracing Options. A new dialog opens where you can tweak the Live Trace settings. Select the Preview check box to see your work.

5. Change Mode to Color to create a colored vector file. Modify the Max Colors setting to taste. You can have up to 256 levels of color (which is very realistic but slow to create). Experiment with options between 20 and 256 colors depending on your needs. This call is subjective and is based on the look you want to achieve. For this footage try setting Max Colors to 75.

6. You can also modify some other options in the Tracing Options dialog. To get a smoother image, try using a slight blur (often values less than 1 will work best). For this footage enter a value of 0.5 px.

▲ TIP: Custom Is King

Even though you can reuse presets, you'll get better results by tweaking your settings for each project.

7. You can dramatically change the look of your footage by tweaking the Trace Settings. Path Fitting controls the tightness of the strokes. Increase the Minimum Area slider to simplify the image. Each tweak will take a moment to redraw, so be sure to wait for the screen to refresh. For this footage enter the following values: Path Fitting: 4 px, Minimum Area: 50 px, and Corner Angle: 40.

8. When you're happy with a look, you'll need to store it. Click the Save Preset button, and in the dialog that appears, give the Live Trace preset a name that's easy to remember. For this project, name it Newspaper Scene and click OK.

9. Click Cancel and skip applying Live Trace for now. Close the open document without saving. Then quit Adobe Illustrator.

Process with Adobe Bridge

Once you've taken the time to create your custom preset, you can process your image sequence using Adobe Bridge. This batch process allows you to open and apply the preset to several images with minimal work.

1. Launch Adobe Bridge CS4 and navigate to your folder where you saved your image sequence.

2. Select the first image in the folder, and then press Command+A (Ctrl+A) to select all the images in the folder.

3. Choose Tools > Illustrator > Live Trace to open a Live Trace dialog that you can use to batch process your files. Choose the Live Trace preset that you created earlier.

4. From Document Profile choose Video and Film. Enter a document size of 1280 × 720 pixels.

5. Click the Choose button for a Destination. Create and choose a new folder on your desktop named Live Trace Results.

6. When you're ready, click OK to start the conversion (you can leave your computer for a while because the process is somewhat time intensive).

Import into After Effects

After Illustrator finishes processing all the still images into vector files, they can be imported back into After Effects. Essentially, each animated frame will come into After Effects and form a new movie clip. Once in After Effects, the clip can be resynced with sound or scaled to a new, finished size.

1. Choose File > Import > File and select the first processed Illustrator file.

2. Choose Footage from the Import As menu and leave the Illustrator/PDF/EPS Sequence check box selected. Click Open to bring the clip into After Effects.

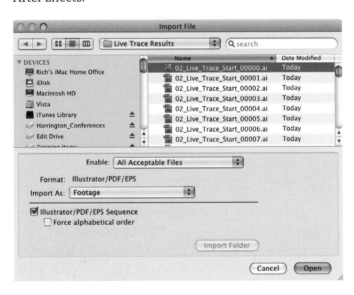

▲ **TIP: As Big as You Want to Be**

Because the image sequence is vector based, you can output at any size. Scale the vector clip up to fit the frame, and then be sure to click the Continuously Rasterize switch in the Timeline. When you render, the file will be perfectly clean because vectors scale to any size.

3. Select the composition **02_Live_Trace_Start** and make its Timeline panel active. Then drag the newly imported vector image sequence into the selected composition.

4. Press Command+Option+F (Ctrl+Alt+F) to force fit the vector file to the document dimensions.

Make Your Footage Match

The imported clip will not play at the same speed as the original footage without a little intervention.

1. Select the original footage clip in the Project panel that you based the Live Trace on.

2. Choose File > Interpret Footage > Remember Interpretation.

3. Select the newly created vector clip and choose File > Interpret Footage > Apply Interpretation.

4. If you have advanced options in use (like 3:2 pulldown for 24 fps material), you should select the clip and press Command+F (Ctrl+F). This allows you to change the new footage's frame rate to match the original.

Both clips now have the same duration and playback speed. Additionally, any audio in the original clip will "sync up" if you place both clips into a composition together.

Silhouette with Auto-trace

If you want to create animated vector shapes from video, using Auto-trace is the way to go. You can choose to convert the alpha, red, green, blue, or luminance channel of a layer to a vector mask by using the Auto-trace command. Additionally, the mask can be applied to an empty solid to create a simple silhouette.

The Auto-trace command is very efficient. It creates only as many Bézier masks as is necessary to outline the specified channel. The masks it creates use the smallest number of vertices possible.

● **NOTE: Best Quality**

When you use the Auto-trace command, all affected layers are automatically set to Best Quality to ensure the most accurate results.

Shooting Advice

You don't have to shoot Auto-trace shots with a chroma key background, but it certainly helps. When you use green screen technology it is easy to key and isolate the footage with accurate transparency. If keying is not possible, be sure to have a high-contrast, monochromatic background.

Tracing in After Effects

For this lesson you'll use a piece of footage that has already been keyed using the Keylight plug-in. Keying is covered in-depth in Chapter 4, "Creating Transparent Video with After Effects."

1. Double-click the After Effects composition **03_Auto-trace_Start** to open the starting composition. This comp contains one shot nested in a pre-composition.

2. To Auto-trace multiple frames, you must set the work area. Press the Home key to move the Current Time Indicator to the start of the comp, and press B to mark the beginning of the work area.

3. Move the Current Time Indicator to 0;00;15;00 and press N to mark the end of the work area.

4. With track 1 highlighted, choose Layer > Auto-trace.

5. In the new window click the Work area radio button, specify that you want to use the work area to create masks for all of those frames. Be sure the Preview check box is selected so you can see your results.

6. Adjust the Blur value to reduce artifacts in the image and reduce jagged edges in the Auto-tracing results. A larger value results in more blurring. For this image use a value of 4 pixels.

7. Multiple options are available for refining the mask further:

   - **Tolerance.** Specifies how much a traced path can deviate from the contours of the channel. For this footage the default values are fine.

   - **Threshold.** Adjusting the threshold moves the midpoint at which a pixel is considered to be part of the edge used for tracing. Pixels with values over the threshold are treated as opaque; pixels with values below are treated as transparent. For this footage use a value of 65%.

   - **Minimum Area.** Increasing the Minimum Area limits the smallest feature in the original image that will be traced. For this image leave the value at 10 to specify a minimum area of 10 × 10 pixels.

   - **Corner Roundness.** Using higher values ensures smoother curves in the mask. For this footage use a value of 65%.

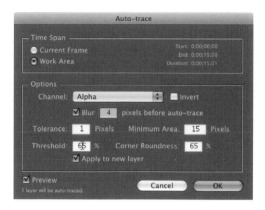

8. Make sure the "Apply to new layer" check box is selected. This applies the mask to a solid colored layer. Click OK to create the Auto-traced layer. The conversion process will take a while (you can see progress in the Info panel).

9. With the new layer selected, choose Layer > Solid Settings. Click the color well and specify a value of R=20 G=0 B=225. Click OK to capture the change in color, and click OK again to update the solid.

10. Disable the visibility of the original footage layer. Then click the RAM Preview button to view your results.

Exporting a SWF

Once your vector animation is complete, it can be exported as a vector file for use in Flash. The best format for this pure vector output is a SWF file. When you render or export a SWF file from After Effects, the program will maintain vector graphics as vector objects as much as possible. If After Effects encounters items that can't be treated as vectors (such as most effects), you can choose to either ignore the effects or rasterize them as JPEG-compressed bitmap images, which will reduce the efficiency of the SWF file.

1. Select the composition **03_Auto-trace_Start**. Choose File > Export > Adobe Flash Player (SWF). Enter the filename Newspaper Reading.swf and save the file to the desktop.

2. The SWF Settings panel opens with several options for the SWF file. Specify the options as needed:

   - **JPEG Quality.** This option specifies the quality of rasterized images. Since you are exporting vectors, this doesn't affect this output.

   - **Unsupported Features.** Set this option to Ignore so unsupported features are not utilized in the finished file. If rasterization is used, the file size will be significantly larger.

   - **Audio.** After Effects offers precise control over audio embedded in SWF files. This file has no audio, so leave the Export Audio check box deselected.

   - **Loop Continuously.** Because this is not a looping animation, deselect the Loop Continuously check box.

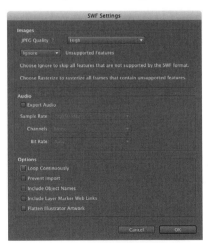

3. Click OK to write the SWF file to disk. The Export dialog provides progress information.

4. When the export completes, you'll find a SWF file and a report named Newspaper ReadingR.htm on your desktop. Double-click the new HTML file to view it. You can view the SWF file and details about the file using the report.

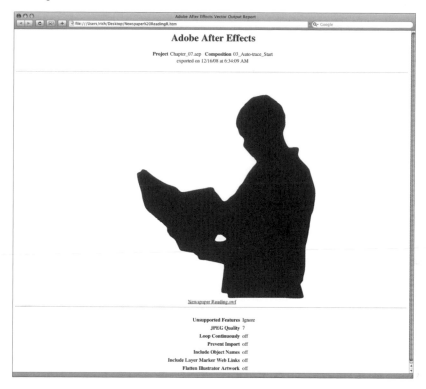

5. When you're finished, switch back to After Effects. Close the document and save your progress.

What's Next?

You discovered three very different ways to convert video into Flash-ready content in this chapter. Next, you'll explore important animation techniques that will help both the Flash and After Effects artist. Powerful options like the Puppet tools in After Effects and the Bones tool in Flash offer new ways to create animated content. Learning to harness the full toolset on your computer will give you more options and better results. Let's explore new ways to make things move.

8 ADVANCED ANIMATION TOOLS IN AFTER EFFECTS AND FLASH

At this point, you've learned most of the essentials. So, your reward is a tour of some of the power animation tools in After Effects and Flash. You'll start in After Effects, where you'll use Motion Sketch, Smoother, Wiggler, and the Puppet tools. Then you'll hop over to Flash and check out the Bones tool, shape tweening, and sound. Even if you're more comfortable in After Effects than Flash—or vice versa—you should learn a few things about your favorite application.

Motion Sketch

Sure, tweening is your bread and butter. But have you ever wished you could avoid plodding from keyframe to keyframe and just drag a layer around? Wouldn't it be awesome if After Effects recorded your drags and automatically laid down keyframes for you? Well, guess what? After Effects will do just that with a tool called Motion Sketch (Window > Motion Sketch). To test this feature, you'll use a ready-made file from the DVD.

For a news show, you'll animate the movements of a suspected criminal, who is represented by a little red man. He'll walk from the bottom of Main Street to the first intersection, turn left, walk around the block and then back onto Main Street. Then he'll start walking downward, stopping briefly in front of the first building, and come to rest in front of a second building.

1. From the DVD, copy the **Chapter_08 Project Files** folder to your hard drive.

2. Open the file **08_start.aep** from the **Chapter_08 Project Files** folder. You'll find a neighborhood map in the comp called Final. Select the criminal.

3. If you don't see the Motion Sketch panel, choose Window > Motion Sketch. In the Motion Sketch panel, select the Background option.

   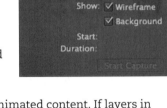

   If you leave Background deselected, you won't be able to see the neighborhood while you're dragging the criminal around (you'll just see the criminal against a blank background). Note that even with Background selected, you won't see any animated content. If layers in addition to the criminal are moving, they'll remain stationary while you're recording with Motion Sketch.

4. To begin the recording process, click the Start Capture button in the Motion Sketch panel.

   This button is misnamed. When you click it, After Effects doesn't start recording, it's just ready to record. Once you begin dragging the criminal around in the Composition panel, it records.

5. Drag the criminal and walk him around the neighborhood as planned. Drag him from the bottom of Main Street to the first intersection, drag him left, and then walk him around the block and back onto Main Street. Then drag him downward, stopping briefly in front of the first building, and bring him to rest in front of a second building. If you make a mistake, stop dragging, press Command+Z (Ctrl+Z) to undo, and then try again. Release the mouse button when you're done recording.

● NOTE: Lengthen the Timeline

When using Motion Sketch, make sure you have enough composition duration to work with. If you run out of time, Motion Sketch won't make your composition longer automatically. Before a Motion Sketch session, it's best to choose Composition > Composition Settings and make your composition a little longer than you think it needs to be. You can always shorten it later.

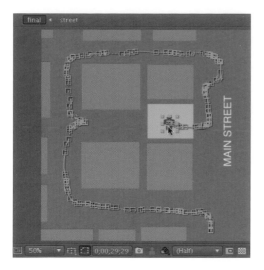

6. Preview the comp and watch the criminal creep around town.

Smoother

As cool as Motion Sketch is, it has a drawback. To see the problem, follow these steps.

1. Select the criminal layer and press P to reveal the Position property.

As you can see, Motion Sketch got a little overenthusiastic about key-frames, putting one on almost every frame. It was just trying to be thorough, recording every little nuance of movement.

It's great to know such fidelity exists if you need it, but with so many keyframes, it would be hard to edit the criminal's movement. You could prune many of them and still see what you want to see. This is where Smoother comes in handy. It intelligently deletes unnecessary key-frames. We often run it after using tools that generate keyframes automatically, such as Motion Sketch or Motion Tracking.

> ▲ TIP: A Smoother Motion Sketch
>
> One way to get smoother strokes is to use a graphics tablet (such as those from Wacom). This will minimize mouse jitters and result in smoother sketches.

2. Click the word Position on the Timeline to select all the Position keyframes.

3. If you don't see the Smoother panel, choose Window > Smoother. In the Smoother panel, set the Tolerance value to 20.

Tolerance is set to 1 by default. This means that if it finds two keyframes in a row and they only move the criminal one pixel, Smoother deletes one of them.

A Tolerance of 1 is usually too conservative. It's best to increase it to 10 or even 20. At 20, if two consecutive keyframes move the criminal 20 or fewer pixels, Smoother deletes one of them. The higher you set Tolerance, the more keyframes Smoother removes (just don't get too aggressive).

Removing keyframes may seem dangerous, but never fear. You can always undo by pressing Command+Z (Ctrl+Z). It's amazing how many keyframes you can delete without noticing a difference. Keep in mind that After Effects interpolates (tweens) between keyframes, so you don't need that many to describe most paths.

4. Click the Apply button to remove keyframes.

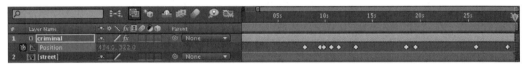

5. Preview the animation and see if it still looks good. If it doesn't, undo and try a lower Tolerance. If it looks fine but there are still too many keyframes, try running Smoother again with a higher Tolerance. You can also manually delete a jitter-causing keyframe by selecting it in the Timeline panel and pressing Delete.

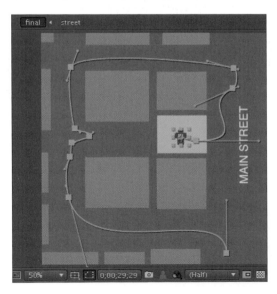

Wiggler

The Wiggler panel is the opposite of the Smoother panel. Using the Wiggler you can add random motion to a range of keyframes. A ready-made project is provided to help you understand this powerful command.

1. Open the project **08_pedestrians.aep** from the **Chapter_08 Project Files** folder.

2. Double-click the comp called Final to load it.

   Here you'll find the same crime scene we just created with the Smoother with some new layers added. These layers contain pedestrians who are all going about their business, oblivious to the dangerous criminal in their midst. If you preview the comp, you'll see them walking about stiffly, more like robots than people. This is because we animated them on simple, straight-line paths.

   Let's loosen up their movements a little, adding some natural bounce to them. Basically, you want After Effects to add some random keyframes—keyframes that make the people veer from their paths a bit without straying too far.

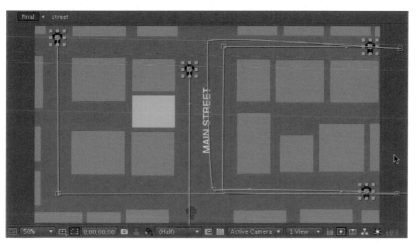

3. Select the topmost pedestrian in the Timeline and press P to reveal its Position keyframes.

4. Click the word Position on the Timeline to select all the keyframes.

5. If necessary, reveal the Wiggler panel by choosing Window > Wiggler.

6. From the Dimensions drop-down menu, select the All Independently option.

   This ensures that the Wiggler will perform separate randomizations on X and Y. After all, it would be odd if a person moved 10 pixels to the right every time that person moved 10 pixels down. However, if for some

For a more sophisticated alternative to Wiggler, see the Expressions video demo in this chapter's Project Files folder. In the video, we show off the versatile Wiggle Expression.

● NOTE: Wiggle for Randomness

You can wiggle any keyframeable property. The Wiggler is great to use whenever you want to add randomness to your comp. For instance, you can wiggle the blurriness setting of Gaussian Blur to make it seem as if an image is moving in and out of focus.

reason you want X and Y to be randomized together, choose the All Together option. You can also choose to randomize just X or just Y.

7. Set Frequency to 1.

   Frequency controls how many times the person wanders from the path each second. If you want the person to appear spastic, set Frequency high; if you want the person to keep to the path most of the time, set Frequency low. Note that if you want the person to veer every other second, you need to set Frequency to 0.5.

8. Set Magnitude to 10.

   Magnitude controls how far the person can veer from the path each time the person moves away from it. If you want the person to fly wildly all over the place, set Magnitude to a high number like 300. If you only want the person to quiver a little, set it to a low number like 2.

9. Click the Apply button to add random keyframes.

10. Preview the comp. If you don't like the amount of randomization, undo and try again with different settings for Frequency and/or Magnitude.

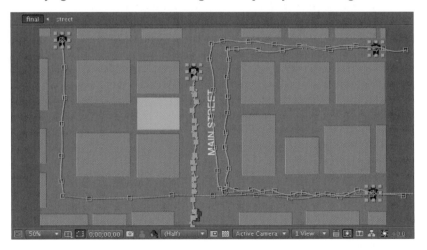

11. Repeat steps 1–8 with the other pedestrian layers.

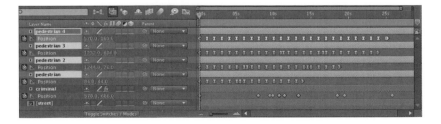

The Puppet Tools

The Puppet tools are a series of tool that you can use to quickly add natural motion to photos or vector artwork. The tools use an effect (called the Puppet effect) that is automatically applied when you use the tools. The Puppet tools warp the image based on the positions of pins that you place. You can use pins to define what parts of the image should move (or shouldn't) and what parts should be in front when other parts overlap. The Puppet tools include:

- **Puppet Pin tool.** Use to place and move Deform pins.
- **Puppet Overlap tool.** Use to place Overlap pins that indicate which parts should appear in front of others when a distortion causes parts to overlap.
- **Puppet Starch tool.** Use to place Starch pins to stiffen parts of the image so they are less distorted by the warp.

Placing Pins

A small flag has been added on the right edge of the screen. It would be very appropriate for the flag to blow in the wind and wave. To do this, you'll need to add some pins to create a mesh and control movement.

1. Open the project **08_flag.aep** from the **Chapter_08 Project Files** folder.
2. Double-click the comp called Final to load it.
3. Select the flag layer.
4. Press Home to move the Current Time Indicator to the start of the Timeline.
5. On the Tools panel, select the Puppet Pin tool, which looks like a thumbtack.

You must add pins to define the joints and bending points for your puppet.

6. Click to place a pin on the point of the flag (on the left).

   By placing the first pin, After Effects automatically attempts to break the image into a triangular mesh. You can see this mesh when a Puppet tool pointer is over the area that the outline defines.

7. Click again to place a pin on the flag's upper-right corner.
8. Click again to place a pin on the flag's lower-right corner, completing a triangular arrangement of pins.

● **NOTE: Visible Mesh**

To show the mesh, select Show in the Tools panel.

Understanding the Puppet Pin Tool

The mesh and the image pixels are interconnected, so moving the mesh will move the pixels. Here are some things to keep in mind:

- If you move a Deform pin, the mesh changes shape. After Effects attempts to keep the overall mesh as rigid as possible to produce natural, life-like movement.

- A layer can have multiple meshes, so use more than one mesh if you want to control distortion independently.

- The meshes do not recognize moving footage (such as video) and will not update.

9. Click to place six pins running down the flagpole. These will help hold it in place, but you'll ensure that it stays in place by using the Puppet Starch tool (explained in the next section).

Puppet Starch Controls

When distorting one part of an image, you may want to prevent other parts from being distorted. Use the Puppet Starch tool to apply Starch pins to keep parts rigid. You must apply Puppet Starch pins to the original outline and then specify the following options:

- **Amount.** The strength of the stiffening amount. The Amount values are added together for places on the mesh where extents overlap. You can use negative Amount values. Small Amount values prevent image tearing without introducing much rigidity.

- **Extent.** How far from the Starch pin its influence extends. The Extent is indicated by a pale fill in the affected parts of the mesh.

1. Select the Puppet Starch tool.

2. Click the pole at the bottom and in the middle to place red Starch pins.

3. Select the top point and raise the Extent property value in the Tools panel. Also, raise the Extent property value on the bottom point. Raise the values until you see gray shading covering the whole pole.

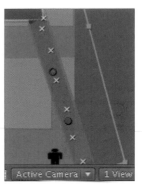

Sketching Motion

The pins on the right of the flag and those on the pole will hold the left edge of the flag in place, as if they're pinning it to the comp's background. You'll be able to animate the flag waving by dragging the leftmost pin.

Instead of keyframing the animation, you can use a built-in Motion Sketch with the Puppet tools. With Motion Sketch, you can animate the motion path of one or more Deform pins in realtime (or a specified speed). This makes it easy to create natural movement and to sync it with audio or other elements. The Motion Sketch options include:

- **Speed.** This is the ratio of the speed of recorded motion compared to playback speed. If Speed is 100%, the motion is played back at the same speed at which it was recorded. If Speed is less than 100%, the motion plays back faster than it was recorded. This is a useful way to draw elaborate paths.

- **Smoothness.** Use a higher value to remove extraneous keyframes from the motion path. It is in fact better to have fewer keyframes if you want smoother motion.

- **Use Draft Deformation.** If your system is lagging, select this option. It ignores Starch pins when sketching, which improves system performance.

1. Switch back to the Puppet Pin tool.

2. Click Record Options in the Tools panel.

3. Move the Current Time Indicator to the start of the Timeline.

4. Hold down the Command (Control) key and begin dragging the left most pin on the flag, making it wave in realtime. As you drag, notice the Current Time Indicator moving through the Timeline. After Effects is recording your movements and automatically laying down keyframes in the Timeline. (If you make a mistake, select the flag layer, type U on the keyboard, and delete the keyframes.) Continue making the flag wave until the Current Time Indicator reaches the end of the Timeline.

5. Preview to watch the flag wave.

The Puppet Tool—Learn by Watching

The Puppet tool can get pretty intense. There are several features to wrap your head around, and this is one tool that just makes sense to learn visually.

On the book's DVD, a video tutorial and some extra files have been included so you can explore the Puppet tool and get more comfortable with it. This powerful tool can be a lot of fun but is difficult to understand by just reading about it.

The Bones Tool

A new addition to the Flash animation toolbox is the powerful Bones tool. This tool is designed for creating chain-like animations (which previously required tedious script writing). The Bones tool lets you quickly draw links between symbols. You can then apply inverse kinematics (IK) to create a natural animation.

In this exercise, you'll create an animation to help illustrate the growing robotic workforce and compare it in size to the human workforce. This animation is a concept that can then be refined and combined with a chart background, some gridlines, and a Y axis to help convey the magnitude of the change.

The animation starts with a simple column chart—just a partial animation intended for you to later finesse in After Effects.

To illustrate the fact that robots will soon put more people out of work, you'll harness several animation tools to animate a robot arm pulling the Robot Workers bar upward to make it taller:

- You'll use the Bones tool to rig the arm, giving it a skeletal structure.
- To make the bar grow, you'll use shape tweening.
- You'll also add a mechanical sound so that the robot arm will seem a little more robotic.

1. Open the project **08_start.fla** from the **Chapter_08 Project Files** folder.
2. Select the arm layer. A series of movie clips is on this layer, one of each arm segment.
3. Select the Bones tool.

   This tool allows you to add a skeletal structure to the arm, indicating to Flash how all the parts connect together—as in the song lyrics, "the head bone's connected to the neck bone."
4. Click the right edge of the rightmost arm segment and drag to the right edge of the arm segment on its left.

● **NOTE: Not Just for Flash**

Even After Effects users will find the Bones tool useful. If you need an IK style animation, you can always create it in Flash and export a SWF or QuickTime file for use in After Effects (see Chapter 11, "Converting Flash to Broadcast Standards").

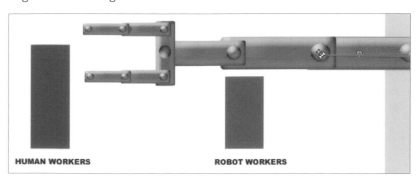

This will lay down a bone from the pivot point of the first segment to the pivot point of the second segment.

5. Continue to create bones from segment to segment until you've reached the final segment of the top pinchers.

● NOTE: A
Completed Version

You'll find a fully rigged (but not animated) version of the robot arm in the file 08_rigged.fla. You can check your work against this file or use this one if you like.

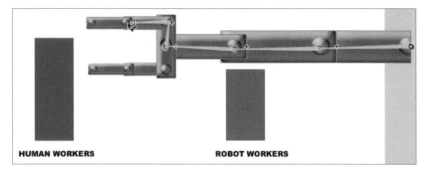

6. Go back and add segments from the pivot in the center of the vertical "hand" segment to the bottom pinchers as shown in the figure.

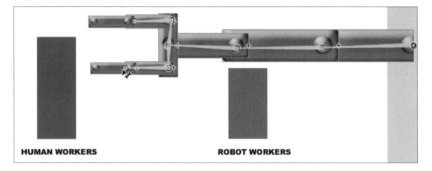

7. Switch to the Selection tool and drag the segments into their initial pose.

8. Farther along on the Timeline, right-click a frame in the Armature layer and choose the Insert Pose option.

● NOTE: Armature Layer

Flash adds an Armature layer when you start using the Bones tool. It moves all the segments to this new layer. Feel free to delete the now empty arm layer in the exercise.

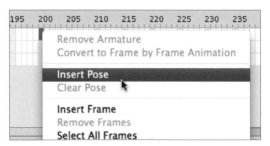

9. Move the arm segments into another pose. Then preview the movie to watch the arm tween from pose to pose.

10. Repeat steps 7 and 8 until you make the arm look like it's reaching over, grabbing the Robot Worker's bar, and pulling it upward. Then make it look like it's releasing the bar. Be sure to animate the pinchers closing around the bar. Extend the "Robot Worker Bar" and "Rest of Graph" layers so they persist for the entire animation.

Of course, the bar won't actually move (or get squeezed by the pinchers), because it's on its own layer and hasn't been animated yet. You'll fix that next.

Shape Tweening

Shape tweening is an odd technique. Generally, you can't animate anything in Flash unless it's saved in the Library as a symbol. Shape tweening is the exception to this rule. In fact, you can't shape tween an instance of a symbol. You can only shape tween vector shapes that haven't been added to the Library.

A shape tween is a morph, but note that it's a vector morph (you're out of luck if you want to morph a photo). Shape tweens work by moving the vector control points around.

1. In **08_ArmAnimated.fla**, unlock the Robot Workers bar layer by clicking the lock icon in the Timeline.

2. Lock the Armature layer so you don't accidentally nudge the robot arm while you're shape tweening the bar.

3. Right-click the robot worker bar's initial keyframe and choose Create Shape Tween.

4. Find the frame where the pinchers first make contact with the bar, right-click the frame, and choose Insert Keyframe.

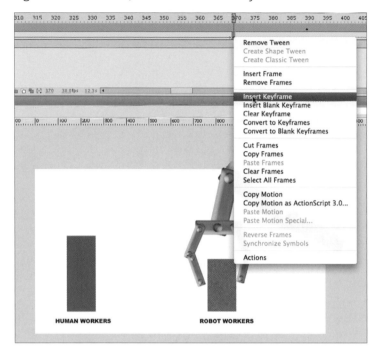

5. Find the frame where the pinchers are digging the farthest into the bar, right-click it (the frame) and choose Insert Keyframe.

6. Select the Subselection tool (the white arrow).

7. Click the edge of the bar, revealing its vector control points.

8. Select the point in the middle of the left edge, and use the right arrow key on your keyboard to nudge it inward until it looks like it's being pinched by the pinchers. Do the same with the right-middle point.

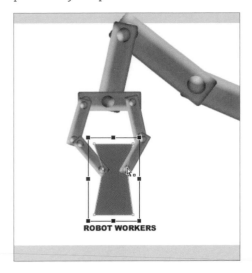

9. Add a keyframe to the frame when the arm starts pulling upward. Then add a keyframe to the frame when the arm has pulled all the way up.

10. Make a selection with the white subselection tool around the upper four vector points, and using your up arrow key, nudge them up until they look like they've been dragged upward by the pinchers.

11. Add a keyframe when the pinchers have released the bar and nudge the middle points outward until the bar forms a clean rectangle again.

12. Preview the animation to watch the robot arm manipulate the bar. (If you're unlucky like us, you may get to see something unpleasant.)

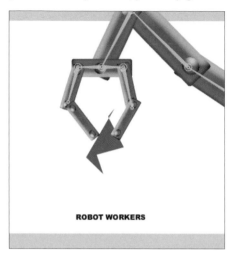

ROBOT WORKERS

Flash runs shape tweens by moving vector points around. Sometimes it gets confused about which point to move and where to move it. When this happens, you get what we like to call a misshapen tween. You can fix these glitches by adding shape hints.

13. Click the start keyframe of a misshapen tween range.

14. Choose Modify > Shape > Add Shape Hint.

Flash places a shape hint in the middle of the bar. Shape hints are small circles with letters in the middle. The first one you add will have an "a" in the middle, the next one will have a "b," and so on.

15. Drag the hint to the bar's lower-left corner. Add hints b, c, and d. Drag them to the other three corners.

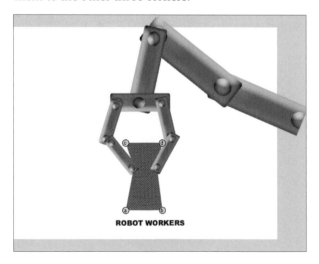

ROBOT WORKERS

● NOTE: Shape Hint Suggestions

There's no rule as to how many shape hints you should add to a misshapen tween. Try to add enough to define a rough outline of the shape you're morphing. It's a trial-and-error technique. Sometimes you might think you've added enough, but when you view the animation, it's still misshapen. You'll then need to go back to the start keyframe and add more hints.

16. Click the next keyframe to the right. On this keyframe—the end of the misshapen range—you'll find identical shape hints to those on the previous keyframe. It may look like there's just one hint, because initially the hints are on top of each other.

17. Drag the copy hints to the same locations as in the previous keyframe.

ROBOT WORKERS

18. Repeat steps 13–17 for any misshapen tweens.

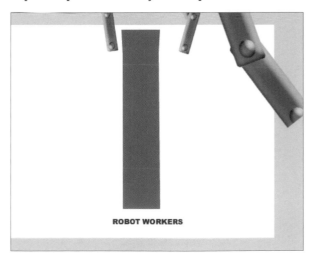

ROBOT WORKERS

Adding Sound

What's a robot without a little whirring? A killer robot that can sneak up on you, that's what! Let's put the proverbial bell around the neck of the kitty. A little sound will help complete the animation.

● NOTE: To
Delay a Sound

If you don't want a sound to start immediately, select a later frame, right-click it, and choose Insert Keyframe. (You don't have to do this if you want the sound to start immediately, because Flash automatically adds a keyframe to frame one of every layer.) With the keyframe selected, drag a sound from the Library and drop it on the Stage.

1. Open the file **08_shapeTweenComplete.fla** from the Flash Stages folder in the **Chapter_08 Project Files** folder. Choose File > Import > Import to Library. Import **robot. mp3** from the **Chapter_08 Project Files** folder.

2. Add a new layer to the Timeline.

3. Drag the robot sound from the Library and drop it on the Stage. You can drop it anywhere.

4. Select the sound's start keyframe.

5. In the Properties panel, you can set the sound to Loop if you want it to play over and over until the movie ends. If you want it to just repeat a few times, set the sound to Repeat and then edit the number of plays.

● NOTE: **What's with the Repeat Option?**

The Repeat option is poorly named. By default, it's set to Repeat × 1. Call us crazy, but if something is repeating once, it's playing twice. However, in the world of Flash, repeat really means "play," so if you want the sound to just play through once, set it to Repeat × 1. If you want it to play twice, set it to Repeat × 2.

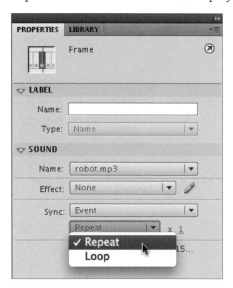

6. Press Command+Return (Ctrl+Enter) to watch the movie.

Prepare the Movie for After Effects

To prepare the movie for import into After Effects, extend all the layers in time so that they hold for five seconds.

1. Right-click the last keyframe in the animated bar layer and choose Remove Tween. The goal here is to hold everything still for five seconds, so that other animations can be added to the end in After Effects. You don't want any tweening from this point on.

2. In the Timeline, scroll out to frame 865 (about five seconds after the animation ends), click the top-layer's 865th frame, hold down the Shift key, and click the bottom layer's 865th frame. This will select frame 865 in all layers.

3. Right-click the selected group of frames and choose Insert Frame.

    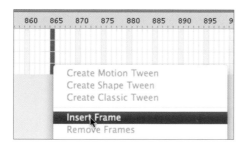

To finish this animation for broadcast, you could export it as a SWF file or QuickTime movie. Then you could bring it into After Effects and composite it over a motion background. For more on exporting Flash Video to use in After Effects, see Chapter 12, "Professional Encoding of Flash Video."

What's Next?

In the next chapter, you'll move into one of the most rewarding and complex features of After Effects—3D. Working in three dimensions is so involved that you'll actually spend the next two chapters on the subject. The next lesson teaches you how to build and craft 3D worlds using source images and footage. You'll learn how to put it all in motion by animating cameras and lights to make it look fantastic. Let's go!

9 CREATING 3D ENVIRONMENTS

One of the primary benefits of animating in After Effects is its support for 3D space, which makes it easy to position and animate objects along their X, Y, or Z axes. Additionally, After Effects supports a rich system of lights and cameras, making believable 3D animation even easier.

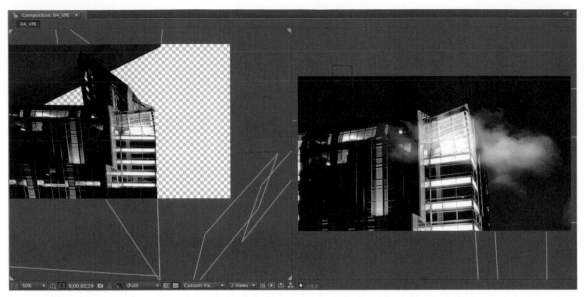

By positioning layers in 3D space, you can create realistic animation that can include depth of field.

● NOTE: Need Photoshop?

This chapter utilizes Adobe Photoshop several times and in one case, Photoshop Extended. If you need to, you can download a 30-day demo from Adobe.com. Additionally, you'll find files with the designation _end in the Chapter_09 Project Files folder that you can use in After Effects. Adobe After Effects and Photoshop have several interdependencies, and the two are used together often for real-world workflow.

You'll explore the 3D animation process in-depth in Chapter 10. In the following pages, you'll learn about the process of creating elements and environments that can be used with 3D cameras or animated in 3D space. The next two chapters are interdependent, so be sure to investigate both fully (and in a linear fashion).

Creating Seamless Textures

A common element you'll need to create for animated environments is seamless textures. These patterns can be repeated or looped to create a background animation, which can be anything from a looping pattern for a road or a gentle group of clouds floating in the sky. The key is to make a pattern that is seamless and large enough that the viewer doesn't detect the loop.

Process in Photoshop

The first step to creating a seamless texture loop is to process the image using Photoshop. Essentially, you'll wrap the image on itself (much like a flat ribbon turned into a loop). Where the image wraps, blending must occur. Fortunately, Photoshop offers several tools that make this process a snap.

1. From the book's DVD, copy the **Chapter_09 Project Files** folder to your computer. If it's not already running, launch Photoshop CS4.

2. Open the folder **01_Background Sources**, and then open the file **cloud_start.psd**.

3. Choose Filter > Other > Offset. A new dialog opens to control the filter.

4. Enter a value of 1000 in the Horizontal pixels right field.

5. Select Wrap Around for Undefined Areas. The photo slides to the right and wraps around to the other side. The image now has a seam in the middle that must be removed. Click OK.

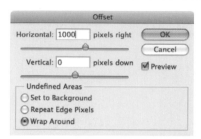

6. Select the Clone Stamp tool and choose a large brush (100 pixels or greater) with a soft edge.

7. Option-click (Alt-click) near the seam to set a sample point.

8. Clone the seam to try to hide the edge. In some cases you'll be removing clouds; in other cases you'll add them in. You can use the image **cloud_end.psd** as a reference. Be sure to occasionally reclick to set a new sample point (by Option-clicking or Alt-clicking).

Be sure to frequently change your sample point. The goal is to blend the two sides of the image together with soft-edged cloning strokes.

9. Cloning will not entirely hide the seam. You'll need to use the Healing Brush. Select the Healing Brush from the Tools panel. Use a soft-edged brush sized at 200 pixels or bigger.

10. Option-click (Alt-click) near the seam to set a sample point.

11. Brush over the visible seams that remain. The most problematic areas are the blue sky regions with different tonal values.

12. Combine Healing Brush and Clone Stamp strokes until the seam disappears.

13. To soften the image a little, choose Filter > Blur > Gaussian Blur.

14. Enter a Radius value of 5 pixels and click OK.

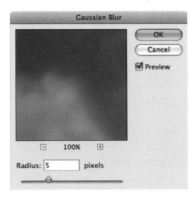

15. Choose Image > Adjustments > Levels to invoke the Levels command.

16. Click the 3rd eyedropper (sample in image to set white point) and then click an area of a cloud that should be white to properly set the white point. If you misclick, hold down the Option (Alt) key to change the Cancel button into a Reset button. Click OK.

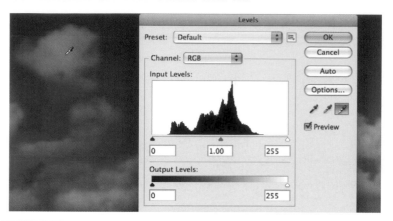

17. Boost the color in the sky by choosing Image > Adjustments > Vibrance.

18. Enter a Vibrance value of 60 and a Saturation amount of 20. Click OK.

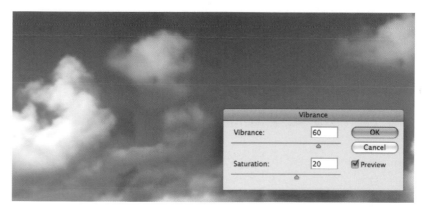

19. Choose File > Save As and navigate to the **Chapter_09 Project Files** folder to save the file.

20. Name the file cloud_pattern.psd and click Save. Close the file. You are now ready to animate the file in After Effects.

Offset Effect in After Effects

Photoshop and After Effects have many similarities, from layers and blending modes to layer styles and effects. Just as you used to use the Offset filter in Photoshop to wrap an image, you can use the same effect in After Effects to animate the Offset, making it possible to animate a seamless pattern.

1. If it's not running already, launch After Effects CS4 and at the Welcome screen, click the New Composition button.

2. From the Preset list, choose HDV/HDTV 720 29.97.

3. Name the Composition 01_Clouds.

4. Set the Duration to 0;00;30;00 and click OK.

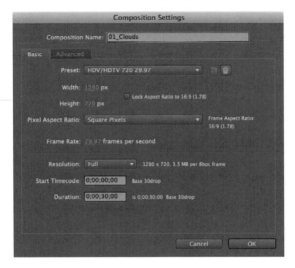

5. At the bottom of the Project panel, click the New Folder icon. Name the folder 01_Background.

6. Choose File > Import and import the file **Cloud_Pattern** from the **Chapter_09 Project Files** folder.

7. Drag the cloud_pattern.psd file into the composition 01_Clouds.

8. Place both the composition and the PSD file into the folder 01_Background.

9. Highlight layer 1 in the Timeline and choose Effect > Distort > Offset.

10. Press the Home key to return to the first frame of the composition.

11. Press E to see the effects applied to the layer.

12. Click the disclosure triangle next to the word Offset to see the controls for the effect.

13. Add a keyframe by clicking the stopwatch for the Shift Center To property.

14. Press the End key to move the Current Time Indicator to the last frame of the composition.

15. Add a keyframe to the Shift Center To property and double-click the newly added keyframe to adjust its value.

16. Click the Units drop-down menu and change it to % of source.

17. To make the image slide one full rotation, add or subtract 100% from the value of the keyframe. To move the image to the left, enter a value of –50%; to move it to the right, enter 150%. Enter 150 and click OK.

18. Let's preview the animation at a lower quality to see it more quickly. In the Preview panel, set the Resolution to Quarter and click the RAM Preview button. Watch the preview of the animation; notice how the clouds seamlessly loop.

Layering Images to Create Depth

Now that you have one instance of the clouds animated, you can add a second to create the illusion of depth. Simply duplicating the layer is not enough. Instead, you must set a different loop point and adjust the scale to create a difference in size. Then the two layers can be blended together to seamlessly mix.

1. Select the layer in the Timeline and choose Edit > Duplicate. A second copy is added.

2. Press U to select all the user-added keyframes. Two frames for the Offset property appear.

3. Double-click the first keyframe for the topmost layer. The X value is set to 50%. Change the X value to 0% and press Return (Enter).

4. Double-click the second keyframe for the topmost layer. The X value is set to 150%. You need this keyframe to be +100% from the first. Change the X value to 100% and click Return (Enter).

5. If blending modes aren't visible, click the Toggle Switches/Modes button at the bottom of the Timeline. Keep in mind that blending modes allow you to mix layers together based on values like color or luminosity.

6. Click the Blending Mode list and set the top layer to Lighten. This mode works best in this scenario because it drops out the darker areas of the sky without changing the intensity of the blue areas much.

7. Let's mix the layers together with a little Opacity change. Press T to view the Opacity controls for the top layer. Set the Opacity property to 80%.

8. Now let's adjust scale so the top clouds appear closer. Since the layer is at 100% scale already (the default size), let's avoid scaling up, which can pixelate the image. Select layer 2 in the Timeline.

9. Press S to view the Scale controls for the bottom layer. Set the Scale to 70% so the bottommost clouds look smaller (hence farther away).

10. In the Preview panel, click the RAM Preview button. Because the clouds have different scales and offset points, the animation appears seamless and fluid.

Stylizing with Adjustment Layers

Adjustment layers have two major benefits. They speed up your design process, allowing you to quickly apply the same effect to multiple layers. Rendering is also faster because the adjustment layer creates a composite of the layer below and applies effects to it. The use of adjustment layers improves rendering speed compared to applying the same effect separately to each of the underlying layers.

1. Click the topmost layer in the Timeline.

2. Choose Layer > New > Adjustment Layer. An adjustment layer is applied to the top of the layer stack.

3. Let's simplify the animation for Web compression using the Cartoon effect. Choose Effect > Stylize > Cartoon.

4. In the Effect Controls panel, change the Render drop-down menu to Fill to avoid any dark strokes appearing in the shot.

5. Change Shading Steps to 12 and Shading Smoothness to 100.

6. In the Preview panel, click the RAM Preview button. Because the clouds have different scales and offset points, the animation appears seamless and fluid.

7. Choose File > Save to store the file. Navigate to the **Chapter_09 Project Files** folder and name the project 09_Progress.aep.

This animation is complete. You can export it as an FLV video for use in Flash or render it to a movie file for use in a video project. For now, just leave it in the After Effects project for later use.

Assembling Virtual Environments from Photos

An emerging technique in the special effects industry is the use of photographic elements to create virtual environments. By combining high-resolution digital images in 3D space, you can create entire environments. You can then combine live action footage with green screen techniques or animate a 3D camera to create moving footage. Let's create a virtual world using Photoshop and After Effects.

Compositing in Photoshop

The first step is to separate elements into their own layers. This technique typically involves making a selection in Photoshop and then moving or duplicating elements to their own layer. To improve flexibility in the compositing process, you'll use layer masks to create "editable" transparency.

1. Switch back to Adobe Photoshop (if it isn't open, launch Photoshop CS4). Choose File > Open, and then navigate to the **Chapter_09 Project Files** folder. Open the folder **02_Environment Sources**, and then open the file **Skyline_start.psd**.

2. The image that opens is sized much larger than the output resolution (which is a good thing). It is about 3,000 pixels across (to view this information quickly, hold down the Option (Alt) key and click the Document Statistics area for the window). The composition you'll be working with is in HD at 1280 × 720 pixels. The extra pixels in the source image means the 3D camera can zoom without seeing pixilization in the image.

● **NOTE: Check the Reference File**

We've included the completed file, Skyline_end.psd, for you to reference when you're compositing during this lesson.

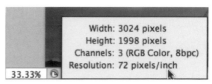

3. Double-click the Background layer in the Layers panel. The New Layer window opens. Name the layer Clouds and click OK.

4. You now need to duplicate the layer and isolate the building silhouettes. Choose Layer > Duplicate Layer, name it Skyline, and then click OK.

5. With the Skyline layer selected, choose Select > Color Range. The Color Range command allows you to select a specified color within the document. You can then easily add to the selection to refine it. All of its speed and power is complemented by a very intuitive user interface.

6. With the eyedropper, click the blue sky.

7. Examine the Color Range dialog. You'll see an initial selection created in the dialog. A black and white matte is shown to preview the selection. The white areas indicate the selection you are creating.

8. Hold down the Shift key and click more of the sky to build a larger selection. You can also hold down the Shift key and click and drag through the image to make a selection.

9. Adjust the Fuzziness slider until you have a good silhouette of the building. If you need to, repeat the Shift-click selection to add more to the Color Range selection.

▲ **TIP: Modifying the Color Range Selection**

If you need to add to the Color Range selection, hold down the Shift key. If you select too much, you can hold down the Option (Alt) key to subtract from the selection. You can also enable the Localized Color Clusters option to require similar pixels to be located closer together in the image.

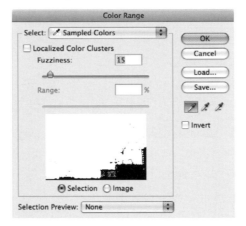

10. Since you actually want the buildings selected, select the Invert check box. The clouds were selected because they had intense color. The Color Range command doesn't work as well with little color to choose from. Sometimes it's easier to select what you don't want, and then invert the selection. When you're satisfied, click OK to create the selection.

11. Let's mask the Skyline layer to hide the clouds. With the Skyline layer selected, click the Add layer mask button at the bottom of the Layers panel. A new mask is added to the layer.

12. Click the eye icon for the Clouds layer to disable it. Examine the layer closely to see the extracted skyline image.

13. Restore the visibility for the Clouds layer.

14. Choose File > Save As. Navigate to the **Chapter_09 Project Files** folder. Name the file Skyline_progress.psd and click Save.

Cloning and healing to remove items

Now that the skyline is on its own layer, you need to remove it from the Clouds layer. Deleting it would be the quickest method, but that would leave holes that would show through when the layers or cameras were animated. Fortunately, you can employ the Clone Stamp and Healing Brush tools you used at the start of the chapter.

▲ **TIP: Clone First, Heal Second**

The first pass in hiding part of a layer is cloning, which will take pixels from one part of the image and move them to another. When cloning is complete, use the Healing Brush to blend the seams and hide any visible patterns.

1. Select the Clouds layer in the Layers panel.

2. Turn off the visibility for the Skyline layer by clicking its eye icon. You'll still see the original skyline on the Clouds layer. This needs to be removed.

3. Select the Clone Stamp tool, and choose a large brush with soft edges.

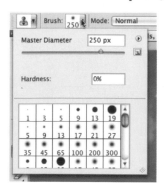

4. Hold down the Option (Alt) key and click in the middle of a large, soft cloud. Make sure the Aligned check box is selected in the options bar.

5. Click and start to clone to remove the buildings. Occasionally, set a new sample point and clone from a different area to avoid repeating too much of the same pattern. Try to sample close to the area you are cloning to avoid problems with sky variation.

6. After cloning, identify any areas that stand out with visible repeating patterns or irregular tones.

7. Select the Healing Brush and choose a large, soft-edged brush. Be sure to select the Healing Brush, not the Spot Healing Brush. Additionally, make sure the tool's Blending Mode is set to Normal.

8. Hold down the Option (Alt) key and click in the middle of a large, soft cloud.

9. Click and paint over a small area that needs healing. When you release the mouse, Photoshop blends the pixels to create a better blend.

10. Repeat the use of the Healing Brush for any areas in need of touch-up.

Organizing content for animation

Now that the two layers are cleaned up, you can prep the file to animate in After Effects. Properly organizing your files in Photoshop makes them easier to animate in After Effects.

1. Turn on the visibility for all layers.

2. Create a new empty layer by clicking the Create a new layer button at the bottom of the Layers panel.

3. By merging a flattened copy of the layered file to the topmost layer, you can use the new layer as a reference layer during the animation stages. This reference layer can be used to check the position of the layers once they are converted to 3D space.

4. Double-click the layer's name, rename the layer Reference, and press Return (Enter).

5. Drag the layer to the top of the stack.

6. Hold down the Option (Alt) key and choose Layer > Merge Visible. A flattened copy of the layered file is created at the top, but the original layers are preserved. Holding down the Option (Alt) key provides this useful alternative of the Merge Visible command.

7. Choose File > Save to capture the changes made.

Importing to After Effects

After the layers are prepped, you can import them into After Effects. The easiest way to do this is as a layered Photoshop file. Because your layers are uniquely and clearly named, they'll be easier to manage in After Effects. Let's create a scene using 3D space and cameras. In the next chapter you'll animate the cameras and elements within the scene as well as adjust lighting and camera settings to get the best results.

1. Switch back to After Effects and choose File > Import > File.

2. Navigate to the **Chapter_09 Project Files** folder, select the **02_Environment Sources** folder, and then choose the file **Skyline_progress.psd**.

3. At the bottom of the Import File window, click the Import As pop-up menu and choose Composition.

4. Click Open; a new dialog opens asking how you want to interpret layer styles applied to the Photoshop layers. Since there are no styles in use,

choose Merge Layer Styles into Footage and click OK. A new composition and a folder (that both contain all the layers in the document) are added to your project.

5. In the Project panel, click the Create a new folder button. Enter the name 02_Environment and press Return (Enter).

6. Drag the composition and folder named Skyline_progress into the new folder.

7. Click the disclosure triangle next to the folder 02_Environment.

8. Select the composition Skyline_progress.psd and choose Edit > Duplicate. A new copy of the composition is created. Adding additional compositions takes up very little space and ensures you have a file to return to for reference or to backtrack.

9. Select the duplicated composition; press Return (Enter) to edit its name. Name the composition 02_Environment and press Return (Enter).

10. Double-click the new composition to load it. Then choose File > Save to capture your work so far.

Positioning layers in 3D space

Now that the composition is imported, you can utilize 3D space to arrange layers. Normally, After Effects works in two dimensions, which means objects can be moved along their X axis (horizontal) or Y axis (vertical). After Effects can work in three dimensions as well, which adds the Z-axis (depth) to the X- and Y-axis controls for horizontal and vertical movement.

Choosing to work in 3D space opens up new options like depth of field, parallax motion, lighting, and shadows. The switch to 3D also brings an increase in preview and render times. Be sure to use a lower-quality setting for RAM previews to speed up your initial animation. You'll learn more about animating in 3D space in the next chapter. For now, let's just "set the stage."

1. Zoom out so you can see the entire composition. Click the Magnification ratio pop-up menu and choose Fit.

2. Turn off the visibility for the Reference layer by clicking the eye icon.

3. If your switches aren't visible, click the Toggle Switches/Modes button at the bottom of the Timeline.

4. Click the 3D switch (the cube column) for the Skyline and Clouds layers. The 3D Layer switch allows the layers to be positioned in 3D space. The Reference layer is not converted to 3D, because it will be toggled off and on for reference during the positioning process.

5. Arranging layers in 3D is easiest when you add a camera and use two views. To add a camera, choose Layer > New > Camera. From the Preset list choose 35 mm and click OK. A full discussion of cameras and their controls is in the next chapter.

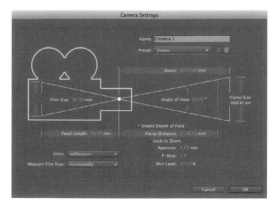

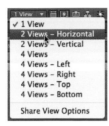

6. Cameras are easy to understand when two views are used. You can look through the camera's "viewfinder" as well as take a global "director" view. Click the Select view layout button at the bottom of the Composition panel and choose 2 Views – Horizontal.

7. The right side currently shows the Active Camera view; the left side shows a top view. Click the left-side viewer to select it (gold triangles in each corner indicate the selected side.)

8. Click the 3D View pop-up menu (currently labeled Top) and choose Custom View 1.

9. Click the Magnification ratio pop-up menu and choose Fit.

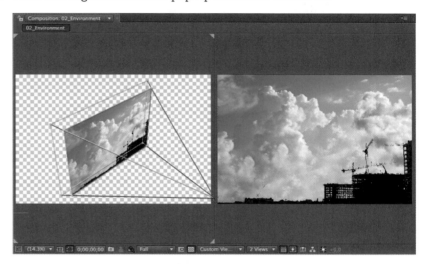

You can now position the layers within 3D space. By spreading layers apart you can create a world that resembles a "shoebox diorama." That is to say that flat layers are cut out and spaced apart within a specified area. The goal is to build a 3D world, and then animate the cameras within the space. Because the layers are spaced apart, camera movement will display a parallax style effect, and objects that are farther away will appear to move slower than those closer to the camera.

10. To begin, access layers in 3D space. Select layer 4 and press P to access its position.

11. Because the layer is 3D, it has three coordinates to modify (X, Y, and Z). A positive value moves the image farther away from the camera, whereas a negative value moves it closer. Enter a value of 8,000 pixels into the Z field to push the cloud layer away. As the layer moves away, it appears to get smaller.

12. Hold down the Shift key and press S to add the Scale property. Scaling up the image is okay because the Scale property will combine with the

distance of the Z axis. Essentially, the image appears smaller because moving it along the Z axis makes it appear to scale down. Scaling the image above 100% until the layer looks like its "original" size is the goal.

13. Scale up the layer by dragging the Scale slider. When the image reaches the edges of the window frame, you can stop scaling (for this image, a value of approximately 372 is correct). By scaling until the active camera view matches, you can restore the appearance of the original image.

▲ **TIP: Check Your Reference**

You can toggle the visibility of the Reference layer to check the position and scale of your layers.

14. Let's add the Cloud layer you created earlier. Click the disclosure triangle next to the folder 01_Background in the Project panel.

15. Drag the composition 01_Clouds to the Timeline and drop it between layers 3 and 4. You can place a composition into another composition.

16. Click the 3D switch for the newly added layer.

17. Press S for Scale, hold down the Shift key, and press P for Position.

18. Enter a position value of 4,000 pixels into the Z field to push the cloud layer away.

19. Scale the 01_Clouds layer to 700%. Then click the Toggle Switches/Modes button.

20. Set the layer to Lighten and lower its opacity to 15%. This creates a gentle overlay texture, adding depth to the clouds.

Changing comp size

After the layers are positioned in 3D space, you can change the size of the composition to match a standard output size. This reduces the amount of the image shown in the window but can be adjusted by modifying the framing camera.

1. Choose Composition > Composition Settings.
2. Click the Preset list and choose HDV/HDTV 720 29.97 to create an HD composition sized for broadcast.
3. Click OK. The skyline disappears and only a small area of the composition is now showing.
4. Select the camera layer (the topmost in the Timeline), and click its disclosure triangle to view its properties.
5. Enter a value of –6,900 into the Z property of Position for Camera 1. This adjusts how far away the camera is from the scene.
6. Enter a value of 500 into the Y property for Point of interest (where the camera is looking). This tilts the camera to see the skyline.

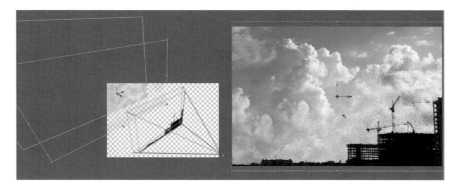

There is a lot more to working with 3D cameras. You'll explore animation and additional properties in the next chapter.

Creating Seamless Backgrounds with Photomerge

Panoramic photography is the practice of shooting multiple photos and then stitching them into a larger photo. If enough photos are taken, you can create a large panoramic image. These photos can then be brought into After Effects to serve as a backdrop for chroma key footage.

Shooting Panoramic Photos Right

Do you want to start shooting your own panoramic photos? Here are a few tips to get the best results.

- For best results use a tripod. Pros know that it's better to use a tripod and slightly move the camera to create overlap.

- For even better results, get a tripod head that rotates and has degree markers. There are even specialized tripod heads that you can purchase from companies like Kaidan (www.kaidan.com) and Really Right Stuff (www.reallyrightstuff.com) that make leveling and rotation much more precise.

- Set the camera into a portrait aspect ratio.

- Switch the camera out of auto mode and lock the exposure to help minimize the amount of changes as the camera pans.

- Make sure there is at least a 15 percent overlap between each shot. Depending on the type of lens you use, you will use between 2 and 24 exposures. More exposures mean less distortion and cleaner panoramic photos.

▲ **TIP: Learn More About Photomerge**

For a video tutorial on Photoshop's Photomerge command, visit www.csfour.com.

Merging Photos

Let's try piecing together a full 360° VR photo. This particular shot is composed of 24 exposures that capture an entire environment. These types of shots are very useful because they allow for great flexibility in creating virtual sets. When combined with green screen footage, you literally have an entire location viewable from 360°. Photoshop makes the combining of multiple shots easy using the Automation command called Photomerge.

1. Choose File > Automate > Photomerge. Photomerge is a specialized "mini-application" within Photoshop that assists in combining multiple images into a single photo.

2. Click the Browse button and navigate to the **Chapter_09 Project Files** folder. Open the folder **03_Photomerge**, and then open the folder **Panoramic Photos**, which contains 24 images. The originals were much higher resolution but have been compressed to save space for this lesson.

3. Click the first photo then press Command+A (Ctrl+A) to select all the pictures in the folder and click Open.

4. Several Layout options are available that attempt to fix problems caused by panoramic photography (such as distortion). A good place to start is Auto, which attempts to align the images but will bend them as needed.

5. Select Blend Images Together and Vignette Removal. These two options will attempt to blend the edges of the photos together and hide subtle differences in exposure.

6. Click OK to build the panoramic image. Photoshop tries to assemble the panorama based on your choices in the dialog. Due to the number of images, the process may take a few minutes.

Notice that the tree trunk appears on both the left and right edges. This image needs a bit more processing to create a completely seamless 360° photo.

Creating a Seamless Loop with an Action

The resulting image from the preceding exercise is quite large but is not a perfect loop. The image can be seamless, but the left and right edges have not been properly cropped to use the image as a circular loop. To fix this process would normally take several (tedious) steps. To solve this problem, you can use an action (we've created one) that will finish processing the full 360° panoramic image. (An action stores and plays back several commands with one click.)

1. Choose Window > Actions to call up the Actions panel.

2. Click the submenu of the Actions panel and choose Load Actions. A new browser window opens.

3. Navigate to the **Chapter_09 Project Files** folder and open the folder **03_Photomerge**.

4. Select the action **Panoramic.atn** and click Load.

5. In the Actions panel, locate the Panoramics set (folder) and choose the Seamless Loop action.

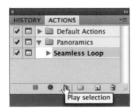

6. Click the Play selection button in the Actions panel. The action splits the layer near the middle and then uses Photoshop's ability to auto-align layers and blend them back together.

7. The image is now seamless on the left and right edges. A new dialog invites you to crop the image as needed.

8. Click Continue. The image needs a bit cropped from the top.

9. Choose Image > Canvas Size. Enter a new height of 1950 pixels and set the Anchor point as shown.

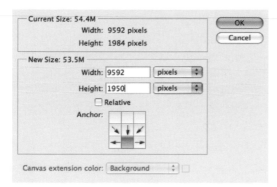

10. Click OK. A dialog warns you that some clipping will occur. Click Proceed.

11. Choose Layer > Flatten Image to discard any layers.

12. Choose File > Save As. Name the file Pano_360 and save it as a TIFF file to the folder **03_Photomerge** inside the **Chapter_09 Project Files** folder.

13. Click Save to write the file to your hard drive. A new dialog pops up for TIFF options. Apply LZW image compression to reduce the file size.

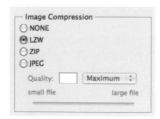

▲ TIP: Why
Choose TIFF

After Effects likes TIFF files as they are a good balance for file size to image quality. TIFFs do support Alpha Channels, but import as flattened files when brought into After Effects.

Importing into After Effects

Now that you've created a full 360° VR photo, you can bring it into After Effects. By turning the image into a cylinder, you can place a 3D camera into the scene and add green screen footage to create a virtual world. Because you have a full view, it makes it easy to simulate being at the particular location.

1. Switch back to After Effects and choose File > Import > File.
2. Navigate to the **Chapter_09 Project Files** folder, select the **03_Photomerge** folder, and then choose the file **Pano_360.tif**. Click Open.
3. In the Project panel, click the Create a new folder button.
4. Enter the name 03_Photomerge and press Return (Enter).
5. Drag the file Pano_360.tif into the new folder.
6. Click the disclosure triangle next to the folder 03_Photomerge. Choose File > Save to capture your work.

Using the Panorama Script

▲ **TIP: Get the Latest Script**

You can find a detailed discussion of the pt_Panorama-Maker.jsx script at http://aenhancers .com/viewtopic .php?f=9&t=435.

To create a panorama, you'll use an After Effects script. The use of scripts allows for programmers to customize After Effects and streamline the creation of complex effects. In this lesson, you'll add a third-party script that coverts a panoramic photo into a cylinder and adds a 3D camera to the scene. The script pt_PanoramaMaker.jsx was created by Paul Tuersley and posted on www.aenhancers.com, a Web site dedicated to sharing After Effects scripts and Expressions.

1. To install a script, you must quit After Effects. Quit the application and save your progress.
2. In the **Chapter_09 Project Files** folder, locate the script **pt_Panorama-Maker.jsx**, which is stored inside the folder **03_Photomerge**.
3. Navigate to the After Effects application folder. Open the folder Scripts, and then open the folder ScriptUI Panels.
4. Copy the file pt_PanoramaMaker.jsx to the ScriptUI Panels folder.
5. Relaunch After Effects. At the Welcome screen, look in the recent projects list and reopen 09_progress.aep by clicking its name.
6. Choose Composition > New Composition. Name the comp 03_Photomerge and choose the HDV/HDTV 720 29.97 preset.
7. Enter a Duration of 0;00;15;00 and click OK.
8. Drag the new composition into the folder **03_Photomerge** and double-click the composition to load it.
9. Drag the file Pano_360.tif into the new composition and select the photo layer in the composition.

10. Choose Window > ptPanoramaMaker.jsx to open a controller window for the script. Inspect the first field, which is how much of a panoramic photo you have. In this case 360 is correct because the photo is a complete arc.

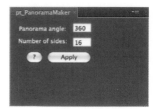

11. In the second field, enter the number of sides to divide the panorama into to create the cylinder. More sides mean a smoother curve (but increased render time). Enter 24 to match the original number of exposures and then close the script UI window. Click Apply.

12. Examine the Viewer. You should have two views set from earlier in the chapter. If not, click the Select view layout and choose 2 Views – Horizontal.

13. Click the left viewer to select it.

14. Double-click the pre-composition called Panorama Precomp to open it. Inside you'll find a Null object to control the panorama and layers to make each face. You'll explore this set more in the next chapter.

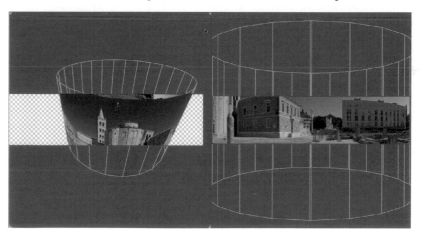

15. Close the Panorama Precomp by clicking the X in its Timeline tab.

16. In the 03_Photomerge composition select Layer 1.

17. Press R for rotation controls. Drag the Y slider to rotate the image on its Y axis. Experiment with different values to explore your options.

18. Choose File > Save to capture your work.

Using Vanishing Point Exchange

Vanishing Point is a feature in Photoshop that allows you to identify planes within a photo. Its original purpose was for users to utilize this information for cloning (or mapping new objects using perspective). As the technology evolved, Adobe added support to Photoshop Extended to export the information as a basic 3D model. You'll learn to complete the following scene and animate your camera in the next chapter.

A flat photo is converted to a basic 3D model using Vanishing Point Exchange. The scene is then enhanced with a nighttime sky and some floating clouds.

Selecting Images

● NOTE: Download Photoshop Extended for 30 Days

If you don't have Photoshop Extended, you can download a 30-day trial copy or use the completed files in the Chapter_09 Project Files folder.

Vanishing Point is fairly tricky and won't work with every photo. You may need to experiment (by trial and error) as you create 3D planes. Still, it's a very cool technique that can save you time and help you to quickly create 3D environments. The integration of Photoshop Extended and After Effects allows for Vanishing Point Exchange.

Photoshop uses Vanishing Point Exchange to convert photos into a series of flat planes and a 3D model. After Effects can then import the Vanishing Point Exchange file and reassemble the objects within 3D space in After Effects using the planes you drew to guide the assembly. (Thanks to Bob Donlon at Adobe for helping us perfect this technique.)

1. Switch back to Photoshop CS4 (you must be using the Extended version for this technique). Choose File > Open and navigate to the **Chapter_09 Project Files** folder. Open the subfolder **04_VPE**, and then open the file **VPE_start.psd**. To save time, this file has been masked using the

Polygonal Lasso tool and the same masking techniques you learned at the start of the chapter.

2. Turn off the visibility icon for the Background layer. Then select the Building layer in the Layers panel.

3. Choose Filter > Vanishing Point. The Vanishing Point interface opens.

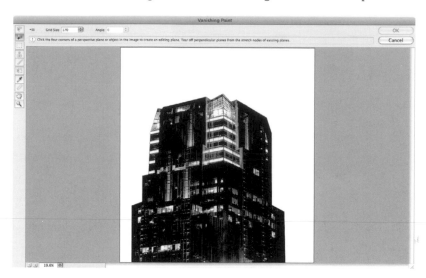

▲ **TIP: Using Vanishing Point Exchange with Photos**

We've found that Vanishing Point Exchange works best when a photo has a clean angle of about 45° with the subject. You should also try to keep the frame as clear as possible to minimize masking and cloning issues.

Creating Planes

After the Vanishing Point interface is open, you need to draw planes on the image. These are represented with grids on your image. You should draw the grid for the largest surface of the object first.

1. Look for a straight line to use as reference. If you need them, you can extend the boundaries to accommodate extruding objects.

2. Define the four corner nodes of the first plane. The Create Plane tool is selected by default. Click in the preview image to define the four corner nodes.

   • Use a rectangle object in the image as a guide when creating the plane.

   • Zoom in with the zoom controls in the bottom-left corner as needed.

   • Try to line up each edge of the plane with the perspective of the photo.

   • Take your time on this step because it is the most crucial part (look closely at the figure for guidance). If you don't get a blue plane on your first try, drag the corners and tweak their position. A yellow or red plane indicates perspective problems.

3. Once the first plane is created, you'll need to generate a second plane for the other wall. You can create a new plane by holding down the Command (Ctrl) key and dragging from the center of a plane's edge and "tear off" a new plane. It is crucial that you "tear off" planes rather than create new ones so the model can stay attached. For this sample, drag from the right edge of the initial plane to create the second wall.

4. Adjust the angle of the second plane so its lines follow the angle of the photo. Experiment with the angle so the plane and building edge line up properly.

5. Drag the right and bottom edges to size the grid to cover the second surface.

Exporting for After Effects

When you've completed the planes in the image, you'll need to export a specialized set of files for After Effects. Photoshop Extended will create a series of PNG files for each plane, a 3DS file for the model, and a Vanishing Point Exchange file to facilitate the import into After Effects.

1. In the submenu in the upper-left corner click and choose Export for After Effects (.vpe).

2. Navigate to the **Chapter_09 Project Files** folder and the **04_VPE** subfolder. Create a new folder named Building, which will serve as a destination for the PNG files and 3D data that Photoshop will generate. Name the VPE file Building and click Save.

3. When the export is complete, click OK to store the Vanishing Point filter information. You can then close and save the Photoshop file. If you need to revisit the planes for tweaking, just open the PSD filter and run the Vanishing Point filter again. Your previous planes will be there for editing.

Importing to After Effects

After you've successfully exported your VPE data, you'll need to import it into After Effects. After Effects offers a dedicated Import command.

1. Switch to After Effects; make sure no items are selected in the Project panel (click in an empty area).
2. Click the New Folder icon at the bottom of the Project panel and name the folder 04_VPE.
3. Choose File > Import > Vanishing Point (vpe).
4. Navigate to the **Chapter_09 Project Files** folder, open the folder **04_VPE**, and then open the folder **Building**. (If you didn't complete the VPE export in Photoshop Extended, use the folder called VPE Export.)
5. Select the file **Building.vpe** and click Open. Then double-click the composition Building.vpe.

6. Drag the newly imported items into the folder **04_VPE**.
7. After Effects creates a new composition and reassembles the 3D objects based on the VPE file by arranging all the planes (each on an individual layer in the PNG format) in 3D space.
8. Click in the Active Camera view to select it.
9. Use the Orbit Camera tool (C) to rotate around your scene. Click and drag in the window to change your view. When finished, choose Edit > Undo. You'll animate the camera in the next chapter.

Camera Positioning Advice

- You can rotate the camera about 40° left or right before the scene looks "too fake."

- The model in the Vanishing Point exercise does not have a roof, so be careful not to pull the camera too high.

- By framing the camera tightly and using keyframes you can create a useful animation.

Cleaning Up Layers

You'll notice that Photoshop inserted white pixels into the transparent areas when it exported the PNG files. You'll need to clean up the individual files using Photoshop. By opening the files again, you can select the unwanted pixels and erase them.

▲ **TIP: Hate Selecting White?**

Do you want an easier color to clean up? Try putting a layer filled with bright red or green behind the layer you are using Vanishing Point with. This makes it easier to select pixels for deletion.

1. Select the layer Build0.png and press Command+E (Ctrl+E) to edit it. The individual file opens in Photoshop for touch-up.

2. In Photoshop, use cloning and erasing to clean up unwanted pixels or blank areas. You can also use the Quick Selection tool and press Delete to erase unwanted pixels.

▲ **TIP: Don't Change the Canvas Size After Export**

Do not change the canvas size when touching up your PNG files. Rather, if you want to extend the photo's edges, you should do that prior to creating the Vanishing Point planes in Photoshop.

3. After fixing the image, close and save it. You are returned to After Effects.

4. Repeat the touch-up for the second layer.

5. Choose Composition > Composition Settings.

6. Choose the HDV/HDTV 720 29.97 preset. Enter a Duration of 0;00;20;00 and click OK.

7. Choose File > Save to capture your progress.

What's Next

You are now ready for Chapter 10, "Using 3D Cameras and Lights." The use of 3D space can be tough. If you had problems with any of the features in this chapter, don't worry, you can use the provided starter project for the next lesson.

10 USING 3D CAMERAS AND LIGHTS

Now that you know how to create virtual sets, it's time for a Hollywood cliché. "Lights! Camera! Action!" And that's just what you'll learn. In this chapter, you'll animate cameras so they move around 3D scenes. You'll delve into some advanced camera topics, such as depth of field and camera orbits, and then you'll hang some lights, move them into place, and maybe even cast a few dramatic shadows.

You'll be working with some of the files you built in Chapter 9, "Creating 3D Environments," adding in a few more elements when you need to. The only file you'll need for this chapter is 3DProjects.aep, which you'll find in the Chapter_10 Project Files folder.

Each comp in the file has a starter version, which you'll open as you work on each project, and a completed version, which you can use to compare your work with our attempts. For instance, the first comp you'll look at is called Skyline. The completed version is called Skyline_Complete. Since 3D is so tough, you can toggle between your design composition and the completed reference version when you want to check your work.

Also in the Chapter_10 Project Files folder is a file called cameraLightTests.aep. You won't be using it in this chapter, but we recommend you take a look at it when you get a chance. Each comp in the file cameraLightTests.aep demonstrates (and isolates) a single feature of cameras or lights. And now, "On with the show!"

Animating a Camera

In the previous lesson you added 3D cameras. Just like other objects in After Effects, cameras support keyframes. You can record key properties like Position or Zoom, and then have After Effects interpolate between two keyframes and move or zoom the camera.

Let's start by animating a camera so that it tracks across a scene from left to right. Doesn't sound so tough, does it? It's not, but there are some nuances you'll want to note, taking special care to recognize the difference between camera Position (where the camera is located) and camera Point of Interest (where the camera is pointing).

● NOTE: Crane Animation

The crane was animated in Flash using one of the techniques you learned in Chapter 8, "Advanced Animation Tools in After Effects and Flash." Do you recall which technique it was?

1. From the book's DVD, copy the **Chapter_10 Project Files** folder to your local hard drive. Then open the project **3DProjects.aep** and double-click the comp called Skyline.

   You will recognize this comp from the previous chapter. (You *did* go through the exercises in Chapter 9, "Creating 3D Environments," didn't you? If not, you *really* need to complete that chapter first.) An animated crane has been added to the comp; but otherwise, it's the same as it was in Chapter 9.

2. At the bottom of the Composition panel, select 2 Views – Horizontal from the Select View Layout pop-up menu. From the adjacent 3D View pop-up menu, set the left view to Top and the right view to Active Camera.

3. In the Timeline, move the Current Time Indicator to the beginning of the Timeline. Click the disclosure triangle for the layer to view the Transform properties. Click the Transform disclosure triangle to open it and turn on the stopwatches for the Camera 1 layer's Transform properties Position and Point of Interest.

4. Remembering that the goal is to make the camera track from left to right while it's pointing at the scene. Try moving the camera to its starting position (on the left) by scrubbing its Position X property.

The camera is now pointing in at a hard angle. Why? Because its Position changed, but its Point of Interest remained the same.

5. Undo the Position change by pressing Command+Z (Ctrl+Z). This time try scrubbing just the Point of Interest to the left.

6. That doesn't work either. The camera is still in its original position. It's just turned to point at something else. Technically speaking, this is a pan (horizontal) or a tilt (vertical). Undo the Point of Interest change. Point to the X axis (the red arrow) of the Camera's 3D manipulator, and drag the camera to its starting position on the left.

● NOTE: Lights Too!

Lights also have Positions and Points of Interest. Everything discussed in the "Animating a Camera" section about moving cameras applies to moving lights, too.

But before dragging, make sure that the Position and Point of Interest properties have their stopwatches turned on in the Timeline. They probably are on now, because we told you to turn them on in step 3. In real-life projects we often remember to turn on the Position stopwatch but forget to turn on the Point of Interest stopwatch.

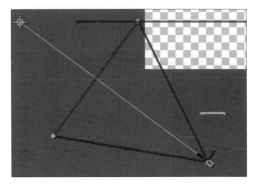

To keep the camera's Position and Point of Interest in sync, remember to keyframe both Position and Point of Interest properties. When you drag the camera in the Composition panel, its Position and Point of Interest move together.

Moving a Camera

You can also move a camera by switching to one of the camera tools on the Tools panel and then dragging in the Composition panel's Active Camera view.

Unified Camera tool. The top tool is the Unified Camera tool. It gives you quick access to the lower three tools via a three-button mouse.

Orbit Camera tool. The tool below the Unified Camera tool is the Orbit Camera tool (with the Unified Camera tool, you can hold down the left mouse button to orbit the camera), which allows you to rotate the camera around its Point of Interest.

Track XY Camera tool. Next is the Track XY Camera tool (middle mouse button), which moves the camera horizontally or vertically.

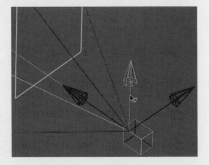

Track Z Camera tool. Then there's the Track Z Camera tool (right mouse button), which moves the camera in and out of the scene along the plane of its Point of Interest.

It's fun to move the camera with its tools, but you'll usually get more precise results by dragging the camera in the Top view (or sometimes in one of the side views).

Position and Point of Interest

Imagine I drove you from left to right past Mount Rushmore, asking you to keep your head turned so you were always staring at President Roosevelt. (From left to right, the heads on Rushmore are Washington, Jefferson, Roosevelt, and Lincoln.) Your body would move from left to right, but you'd have to keep turning your head to remain looking at Roosevelt. If you were an After Effects camera, your body moving would be an adjustment to your Position; your head would stay facing towards Roosevelt, your point of interest.

In the comp in step 4, you left the Point of Interest pointing to the middle of the scene while you moved the Position to the left. That's not what you want. You want to move the Position and Point of Interest together. Doing so is like driving past Mount Rushmore looking at each president as you pass him.

Point of Interest was an alien concept to us at first. But you can think of it this way. Adjusting the camera Position is like moving the physical camera, which is often referred to as:

- a truck (X axis or horizontal move)
- a crane or jib (Y axis or vertical move)
- a dolly (Z axis or physically moving the camera forward or back)

Adjusting the Point of Interest is similar to moving the camera on a tripod head in one of these ways:

- panning (X axis or side-to-side move)
- tilting (Y axis or up-and-down move)
- changing the Z value for Point of Interest is not recommended

Once you get used to Point of Interest, you'll find it very helpful. We urge you to give Point of Interest a shot. However, if you'd rather not work with this property, you can shut it off. If you turn off Point of Interest, you control the camera the way you'd control one in real life—by pointing it (rotating it toward) whatever you want it to "film." To disable Point of Interest, select the camera layer, and then choose Layer > Transform > Auto-Orient. In the Auto-Orientation dialog, select the Off option. In our opinion, this is not a good workflow for most projects.

7. Move the Current Time Indicator to the end of the Timeline, and using the X axis arrow, drag the camera to its end position.

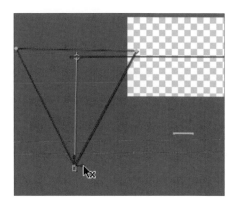

To add a little spice to the move, you can move the camera a little more to the right and in closer to the scene, but leave its Point of Interest staring at the same spot (the spot it ended up staring at in step 6). How do you move just Position (but not Point of Interest) while dragging one of the camera's axes in the Composition panel? Easy: Just add the Command (Ctrl) key.

When you hold down the Command (Ctrl) key and drag, you move Position without moving Point of Interest.

8. Command+drag (Ctrl+drag) the camera's X axis a little to the right. Then Command+drag (Ctrl+drag) the camera's Z axis a little closer to the scene.

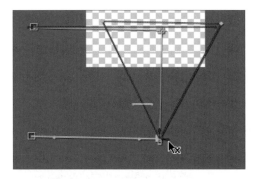

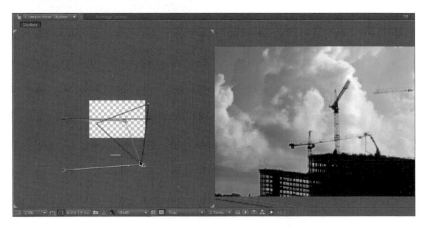

Which Way Is Up?

You can orient the 3D manipulators in three different ways. Each has its benefits but behaves differently.

Local Axis

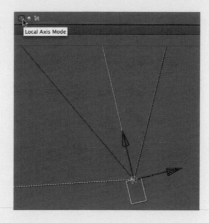

You can use the red, green, and blue arrows that help you move (or rotate) 3D layers, lights, and cameras along an axis. The default orientation is Local Axis mode. In this mode, the arrows are "glued" to their layers.

Imagine a man facing north. Now imagine he has an arrow sticking out of his forehead, pointing straight ahead. Since the man is facing north and the arrow is pointing straight ahead, the arrow is facing north, too. But if the man turns to face east, the arrow will face east, too—it's glued to him.

In Local Axis mode, if you rotate a layer, its 3D arrows rotate, too. The X axis moves the layer to *its* (the layer's) right or left, which isn't necessarily your screen's right or left.

World Axis

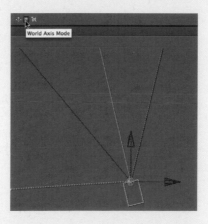

World Axis mode is similar to the way you think of compass directions on earth. No matter where you are on the planet, a compass always points toward the north pole (or, to be precise, the magnetic north pole).

The "world" of World Axis mode is the scene. The Z arrow always points to the back of the scene; the Y arrow always points to the top of the scene; and the X arrow always points to the right of the scene. In the following figure, you're looking down from above (Top view), so the Y arrow (green) is pointing toward you since you're at the top of the scene.

(continued on next page)

Which Way Is Up? *(continued)*

View Axis

View Axis mode is the simplest orientation. It's based on the orientation of your screen. In View Axis mode, the red arrow (X) always points to the right edge of your screen; the green arrow (Y) always points to the top of your screen; and the blue arrow (Z) always points away from you, into the screen. It doesn't matter whether you're looking at the Active Camera view, a custom view, or the Top view: The arrows always point the same ways.

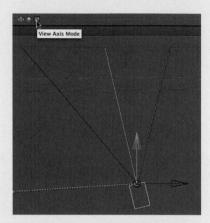

This is potentially confusing, because it means that although the arrows never change the direction in which they're pointing, dragging them in different views gives you different results. For instance, if you drag the blue arrow in Active Camera view, the layer will move toward you. If you drag the blue arrow in Top view, the layer will move upward (as you can see in the following Top view figure shown).

The Bottom Line

Once you get the hang of these modes, they can be very useful. But before you get the hang of them, they'll probably confuse you. So here's an easy way to use them in the meantime: If you want to drag a layer to a new position, see if one of the arrows is facing that position. If it is, great—drag from that arrow.

If it's not, cycle through the view modes until you see an arrow facing close to the direction you want the layer to move. Don't worry about what the modes mean. Just switch modes, watch the arrows, and drag when you see an arrow that points in the right direction.

Use the Active Camera view to make sure the camera isn't filming anything you don't want people to see, such as the edges of layers. If necessary, adjust the camera's position to keep the illusion intact.

9. Invoke a RAM Preview for the comp, watching the camera track from left to right and then in a little.

   Pretty cool, huh? The reason you get that 3D feeling is because the layers are different distances from the camera. This creates a parallax effect, which is a really believable way to add depth to a scene with flat objects. You can see that the crane is very close to the camera, which makes the pan very dramatic, whereas the cloud layer is *very* far away, which makes it seem suspended in space. This technique is essentially an optical illusion, but it works very well.

Animating a 3D Pre-comp

Let's switch to a new exercise. In the previous chapter, you created a 3D panorama and arranged it so the images formed a circle. Now you'll place a reporter (shot in front of a green screen) inside the circle and animate the circle spinning. The result will look as if the background is whizzing by behind the reporter.

1. Open the comp called Field_Reporter. All you can see inside it is a flattened version of the panorama. Actually, this is the 3D circle. It's nested inside a pre-comp. You need to flip a couple of switches to make sure the nested comp passes its 3D information through to the comp it's nested in (Field_Reporter).

2. In the Timeline, enable the Panorama Precomp layer's 3D switch.

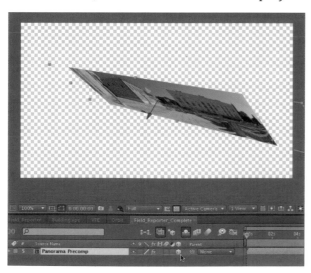

   Don't tilt the layer as you see in the figure. We tilted it to show you that enabling the 3D switch only gets you halfway to the goal: It turns the layer into a 3D layer, but it doesn't pass the nested 3D data (the fact that the layers inside Panorama Precomp are arranged in a circle).

3. Enable the layer's Collapse Transformations switch (also known as the Continually Rasterize switch).

4. Scale the layer up to 2,000% so that it fills the screen.

Which Switch Is Which?

The Collapse Transformations switch has two very different functions. In fact, it has two different names to describe those functions: Collapse Transformations and Continually Rasterize. The latter name/function is useful for keeping vector layers looking smooth at all resolutions. If you scale a vector layer up to 1,000%, it will still look smooth (as opposed to pixilated or blurry) as long as you've remembered to select the layer and flip the Continually Rasterize switch.

The same switch, in this case known as the Collapse Transformations switch, passes 3D information from inside a nested composition (a pre-comp) to the composition it's nested in. In other words, the positions and rotations of 3D layers in the nested comp will be passed upward into the "parent" comp. The pre-comp's 3D layers will be treated as individual 3D layers in the parent comp.

For a pre-comp's 3D layers to be passed upward into the parent comp, you have to enable both the Collapse Transformations switch and the 3D switch for the pre-comp layer. This is a great way to harness the benefits of 3D without having as many layers in the main Timeline.

▲ TIP: 3D Worlds within 3D Worlds

To gain access to the 3D layout of a layer that's nested inside another comp (aka a pre-comp), enable its 3D and Collapse Transformations switches.

5. Press R to access the layer's Rotation properties. With the Current Time Indicator at the beginning of the Timeline, turn on the Y Rotation property's stopwatch. Move the Current Time Indicator to the end of the Timeline and set the layer's Y Rotation property to rotate one time around.

6. Move the Current Time Indicator back to the beginning of the Timeline, and drag the composition Reporter_Keyed footage from the Project panel to the top layer of the Timeline. Enable its 3D switch.

Lighting the Scene

Let's light the reporter so that he blends a little better with the background.

1. Choose Layer > New > Light. In the Light Settings dialog, make sure the Light Type is Spot, and then click OK, accepting the default parameters.

● NOTE: Adjusting Lights in the Timeline

You don't need to worry much about the settings in the Light Settings dialog, because all the parameters in it (including the Light Type) are adjustable on the Timeline after you add the light.

2. In Top view (and a side view if necessary), adjust the light so it's positioned similarly to the light in this figure.

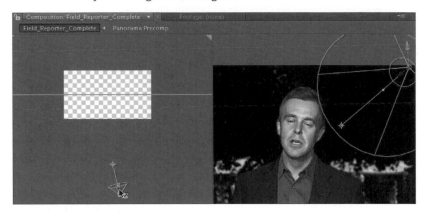

3. Select the reporter layer, and drag it a little closer to the light so it receives more light than the background.

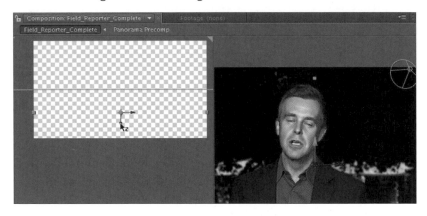

● **NOTE: Raise the Intensity**

You can raise a light's Intensity up to 200%, 300%, or higher. The higher the Intensity, the brighter the light! In light of this (pun intended), we're wondering what 100% signifies. It seems to mean "default brightness."

4. In the Timeline, name the light layer Spot. Click the disclosure triangle to it open it. Then click the disclosure triangle to open its Light Options. Lower the light's Intensity to 30%.

You've now made the reporter blend in with the background by making him as dark as the background. Is there a way to keep the blending but make the scene look a little less gloomy? Sure there is! You'll just add in another light—one that makes both layers brighter by the same amount (now that they're equally dark).

5. Choose Layer > New > Light. Choose Ambient as the Light Type and rename the light to ambient in the Timeline. Click the disclosure triangle to open it and set the Light Options Intensity to 60%.

Ambient lights don't have Transform properties (Position, Scale, etc.). They are just general illumination, adding a wash of light to the whole scene. You can think of them as levels controls. You want to set the ambient light below 100% so you can add other lights to build up the scene and add shadows.

A Type of Light on the Subject

After Effects includes several types of lights: Parallel, Spot, Point, and Ambient. You can choose a light's type from the drop-down menu in the Light Settings dialog. You can also set a light's type in its Light Options layer properties in the Timeline. Keep in mind that like cameras, lights only affect 3D layers.

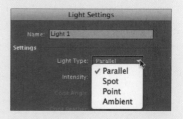

In the following figure you can see a Parallel light shining on a solid. Parallel lights shine in a single direction (specified by their Point of Interest property). The light is hitting the solid on the right but not the one on the left.

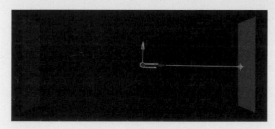

Spot lights are similar to Parallel lights. They only shine in one direction, which is why this spot is only hitting the solid on the right. Spot lights have some additional properties (not shared by Parallel lights), such as Cone Angle (how big the spot is) and Cone Feather (how blurry the spot's edges are).

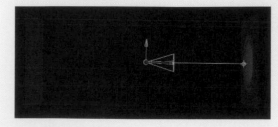

(continued on next page)

A Type of Light on the Subject *(continued)*

A Point light is like a bare lightbulb: It shines in all directions at once. That's why this one is hitting both solids.

An Ambient light has no position. It's just general illumination. In this figure a green Ambient light has been added and its Intensity set to a low value.

Here the Ambient light's Intensity value has been cranked up.

Often, after adding Spot lights, Point lights, and/or Parallel lights, we include an Ambient light as a sort of general levels control for the scene. Some designers choose to add the ambient light first and darken the scene before adding other lights for realism and dramatic effect. Try both approaches and see which works best for you.

Adding a Camera to the Scene

Finally, let's add a camera to the scene and animate it so that it gradually moves closer to the reporter.

1. Choose Layer > New > Camera. In the Camera Settings dialog, select the 50mm preset (the one that's closest to the way the human eye sees), and click OK.

2. In the Timeline, turn on the camera's Position stopwatch. From a Top view, animate the camera along the Z axis so that when the Current Time Indicator is at the start of the Timeline it's far away from the reporter, and when the Current Time Indicator is at the end of the Timeline it's close to the reporter.

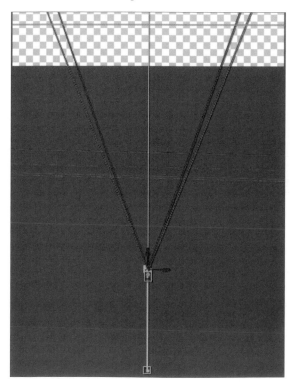

3. Preview the comp, watching the background spin and the camera dolly into the reporter.

   In real execution, the background wouldn't spin (unless you were trying for a frantic merry-go-round effect)—we just made it spin here to teach you the concepts. Rather, you'd adjust the background to give yourself an ideal shot and believable composite for the final effect.

Camera Controls

Cameras have two sets of controls: those in the Camera Settings dialog and others in the Timeline (click the disclosure triangle to open the camera, and then click the disclosure triangle to open its Camera Options property group). There's a bit of overlap, but you can only access some of the properties from the Timeline. The dialog pops up automatically when you first add a camera. Thereafter, you can access it by double-clicking the camera's icon in the Timeline. Or you can select the camera and choose Layer > Camera Settings.

To explore the settings, take a look at **CameraLightTests.aep** in the **Chapter_10 Project Files** folder. It isolates each camera setting it its own comp and shows you what happens when you tweak that setting. For instance, here we've experimented with three cameras, each positioned at the same layer (a row of numbers) and each set to a different preset.

Here's a list of Camera Settings dialog properties and a short explanation of what each property does (see online help for more info). Starred properties are available in the Timeline:

Preset. Sets most of the other properties in the dialog so that as a whole the camera simulates a real-world, 35mm camera with a lens of a specific focal length (specified by the preset's name). The higher the number in the preset's name, the narrower the camera angle. So cameras set to the 200mm preset will see less of the scene's width than cameras set to the 15mm preset.

Zoom*. The distance from the lens to whatever the camera is looking at. If Zoom is set to 1,000, a layer that is 1,000 pixels away from the camera will appear at its full size.

Focus Distance*. If you set this to 1,000, a layer that's 1,000 pixels away from the camera will be in perfect focus.

Lock To Zoom. If enabled, the Focal Distance value will match the Zoom value.

Focal Length. The distance from the film (in the back of the camera) to the camera lens. If you adjust this value, Preset, Angle Of View, and Aperture (below) also change. This property is of greatest interest to professional photographers who are trying to simulate a real-world camera effect in After Effects.

Film Size. How much of the film gets exposed to the light. Adjusting this setting modifies Zoom's value. This is another property that will mostly interest photographers.

Angle Of View. The wider the Angle Of View, the more of the scene you can see. This setting is determined by the Focal Length, F-stop, and Blur Level settings.

Enable Depth of Field*. This has our vote for coolest camera feature and is explored later in this chapter. With Depth of Field enabled, items too close or too far from the camera go out of focus.

Aperture*. In a real camera, this is the size of the lens opening. The higher this setting, the blurrier the Depth of Field effect gets.

F-stop. Has the same effect as Aperture but it uses F-stop units, which are meaningful to photographers.

Blur Level*. This is a cheat to make the Depth of Field illusion more or less intense. With a Blur Level of 100%, Depth of Field simulates a real camera. Raising or lowering the Blur Level value exaggerates the effect.

Camera Orbits

Let's say you want a camera to circle around something. Easy, right? Just move its anchor point to the center of the orbit and rotate. But wait a second. Cameras don't have anchor points! Or rather, you can't adjust their anchor points in the Timeline. Camera's anchor points are forever glued to their positions, so if you rotate a camera, it will spin like it's on the top of a tripod. Rotating it will never make it orbit around something other than itself.

● NOTE: As
with Cameras,
So with Lights

Everything discussed about cameras in the "Camera Orbits" section applies to lights, too. Lights don't have adjustable anchor points, either.

The trick to orbiting a camera is to give it a proxy anchor point, and that proxy is a Null layer. Null layers don't render. Sound useless? They're not. Null layers make great parent layers. If you have 15 flying saucer layers and you want to move them as a single squadron, just add a Null layer, make the Null layer the parent of all the flying saucers, move the Null layer, and its children will follow it. You don't have any flying saucers, so you'll use a Null layer to control a camera.

1. Open the Orbit comp. In it you'll see the panorama. Last time you saw it you made it spin. This time you'll leave it in place and spin a camera around it.

Why spin a camera around a layer instead of the other way around? It makes the most sense when you want to spin a camera around several layers. It's easier to spin the one camera around the layers than it is to spin multiple layers around a camera. To test this theory, we added a second layer to this comp—a red arrow. You'll spin the camera around both the panorama and the arrow.

2. With the Current Time Indicator at the start of the Timeline, choose Layer > New > Null Object.

3. In the Timeline, rename the Null layer to Camera Parent Null and enable its 3D switch. The Null layer will stand in as the camera's anchor point, so you want to make sure it's in the center of the spot you want the camera to orbit. In this case, it went there automatically, because Null layers get placed in the center of the comp, and it so happens you want the camera to rotate around the center.

4. Over the course of the Timeline, make the Null layer spin one time around its Y axis.

5. Grab the camera layer's pickwhip (the curly icon) and point it to the Null layer. This makes the Null layer the camera's parent. Children layers get offset by their parents' anchor points and rotations, so the camera will rotate around the Null layer.

6. Over the course of the Timeline, animate the camera so that it starts far away and gradually gets closer to the panorama. In other words, keyframe its Z axis.

7. Preview the comp, watching the camera spin around the panorama and arrow.

Depth of Field

For our money, the main reason to use cameras in After Effects is Depth of Field—the effect that makes objects go out of focus when they're too close or too far from the camera. Depth of Field is that little oomph of realism that often "sells" a motion graphic. Alas, there's a hefty price to pay in terms of render time (that's true with any blur effect), but Depth of Field is worth it.

1. Open the comp called Depth_of_Field. Make sure the Current Time Indicator is at the beginning of the Timeline. As you can see, the reporter's shoulder and the background are both in focus, even though the shoulder is much closer to the camera than the background.

2. In the Timeline, click the disclosure triangle to open the camera layer. Then click the disclosure triangle to open its Camera Options group. Click the Depth of Field value to toggle it from Off to On.

3. Move the Current Time Indicator to the end of the Timeline. The camera is animated so it pulls out, revealing the reporter from the waist up and moving far from the background. Notice that with Depth of Field enabled the focus is dynamic. Due to the camera move, the reporter is now in focus and the background is blurred.

4. In the Timeline, increase the Blur Level property to exaggerate the effect.

When you select the camera and look at the scene from the Top view, you can more clearly see what's going on. The background is in the camera's focus range first, and then the reporter is inside its focus range.

5. Adjusting the Focus Distance widens or narrows the range that the camera can keep in focus. Preview the comp to see the shift in focus.

Casting Shadows

If Depth of Field is the killer feature of cameras, Casts Shadows is the killer feature of lights. Also like Depth of Field, shadows add to render time. Again, they're worth waiting for.

1. Open the comp called Shadows. A light is animated so it crosses from left to right across the text, but it's not casting any shadows.

● NOTE: **Two More Shadow Properties**

Light layers have two shadow proper- ties besides Casts Shadows: Shadow Darkness (the inten- sity of the shadow) and Shadow Diffu- sion (how blurry the shadow is). Shadow diffusion lengthens render time even more than it has already been length- ened by adding the shadow in the first place—but diffusion sure looks cool and shadowy.

2. Click the disclosure triangle to open the light layer on the Timeline, click the disclosure triangle to open the Light Options, and toggle the Casts Shadows property to On.

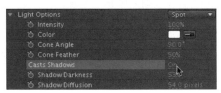

You turned shadows on, but why don't you see any shadows? Because in After Effects, a shadow is like a ball that layers toss to each other. The light is tossing the shadow to the text layer, but the text layer isn't toss- ing it to the background layer.

3. Click the disclosure triangle to open the text layer, click the disclosure triangle to open its Material Options property group, and toggle Casts Shadows to On.

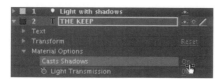

● NOTE: **Casts Shadows Settings**

Casts Shadows switches between Off, Only, and On. The Only setting is useful if you want to create a shadow that has no source, such as a nightmare image of an axe-murderer's shadow on a bedroom wall. When you set Casts Shadows to Only, you'll see just the shadow, not the source layer.

Since shadows lengthen render time, you want as few layers as possible tossing the shadow ball. And because there's nothing behind the background layer, it would be foolish to enable its Casts Shadows property (because it has no layer to throw the ball to). That would increase render time with no visual payoff.

4. Preview the comp. Notice the shadow moving across the back wall.

Practice Makes Perfect

In Chapter 9, you built a 3D scene using Photoshop's Vanishing Point effect. We've finessed it a little with some animated clouds and a moving camera.

1. Open the comps VPE and VPE_Complete.

2. Select the comp VPE_Complete and invoke a RAM Preview.

   Notice how the camera descends and rotates through the 3D scene. Clouds also hover in front of the building (which the camera tracks by).

3. Examine the Timeline and composition carefully. Keep it open for reference.

It's time to earn your 3D pilot's wings. Practice makes perfect, so try moving a camera around the VPE starter comp on your own. It's up to you how you want to complete the task, just make it look good!

If you get stuck and need a hint, just refer to the VPE_Complete comp, select the camera layer, and press UU on the keyboard (the letter U typed twice in rapid succession). This practice step is optional, but if you can fly on your own, you can consider yourself 3D savvy!

What's Next?

Now that you've stretched After Effects into the third dimension, it's time to ride through a wormhole back to Flash. Although Flash was originally built for creating Web animations, it's now often used to create content for broadcast video. Unfortunately, Flash doesn't have a Render for Television option. Flash animators who are used to Web authoring may find themselves lost the first time they're asked to create content for film or video. Good thing this book has Chapter 11, "Converting Flash to Broadcast Standards."

11 CONVERTING FLASH TO BROADCAST STANDARDS

As the worlds of Web animation, cel animation, and broadcast graphics collide, it's more feasible to use an animation created in Flash in a video project, such as an animation used for broadcast or a background for a DVD menu. Flash does have the ability to export a QuickTime movie directly, but this method lacks certain refined benefits such as anti-aliasing, interlacing, and broadcast-safe colors. By spending a little extra time prepping the FLA file, you can export vector-based SWF files.

These can then be recomposited in After Effects as well as enhanced for a better overall look.

The Technical Essentials of Video

When animating in Flash, you have the benefit of designing on a computer, which is also the primary display on which to view that animation. When you decide that video is the path you're going to take, prepare to face a lot of issues unique to video production.

© ISTOCKPHOTO

There are a lot of technical details in the world of video—what follows is not meant to be a full-blown crash course in being a video engineer. Video is a unique (and messy) beast; it has a checkered history filled with compromises and major shifts in standards. To make things worse, there's a standards war going on between multiple formats, digital versus analog, standard versus widescreen, and even the flavor of high definition video. While it sounds confusing, we'll do our best to break it down.

Determining a Frame Aspect Ratio

You first need to determine the frame aspect ratio of your video device. Generally speaking, there are only two sizes in use. Standard Definition television is generally a 4:3 frame aspect ratio, which means the screen is four units wide to three units tall. Another way of expressing this is that television has a 1.33:1 frame aspect ratio.

You will encounter one other frame aspect ratio with increasing frequency—the 16:9 frame aspect ratio, which has its roots in Hollywood. In the early 1950s, Hollywood tried to regain its audience from television. The invention of Cinerama followed by CinemaScope introduced a wider screen to the public. The standard has evolved, and a version called Academy Flat has been adopted by High Definition (HD) television technology.

The image on the left has a 16:9 frame aspect ratio, whereas the image on the right has a 4:3 frame aspect ratio.

When designing for HD video output (or output to widescreen DVD), you'll use a 16:9 frame aspect ratio. This breaks down to a ratio of 1.85:1 (16÷9=1.85)

and is emerging as the new standard for many devices, including televisions, Blu-ray, and even YouTube and iPods.

You'll need to decide which frame aspect ratio you want to use so your Flash project can be conformed to it. During this process, you'll end up cutting off part of the image as you scale layers to fill the frame, unless you know which video-standard dimensions you're going to use before you begin working in Flash. In that case, you can simply set your stage size accordingly. Below, we'll give you specific widths and heights you can use when you pick a Stage size.

Determining a Frame Rate

Although determining an aspect ratio is fairly simple, the same can't be said for frame rates. It used to be simple with only three common frame rates:

- **NTSC.** The National Television Standards Committee standard is used in the United States, Japan, Canada, Mexico, and several other areas in North and Central America. It uses a frame rate of 29.97 fps. It's important to note that Flash cannot export this frame rate.

- **PAL/SECAM.** There are two standards used throughout most of the world. The Phase Alternating Line (or PAL) standard is the most common (used in about 80 countries). The Séquentiel Couleur avec Memoire (SECAM) or its derivatives are used in about 50 countries globally. Both formats use a frame rate of an even 25 frames per second.

- **Film.** Traditional film uses a frame rate of 24 frames per second. And this is why many Flash animators build animations at 12 frames per second— to follow the traditional approach of cel animation, which is "shooting on twos" where a frame of animation is shown for two frames of film.

● **NOTE: Set the Stage**

In many cases, you'll know which video-standard dimensions you're going to use before you begin working in Flash. In that case, you can simply set your Stage size accordingly. In the next section, we'll give you specific widths and heights you can use when you pick a Stage size.

▲ **TIP: The Lowdown on Frame Rates**

You will likely design in Flash using 30 for NTSC projects, 25 for PAL/SECAM, and 24 for film or 24p projects.

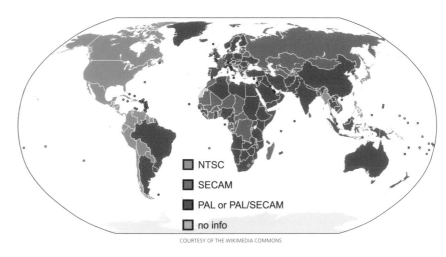

- NTSC
- SECAM
- PAL or PAL/SECAM
- no info

COURTESY OF THE WIKIMEDIA COMMONS

● NOTE: Pixel
Aspect Ratio

When you view
non-square pixels on
a computer, they'll
look distorted. Both
After Effects and
Photoshop offer
Pixel Aspect Ratio
correction that you
can enable. In After
Effects click the Tog-
gle Pixel Aspect Ratio
Correction button.
at the bottom of the
Composition window.
In Photoshop choose
View > Pixel Aspect
Ratio Correction.

Unfortunately, the standards war surrounding HD makes determining frame rates tougher. You'll find both progressive (p) and interlaced (i) formats in use with HD. You also can encounter any of the following frame rates in use: 23.98p, 24p, 25i, 25p, 29.97i/59.94i, 29.97p, 30p, 50p, 59.94p, and 60p. Flash only supports whole numbers, so you'll generally round up (for example, 23.98 to 24). Fortunately, After Effects can interpret the SWF output and make it work for different video outputs.

Using Square or Non-square Pixels

There is nothing fun about pixels when it comes to video, because video (unlike computers and digital photography cameras) often uses non-square pixels. This means that the pixels do not have the same width and height. In a nutshell, computers and Flash work with square pixels (1.0 aspect); most standard definition digital video works with non-square pixels, whereas HD works with both square and non-square pixels.

A video signal that uses the NTSC standard is often interpreted by video boards as an image that is 648 × 486 square pixels. Those countries that use the PAL format use boards that work with images that measure 768 × 576 square pixels. Of course, if you offer a standard, manufacturers will ignore it.

In an effort to pack more pixels and increase resolution, the ITU-R BT 601 video standard was developed. It is often called "D1" (after the D1 format invented by Sony in 1986, which was the first component digital format available). In NTSC, the native "board" size of a D1 frame is 720 × 486 non-square pixels. The PAL format uses 720 × 576 non-square pixels.

The D1 format has evolved into the Digital Video (DV) standard, which is employed in the consumer DV format, as well as DVCAM and DVCPRO tape and DVD authoring. The native size for DV frames is 720 × 480 non-square pixels for NTSC (six less than the D1 format). The PAL DV format is identical to the standard PAL format and remains unchanged at 720 × 576 non-square pixels.

● NOTE: More
Accurate PARs

With the release of
CS4, Adobe slightly
tweaked the pixel
aspect ratio of
non-square pixels.
This has resulted in
new square pixel
equivalents, which
may differ from sizes
you worked with in
the past.

Are you confused yet? Don't worry, we'll break it down into a simple work-flow for you: Flash can only work with square pixels; After Effects, however, is quite versatile and can convert between sizes for you. But it's critical that your Flash document starts out sized correctly for your targeted video format. Here are some standard sizes you may encounter.

STANDARD DEFINITION

Format	Ratio	Video Native Size	Flash Stage Size
NTSC D1	4:3	720 × 486	720 × 534 or 654 × 486
NTSC D1 (widescreen)	16:9	720 × 486	872 × 486
NTSC DV	4:3	720 × 480	720 × 528 or 654 × 480
NTSC DV (widescreen)	16:9	720 × 480	872 × 480
PAL D1/DV	4:3	720 × 576	788 × 576
PAL D1/DV (widescreen)	16:9	720 × 576	1050 × 576

▲ TIP: Don't Be Afraid to Ask Questions

With so many different formats, there's a lot to video. You can always check with your clients or team members to clarify which video format they are using.

HIGH DEFINITION

Format	Ratio	Video Native Size	Flash Stage Size
HD/HDV 720	16:9	1280 × 720	1280 × 720
HD 1080	16:9	1920 × 1080	1920 × 1080
HDV 1080	16:9	1440 × 1080	1920 × 1080
DVCPRO HD 720P	16:9	960 × 720	1280 × 720
DVCPRO HD 1080i	16:9	1440 × 1080 or 1280 × 1080	1920 × 1080

Addressing Interlaced Video

When television was invented, it was decided that 30 frames per second generated smooth motion. However, it took 60 images per second to reduce flicker. The problem was that the broadcast signal could not hold that much information without significant softening, and the slow speed of phosphors in the television tube produced banding.

The image on the left shows progressive video (or whole frame), while the image on the right illustrates interlacing. You can see the tearing in the antenna area the most.

▲ **TIP: The Lowdown on Interlacing**

There's not much you can do from the Flash side for interlacing. Just be sure to avoid using lines thinner than 2 pixels or your image will flicker.

To maintain a relatively crisp picture, the solution of interlacing was decided on by the first National Television Standards Committee in 1940. By showing half an image 60 times per second, all the problems could be solved. The electron beam would scan across the tube, painting every other line. It would then return to the top and paint the remaining lines. These alternating lines are often identified by field dominance and are referred to as upper (odd field first) or lower (even field first). This solution solved the problem between bandwidth, flicker, and smooth motion.

In fact, currently, several HD formats still use interlacing (generally noted with a lowercase i after the format name—such as 1080i). But Flash doesn't offer interlacing, which is a problem. Computer screens (as well as most flat-screen display technology) use a progressive display, which means only a full frame can be loaded. Keep in mind that although interlacing is an issue for many video formats, there's nothing you can do to solve it inside Flash.

Title and Action Safe Zones

▲ **TIP: Action Safe Guides for Flash**

Flash doesn't actually support action safe guides for video, but here's a quick work-around. You'll find a series of PNG files in the Chapter_11 Project Files folder for standard video sizes. You can add these to your Flash project as a layer for guidance. In fact, simply right-click a layer in the Timeline and choose Guide. You can see the layer as a guide, but it won't be included in your final output from Flash.

Whether you are designing in Flash or After Effects, you need to keep one space issue in mind. Not everything on your canvas will make it on the television screen. On any given television set, up to 10 percent of the viewable signal is lost (just like a bleed area in print). This viewable area is called the action safe area. Because of variations in the manufacturing of television sets, this padded region is generally lost.

You'll still design "edge to edge" but can count on losing the outermost 10 percent. Fortunately, After Effects lets you preview this area. Additionally, you must move all text elements in an additional

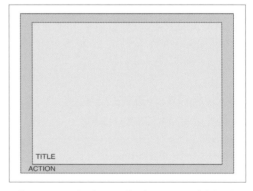

10 percent (or 20 percent total from the outer edge). By placing text within the title safe area, you'll ensure that it is readable because it will have a margin.

Luminance and Color

The color and brightness ranges supported by video are different than those Flash uses. Flash uses the RGB color space, which is common to computers. Each pixel you see on your monitor is composed of light being emitted by a red, a green, and a blue phosphor placed closely together. Your eyes perceive that light as a single-colored dot, or pixel.

So what's the problem? Televisions use the same red, green, and blue phosphors right? Not exactly. Television signals are not transmitted or stored in

RGB due to a final legacy issue: Initially, television was black and white. These images were actually a grayscale signal that consisted of only one channel that contained the brightness information (known as *luminance or luma*). In an effort to keep consumers happy, color television was made backward compatible. An RGB broadcast would not work on a black-and-white television, so broadcasters chose (and still use) the Y, R-Y, B-y color space. The Y is the luminance information, and the other two represent the color components (hue and saturation). These three signals would combine to form the composited pixels. The color space goes by many names: It is often clarified as Y, Cr, Cb, and can also be found (some say inaccurately) as YCC, YUV, or as YIQ.

How does this affect you? Don't worry about the engineering side, but realize that colors will look different on a television screen than they do in Flash or on a computer monitor. The color shift is minor, but present. After Effects does a good job of handling this color shift, and we'll explain how later in this lesson.

Additionally, Flash and video handle luminance values differently. When working in Flash, black is an absolute black and white is an absolute white. Photoshop assigns a value of 0 to black and a value of 255 to white. There is no allowance for anything beyond this range. This process is referred to as computer graphics or RGB mapping. Adobe Photoshop and After Effects also work with RGB mapping.

When you choose to render video in After Effects, the luminance levels will often be adjusted during output by the video compression type you pick. If you choose to export video directly from Flash, this can be a problem. Because After Effects is better at handling the color and luminance issues, we highly recommend processing SWF files in After Effects to make video.

If you must output video directly from Flash (for example, if the animation relies on ActionScript, which is ignored by After Effects), you'll want to pay closer attention to color and luminance. Here are a few simple pieces of advice to follow when outputting video directly from Flash:

- **Certain colors do not look good on video.** Bright reds have a tendency to "bleed" onscreen; light yellows look terrible as well on a video monitor.
- **Oversaturated colors will cause problems.** Consumer televisions ship with the saturation and red tones turned up too high. Muted colors will become more vibrant once they make it out to televisions. When choosing a color in Flash, look at the RGB value. Make sure that each component falls between 16 and 235.
- **Avoid extremely dark colors.** On video there is very little difference between indigo, charcoal, and slate. Dark tones tend to gravitate toward black in the viewer's eyes.
- **Avoid "pure" white.** It will bloom onscreen, making it difficult to read. Instead, use off-white R:235 G: 235 B: 235.

Preparing the FLA File

● NOTE: **Special Shout-out**

A special thanks to RC Concepcion at *Layers* magazine for creating the Flash animation used in this chapter. Be sure to check out his great tutorials and podcast at www.layersmagazine.com.

Once you've identified a Flash project that you want to migrate to video, you'll want to revisit the source project (a FLA file). Although After Effects can work with previously exported SWF files, you won't achieve as high-quality results if you don't tweak the FLA project's settings. By going back to the source, you can achieve the best results.

Configuring the Canvas and Frame Rate

The first two areas you need to focus on are getting your Flash project sized right and using the correct frame rate. Earlier in the section "Using Square or Non-square Pixels," we offered a table for common frame sizes. Let's assume for this exercise that you will convert a Flash animation for use in HD at 1280 × 720 and 29.97 frames per second.

1. If they are not running already, launch both After Effects and Flash Professional. Copy the **Chapter_11 Project Files** folder to your hard drive, open the folder, and double-click the file **Financial Background Start.fla**.

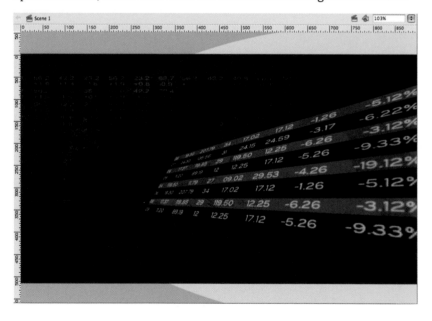

This is an animated graphic produced for a financial news story. The goal here is to convert it to a full motion video background.

2. Test the movie by pressing Command+Return (Ctrl+Enter).

The movie has a motion background, a financial ticker, and text. You'll eventually remove the text and output the other two items as separate SWF files. Let's first get the stage set up correctly.

3. Choose Window > Workspace > Designer to use the common layout for resizing and positioning elements.

4. Choose View > Magnification > 50% to see the entire Stage. Several of the elements extend beyond the edge of the Stage. Click a blank area off the edge of the Stage to make sure no graphics are selected.

5. In the Properties panel, change the Frame rate to 30. This most closely matches the final output of 29.97; After Effects will fix this later.

6. Click the Edit button in the Properties panel.

7. In the Document Properties window, change the dimensions to 1280 × 720, and then click OK.

The Stage is enlarged, but now you must scale the elements.

Scaling Elements to Fill the Frame

It is unlikely that your original Flash project will match the exact frame size or aspect ratio of video. You'll need to scale elements to fill the frame. Sometimes this will mean parts of the image will be cut off; other times you may choose to distort objects slightly to fill the frame. Let's scale the items on the Stage to fill out the new Stage size.

> ▲ **TIP: A Wider View**
>
> You can scale the Timeline via the sub-menu in the Timeline's upper-right corner.

1. Size the Timeline so you can see all the tracks.

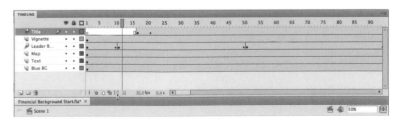

2. Turn off the visibility of all layers except Blue BG.

3. Select the Blue BG layer in the Timeline.

4. Press Q to select the Free Transform tool. Scale the Blue BG layer to fill the entire frame by dragging the lower-right corner.

5. When satisfied, lock the Blue BG layer. Then turn on the visibility for the Text layer and select it.

● **NOTE: Resizing Keyframed Layers**

We're going easy on you by only asking you to resize layers with no keyframes. Resizing tweened layers is a pain, because you have to make sure the artwork is resized at each keyframe. If you resize at just one keyframe, making the artwork larger, it will tween back to its smaller size at the next keyframe. To learn some cool tips that will help you edit multiple Flash frames at once, watch the demo video called onion skinning.mov in this chapters's Project Files folder.

▲ **TIP: Scale Multiple Frames**

If you need to scale a layer that has keyframes be sure to check out the Flash tool called Edit Multiple Frames. It can be helpful in this situation. You can read about it in the Flash online Help.

6. Scale the layer larger so it fits the width of the Stage. Don't worry about the top and bottom edges, because the animation will repeat. Reposition the layer as needed by dragging.

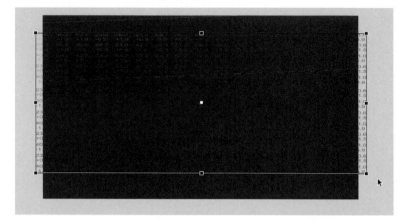

7. When satisfied, lock the Text layer. Then turn on the visibility for the Map layer and select it.

8. Hold the Shift and Option (Alt) keys to constrain the object, and then drag the lower-right corner handle until the map is slightly wider than the Stage.

9. Using similar techniques, resize and reposition the Vignette layer.

10. Right-click the Title layer and choose Delete Layer.

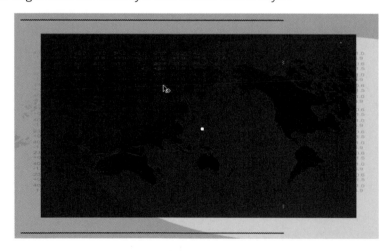

11. Choose File > Save As, name the file Financial Background for AE.fla, and save it to the **Chapter_11 Project Files** folder.

12. Press Command+Return (Ctrl+Enter) to preview the animation.

It looks good, but the leader board should be exported on its own.

Removing Movie Clip Symbols

There's a little gotcha in the project: There are several instances of movie clip symbols. Many Flash animators prefer to use movie clip symbols because they allow for reusable pieces of Flash animation, they can be manipulated in 3D, and they're controllable via the ActionScript language. Using movie clips is a great way to keep file size to a minimum for the Web (because the movie clip only loads once and multiple instances can be repeated in the project). However, the problem is that movie clip animations require the Flash Player to work (and After Effects ignores them).

You have two choices: convert the movie clip symbols to graphics—an older symbol type that doesn't work well with 3D or ActionScript—or export a QuickTime movie. Let's tackle both methods for this project. You'll start by converting movie clips to graphic symbols.

1. Look in the Library; you'll see that there are five movie clip symbols. You only need to convert the ones that are animated (which are the digits and digitscrawl symbols).

2. Let's first update the symbol in the Library. Right-click digits and choose Properties. From the Type pop-up menu choose Graphic and click OK.

3. Convert the digitscrawl symbol using the same approach.

4. Now that the Library is updated, you need to update the instances in the Timeline. To do this, you must select the object. Because the objects overlap, this can be a little tricky. In the Timeline, select the Text layer. Option-click (Alt-click) its lock icon to lock all other layers.

5. Choose Edit > Select All to select the Text layer (because everything else is locked, only the text is selected).

6. In the Properties panel, change the instance of digitscrawl to a Graphic.

   The Leader Board layer cannot be exported as a SWF. Because the file uses 3D in Flash, it must be treated as a movie clip symbol. Recall that movie clip symbols cannot be exported as a SWF for After Effects; you'll revisit this issue in a moment.

> ● **NOTE: Updating Instances on the Stage**
>
> Changing the symbol type of Library items will not update instances you added to the Stage before making the change in the Library. You must make the change both in the Library and to each instance on the Stage.

7. In the Timeline, right-click the Leader Board layer and choose Delete Layer.

Now that the project is prepped, you can export a SWF for After Effects.

▲ TIP: Copy Frames

Sometimes, you may need to move contents from one FLA to another. If you need to copy a range on the Timeline, select the original frames (click the start frame; Shift-click the end frame), Control-click (right-click) the range, and choose Copy Frames from the context menu. In the target FLA, Control-click (right-click) a keyframe and choose Paste Frames from the context menu.

▲ TIP: Another Way to Export

For more control over SWF exports, choose File > Publish Settings, instead of File > Export. We covered Publish Settings in Chapter 2.

▲ TIP: When to Use After Time Elapsed

If your Flash movie contains ActionScript, you should try the After time elapsed option. This allows for dynamic content to be successfully exported.

Exporting for After Effects

You'll export for After Effects in two passes: The first pass will be as a SWF for the background layer. Then you'll have to export the Leader Board animation separately as a QuickTime movie because the 3D layer requires a movie clip symbol, which is ignored by After Effects.

1. Choose File > Export > Export Movie.

2. In the Export Movie window, target your **Chapter_11 Project Files** folder. Name the file Financial BG.swf and choose SWF Movie from the Format pop-up menu.

3. Click Save to write the file to disk. A SWF file is exported, which you'll work with in a moment.

Now that you've written a SWF file, you can complete the second pass and revisit the 3D Leader Board layer. Because this layer uses 3D, it must use a movie clip symbol. Because it uses a movie clip symbol, you can't export a SWF for After Effects; rather, you must export a QuickTime movie.

1. Open the file **3DTicker Export Start.fla** from the **Chapter_11 Project Files** folder. This is just the 3D layer saved as its own Flash project.

2. Choose File > Export > Movie. Target your **Chapter_11 Project Files** folder and choose QuickTime from the Type pop-up menu. Click Save; the QuickTime Export Settings window opens.

3. You now need to specify settings for the exported movie. Select the check box next to Ignore stage color. This creates an alpha channel using the stage color that will embed transparency into the movie file.

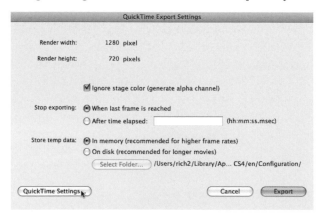

4. The next area allows you to specify how long Flash should export. For this file, choose When last frame is reached.

5. Choose to Store temp data In memory, because this is a high frame rate movie.

6. Click the QuickTime Settings button to adjust the type of file that is written.

7. Deselect the Sound and Prepare for Internet Streaming check boxes. The rest of the default settings are fine for this file.

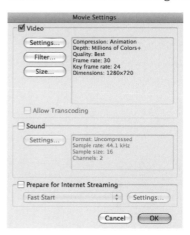

▲ **TIP: Stealing From Yourself**

You can also open one FLA's library into another FLA by choosing File > Open External Library. In the dialog, select the FLA that has the Library you want to access.

8. Click the Size button and change the Dimensions to 1280 × 720 HD to force the correct output size.

● **NOTE: Output Codec**

You must use an output codec that supports embedded alpha channels (such as Animation). This is the default in Flash, but you can double-check and select it in the QuickTime Settings window.

9. Click OK twice to close the open settings windows, and then click Export. Flash takes a few minutes to cache the file and write to disk. When the export is complete, a dialog informs you of this and prompts you to click OK. After reading the dialog, click OK to close it.

You are now ready to complete the project in After Effects.

Finishing in After Effects

After you've successfully exported your animation, you can finish and conform it in After Effects. This process is fairly straightforward but handles some important conversions "under the hood." Essentially, you recomposite your elements together, and then enhance the composite with a few adjustment layers.

● NOTE: **Alpha Channel Types**

There are three kinds of alpha channels in After Effects. None means there is no alpha channel. A premultiplied alpha channel makes the graphic look "normal" when you open it in a Quick-Time player because soft edges are mixed with black to simulate transparency. This is the type of alpha channel Flash writes. The third type, straight alpha channel, does not try to simulate soft edges. This leads to a rough edge when the graphic is viewed on its own, but the alpha channel creates a clean composite when the footage is overlaid on top of another source.

Importing the Assets

You learned how to set up an After Effects project in Chapter 1, "After Effects Essentials for the Flash User." Now you'll bring the two movies into an After Effects project so you can work with them.

1. Switch to After Effects.

2. Double-click in an empty area of the Project panel to bring up the Import dialog. Navigate to the **Chapter_11 Project Files** folder and select the two items you exported from Flash. Click Open to bring in the files.

   The Interpret Footage window opens for the 3DTicker movie. After Effects needs to know how to interpret the footage.

3. Click Guess to let After Effects analyze the footage. It should determine that the footage is premultiplied with black (which is correct). This means there is black in the background, which needs to be partially removed along with the alpha channel for proper transparency. Then click OK.

You are now ready to interpret the footage.

Interpreting the Footage

When you import footage into After Effects, the program uses a set of internal rules to interpret each footage item. This works well because it allows the program to mix square and non-square footage as well as other technical considerations like 3:2 pulldown and fields. However, there will be times when you'll need to manually override this interpretation.

Let's correctly interpret the two items you've just brought in.

1. Select the file **Financial Background.swf** in the Project panel.

2. Click the Interpret Footage button at the bottom of the Project panel.

▲ TIP: **Cycling Animations**

If you are importing a walk cycle or looping animation, you can specify how many times the file should loop in the Interpret Footage window as well.

3. Select Conform to frame rate and enter 29.97 frames per second. Click OK to store the interpretation.

4. Repeat the interpretation process for the file **3DTicker Start.mov**. Set the footage to a frame rate of 29.97 fps.

Compositing the Footage

Once your footage is loaded and ready, it's time to place it into an After Effects composition. In this particular project, there are two footage layers that need to be recombined into a single composition.

1. Drag the file Financial Background.swf onto the Create a New Composition button at the bottom of the Project panel. After Effects creates a new comp that matches the size and duration of the footage item.

2. Select the newly created comp and choose Composition > Composition Settings. Examine the settings in use.

   Because the frame size was 1280 × 720 and the frame rate was conformed to 29.97 frames per second, After Effects correctly identified that this footage should use a composition defined by the HDV/HDTV 720 29.97 preset.

3. Click OK to close the Composition Settings window.

4. Drag the file 3DTicker Start.mov to the Timeline and place it above track 1.

5 Position the 3DTicker layer so the object resides on the right of the screen.

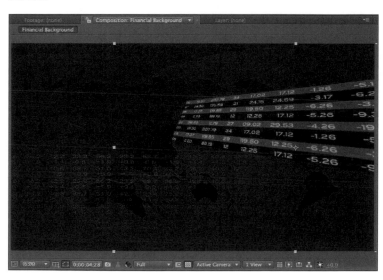

6. Click the RAM Preview button to watch your animation.

▲ **TIP: Identical Interpretation Timesaver**

While it won't work for this project (the two files have different styles of alpha channels), you can save time when dealing with "similar footage." You can use the same settings by copying interpretation settings from one item and applying them to another. Just select the clip with the interpretation settings that you want to apply and choose File > Interpret Footage > Remember Interpretation. Then select the destination clip(s) and choose File > Interpret Footage > Apply Interpretation.

It should look nearly identical to what you saw in Flash, except now it is a video file. Feel free to reposition the 3DTicker movie as desired.

Using Adjustment Layers

Adjustment layers let you apply an effect to multiple layers at once in After Effects. To finalize your animation for broadcast or professional video output, you need to do a little work and add a few adjustment layers with effects. These effects are all optional but generally work well for most Flash to video conversions.

1. Choose Layer > New > Adjustment Layer. Name the layer Blur. A new adjustment layer is added to the top of your Timeline.

2. Choose Effect > Blur & Sharpen > Fast Blur. The Fast Blur effect renders quickly and also offers a unique feature called Repeat Edge Pixels, which keeps the edges opaque when the blue is applied. Set Blurriness to 10.0 and select the Repeat Edge Pixels check box.

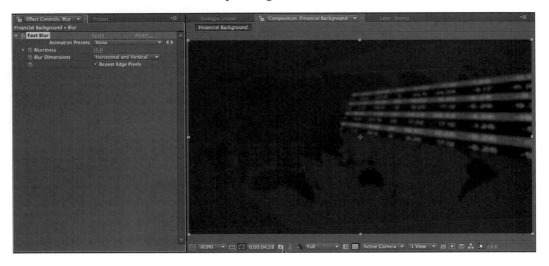

● NOTE: Soften Edges, Reduce Flickering

You can experiment with different blending modes and opacities to achieve different looks for your footage. This particular combination helps soften the hard edges of the animation and reduces flickering.

3. Change the adjustment layer's blending mode to Lighten and reduce its opacity to 80%.

4. Let's add some grain to the image. Choose Layer > New > Adjustment Layer. Name the layer Grain. Choose Effect > Noise & Grain > Add Grain.

   Adding a little grain can make the animation look more organic and less computer generated. This is very much an aesthetic choice and may not look good to all users or on all footage.

   When you first apply it, only a small preview window is shown. Set your zoom level to 200% so you can better see the grain.

5. Change the Intensity to 0.400 to reduce the intensity of the effect.

6. Change both Size and Softness to 2.000 to make the effect gentler.

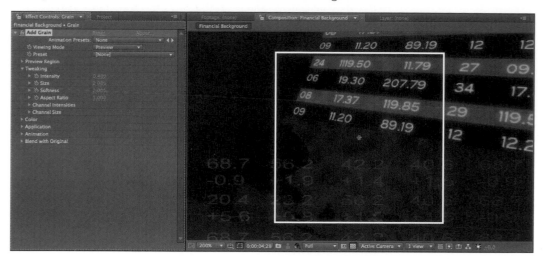

7. Click the Viewing Mode drop-down menu and choose Final Output. Set the zoom level back to Fit.

8. Set the Opacity of the blending mode to 20%.

9. Let's add a vignette or power window to darken the edges a bit more. This is a standard stylization effect that can be used to draw the viewer's eye to the center of the screen. First, choose Layer > New > Solid.

10. With the eyedropper, select the darkest black in your animation. Sampling directly from the animation helps the darker edge blend better. Name the layer Vignette, and click OK.

11. From the toolbar, select the Ellipse tool (you can cycle through the different shapes by pressing the Q key repeatedly). Double-click the Ellipse tool to apply an elliptical mask to the footage.

12. The mask is applied to the footage but needs to be tweaked. Select the Vignette layer in the Timeline and press MM to modify the mask's properties. Select the check box next to Inverted to reverse the mask. Set Mask Feather to 80.0 pixels.

13. Now, let's blend the mask. Change the Vignette layer's blending mode to Multiply and lower the Opacity to 25%.

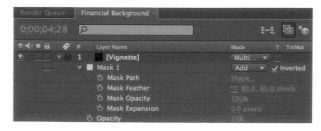

14. Let's add one more adjustment layer. Choose Layer > New > Adjustment Layer. Name the layer Broadcast Safe.

15. Choose Effect > Color Correction > Broadcast Colors. Choose the correct Broadcast Locale for your output (either NTSC or PAL).

16. Change the How to Make Colors Safe pop-up menu to Reduce Saturation. This will gently reduce the saturated areas as necessary to conform the video to broadcast video standards.

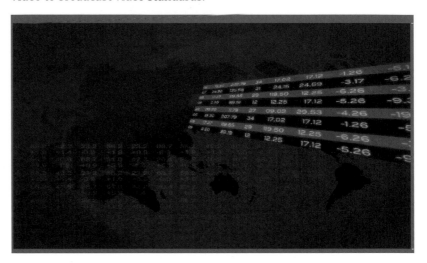

17. Click the RAM Preview button to watch your animation. Then choose File > Save and save your project to the **Chapter_11 Project Files** folder.

When you're satisfied with the project, it's time to render. After Effects can render to several formats including video files for Premiere Pro (or other editing tools) and MPEG-2 files for use in Adobe Encore. You learned how to render in Chapter 1.

What's Next?

Converting a Flash file to a professional video format allows you to integrate animation files into other media projects. But what about when your project is finished? You can deploy a completed video project to the Internet as Flash video or return a video file to Flash for interactive programming. In the next chapter, you'll learn how to professionally encode video to the three different Flash Video formats.

12 PROFESSIONAL ENCODING OF FLASH VIDEO

The use of Flash Video has become tremendously popular. Adobe estimates that more Internet browsers are capable of viewing Flash Video than any other delivery platform. This is due, in large part, to the huge install base of the Flash plug-in but is also influenced by the quality of video that can be delivered.

With the introduction of Creative Suite 4, using video in Flash has become even easier. Flash now supports three different types of video files (each with unique benefits). Additionally, Adobe Media Encoder CS4 makes encoding video for Flash more straightforward and faster than in the past.

Adobe Media Encoder offers precise control over the conversion of media files.

How you approach encoding video depends on your comfort level. Many users remain in the dark as to how video works and find that they are only capable of using the bundled presets. While these options work well, by knowing how to switch from autopilot to manual control you gain significant improvements in quality and flexibility. In this chapter, you'll explore the process of encoding Flash Video files using Flash's Video Import Wizard, the Adobe Media Encoder, and Adobe After Effects.

Delivery Methods for Flash Video

The delivery method you choose to use will influence how you encode Flash Video files. Three primary workflows are used to get Flash Video files to an end user's computer. Each takes a different approach with specific outcomes in mind.

Adobe Flash Media Server

For many situations, streaming video will be your best choice. The three primary benefits to streaming Flash content are that the content is optimized for fast delivery, the servers can adjust to better meet fluctuations in demand,

and the content can be protected because it is never stored on the end user's computer. Additionally, if metrics matter (such as for advertisers), you can get very detailed statistics about video consumption.

Adobe Flash Media Server provides administrative controls over the delivery of Flash Video.

Flash Media Server is a server solution optimized to deliver real-time media. You can host your own Flash Media Server or use a content delivery network provider. Flash Media Server uses bandwidth detection to deliver the right-sized video to the user. For example, a dial-up modem would receive significantly lower quality than a cable modem.

When designing Flash documents using streaming video, you import locally stored video clips into the Flash document. The video files are then moved onto Flash Media Server, and the Flash document updates their location. Video playback is done using the FLVPlayback component or ActionScript. You'll explore interactive controls in Chapter 13, "Creating Interactive Controls."

Progressive Download

The use of progressive download is very common and offers similar performance to streaming files under specific conditions. If the Web site accessing the video is a low-volume site and makes limited use of video, progressive download is a valid option.

A progressively downloaded clip will not stream in realtime from the server. Rather, the end user clicks play, and the file begins to play after enough video has downloaded to the local computer. Progressive download does allow the user to watch a clip before the file has been completely downloaded but does not offer the ability to scale to meet user demands or to protect the files from being permanently saved to a user's computer.

● **NOTE:** Looking for Adobe Flash Media Server Partners?

Adobe maintains two lists of use for Adobe Flash Media Server. One is a list of Flash Video Streaming Service providers who can host Flash video at www.adobe.com/products/flashmediaserver/fvss. The other is a list of publishing partners who provide a full-service solution at www.adobe.com/products/flashmediaserver/fmsp.

This method works well to keep the published SWF files small. Video is then loaded only when the user makes a choice. Video playback is done using the FLVPlayback component or ActionScript.

Embedded Video

If you are using very small and very short files, you can embed them directly into the Flash document. When you publish a SWF file, the video will be included. While easy to author, this approach has several drawbacks: The published files quickly become bloated, audio/video sync can drift, and making updates requires a complete republish of the SWF file.

Video can be embedded directly into a SWF file.

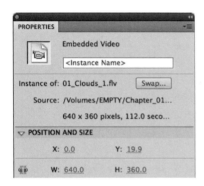

● **NOTE: Dynamic Means More Uploading**

It's important to remember that linked video files need to be uploaded to the server. You can choose to load them first, then create the Flash file, or to upload them when you publish.

The Benefits of Dynamically Delivered Flash Video

Choosing to use the FLVPlayback component or ActionScript offers several advantages over embedded files:

• External video files can have different frame rates than the parent document. This means you can use lower frame rates for the user interface and higher rates for video content.

• Longer video files can be used because they are stored as separate elements. This means they won't require as much RAM as embedded video files.

• Video begins playing as soon as the first segment caches. Other files can load on-demand or in the background.

• Creating captions for your video is easier because you can utilize callback functions to access metadata. This can make the video more accessible. You'll explore accessible video in Chapter 14, "Making Video Accessible."

• During the authoring stage, you only need to publish the SWF file for the interface. You won't need to re-render the video. This reduces preview times.

Delivery Formats

Flash Video is actually an all-encompassing term. The architecture has many different components (including two file extensions and three different compression types). Flash Video has significantly evolved since its introduction in Flash 6. Which format you choose will depend on compatibility with end users and specific technical needs of the author. Let's explore the three options available.

H.264 – F4V

The newest flavor of Flash Video is the F4V video format. These files draw on the open standard of H.264 (also called MPEG-4 Part 10 or AVC) and offer significantly better image quality at a smaller file size. However, they do require more processing power by the end user's computer to decompress and view.

If you want to use an F4V file, the user must be using the Flash Player beginning with version 9.0.r115. While this version of the player will work with older operating systems, it is often not installed in corporate or regulated environments that don't frequently update. The files do not support embedded alpha channels and make using ActionScript cue points more difficult.

These drawbacks are not meant to discourage you. The use of H.264 video is an immensely popular way to encode and deliver. In fact, it allows for video assets to be compatible with the Flash Player and portable media devices like iPods. H.264 video and the F4V format are the future, just make sure your audience can support them in the present.

> ● **NOTE: Not Just F4V**
>
> While the Flash plug-in prefers F4V files, it can in fact handle other file types. MPEG-4 file formats for QuickTime or iTunes often work as well.

The "Ity"s

Four major facets will shape your compression approach.

- **Portability.** How easy is the file to get from one device to another? Is the compressed file small enough to transfer via the Internet (and at what connection speed)?
- **Compatibility.** Can the file be viewed by multiple applications and/or Web browsers?
- **Affordability.** Are the codec or hardware requirements within your budget? Are there any licensing fees involved?
- **Quality.** Does the image or sound quality match your audience's needs?

On2 VP6 – FLV

The On2 VP6 codec (compressor decompressor) is the top choice when you are creating video you intend to work with Flash Player 8 or later. A significant improvement over the original Spark codec, the On2 codec was unveiled with Flash 8.

Compared to the Sorenson Spark codec, the On2 VP6 codec offers higher image quality at identical data rates. It also supports the use of an 8-bit alpha channel, which allows for video to be composited (see Chapter 4).

The On2 VP6 codec does take more processing time to encode than Sorenson Spark. It also places higher demands on the client's processor (although less than H.264). Be sure you consider the audience makeup when deciding between On2 and Spark.

Sorenson Spark – FLV

The introduction of video with Flash Player 6 was powered by the Sorenson Spark video codec. Sorenson, the maker of the compression software Squeeze, has a long history with video compression and codecs.

While the Spark codec is significant for its role in bringing video to Flash, it is now seen as obsolete. The primary reason it is still used is for deploying FLV files to significantly older computers that lack the computational power to process modern video codecs. The following table compares the three options available for Flash Video files.

Codec	SWF Version (publish version)	Flash Player Version (required for playback)
Sorenson Spark	6	6, 7, 8
	7	7, 8, 9, 10
On2 VP6	6, 7, 8	8, 9, 10
H.264	9.2 or later	9.2 or later

Delivery Size

The use of HD video is quickly becoming a standard as broadband connection speeds increase and more powerful computers proliferate. As a result, the move to 16:9 video is also becoming an increasingly common standard (even YouTube recently switched).

Standard Definition

Standard Definition video is generally considered to be NTSC or PAL frame sizes. In square pixel terms, this usually tops out at 860 × 480 pixels for wide-screen and 640 × 480 for traditional 4:3. This style of video can be acquired using several types of cameras, but the use of DV (including DVCAM and DVCPRO) is the most popular.

Here are the minimum system requirements to play back Standard Definition video with Flash Player 10:

Windows

- Intel Pentium 4 2.33 GHz processor (or equivalent)
- 128 MB of RAM
- 64 MB of VRAM

Macintosh

- PowerPC G5 1.8 GHz or faster processor
- Intel Core Duo 1.33 GHz or faster processor
- 256 MB of RAM
- 64 MB of VRAM

High Definition

The use of 720p HD video is the most popular form of HD for Web use. This is due to the size of the displays used with computers and the smaller file sizes compared to 1080i HD. Here are the minimum system requirements to play back a 1280 × 720 Flash file at 24–30 fps:

Windows

- Intel Pentium 4 3 GHz processor (or equivalent)
- 128 MB of RAM
- 64 MB of VRAM

Macintosh

- Intel Core Duo 1.83 GHz or faster processor
- 256 MB of RAM
- 64 MB of VRAM

The requirements for the other flavor of HD are much heftier. Playing back a 1080p file is very taxing on system specs and download bandwidth. Here are the minimum system requirements to play back a 1920 × 1080 Flash file at 24–30 fps:

Windows

- Intel Core Duo 1.8 GHz processor (or equivalent)
- 128 MB of RAM
- 64 MB of VRAM

Macintosh

- Intel Core Duo 2.66 GHz processor (or equivalent)
- 512 MB of RAM
- 128 MB of VRAM

How to Make Better FLV and F4V Files

Here's some direct advice on getting better output with your Flash Video files. Making the video file available to your target audience is your goal, but the challenges of hardware, connection speed, and even operating system can affect the decisions you make. Let's take a common sense approach to getting your video "out there."

- **Deinterlace your video.** Many video files are interlaced, which means that half of one image is blended with half of the next. On a television this produces smooth motion, but on a computer it produces junk. If you can shoot progressive video, do so. The Adobe Media Encoder removes interlacing from all video footage that it processes.

- **Work with video in the native format until your final output.** Avoid the temptation to work with precompressed files. You want to edit video in Premiere Pro at its native quality and work in After Effects this way as well. Compressing video twice produces inferior results including larger file sizes and more noise in the image.

- **Choose elegant transitions.** Using dramatic wipes or transitions will cause the video to pixilate. Try to favor short and simple transitions that will hold up better to compression, or better yet, a simple cut.

- **Reshape the video.** You are very likely working with non-square pixels when you are dealing with video. So the video needs to be reshaped to a square pixel equivalent (for example, widescreen NTSC Digital Video transforms from 720 × 480 to 872 × 480). You must resize video so it properly displays on a computer monitor (see Chapter 11).

- **Shrink the window.** You don't need to make video postage stamp size, but reducing the window to half its original size creates a file that is instantly 25 percent of the file size of the original. That's a BIG savings in space.

- **Lower the frame rate.** Your video file is likely recorded between 24 and 30 fps, which is needed for a television display but not important for most Web video. Reducing your frame rate to one half or one third its original rate (in whole numbers) offers a great savings in file size. Be sure to test the files on the intended devices to see if video playback becomes too "choppy."

- **Avoid mixing aspect ratios.** The Flash encoding tools support both 16:9 and 4:3 video. Placing a 4:3 video in a 16:9 frame results in pillar-boxing (or black bars on the side). The inverse, placing 16:9 video into a 4:3

How to Make Better FLV and F4V Files (continued)

frame, is called letter-boxing, which creates black bars at the top and bottom of the frame. Neither is advisable, so it's important to choose a frame size that matches the aspect ratio of your source footage.

- **Lower your audio standards.** Most users are listening to computer audio on tiny speakers. Cutting your sample rate to 22 or 11 kHz and the sample size to 8 bit will often produce unnoticeable audio changes but huge space savings. You can also encode only mono audio, which takes up less space than a stereo track.

- **Choose the right codec.** Flash supports three different video codecs. You should do your best to limit the use of the Sorenson Spark codec. On the other hand, carefully consider both options when deciding between On2 VP6 and F4V. See the section "Delivery Formats" earlier in the chapter for consideration points.

- **Test it.** Before you compress a lot of video, create a small test file. Try compressing 30 seconds of video with different settings. Find the settings that work best for you and your audience.

Deploying Video

There are three distinct ways to encode video for Flash. The method you choose depends on environment, established workflow practices, and personal choice. Let's explore each option in depth and evaluate its benefits.

The Video Import Wizard

Adobe Flash makes importing video simple by offering the Video Import Wizard. When you import a video, Flash guides you through the process by asking questions and providing options for optimal delivery of the video file. The wizard configures settings for the import and playback method, yet still allows flexibility for future changes.

Initiating import

The process of importing a clip to Flash is straightforward but does require you to make some choices. By exploring the Video Import Wizard, you gain functional knowledge of its use as well as grasp general encoding practices.

1. From the book's DVD, copy the **Chapter_12 Project Files** folder to your computer. If it's not already running, launch Flash CS4 Professional.

2. Choose File > New to open the New Document window. Choose Flash File (ActionScript 3.0) and click OK. A new empty document opens.

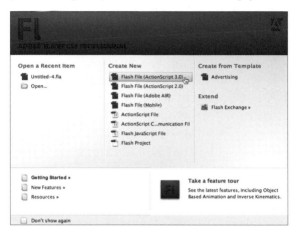

3. Choose File > Import > Import Video. The Import Video dialog opens.

● NOTE: Not Using FLV or MPEG-4?

If you choose a video file that is not a FLV or MPEG-4 video (with H.264 compression), a dialog warns that the video file is not ready for use in Flash. Simply click OK. You should then click the Launch Adobe Media Encoder button at the bottom of the Import Video dialog. You'll explore Adobe Media Encoder in depth later in this chapter.

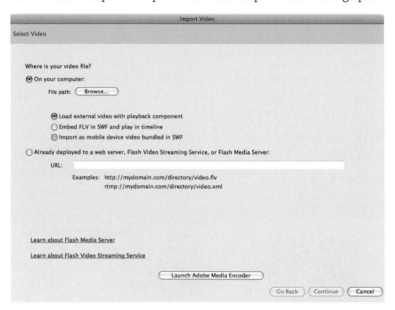

4. Click the Browse button and navigate to the **Chapter_12 Project Files** folder on your computer. Select the file **01_Bumper.mp4**.

Import options

Once a file is selected for import, you need to determine and specify how you want to use the video file. The Video Import dialog provides three video import options.

- **Load external video with playback component.** This option allows you to place the video file onto either a Web server or Flash Media Server. The project also has an instance of the FLVPlayback component to control video playback. This option works well for Adobe Flash Media Server or progressive download.

- **Embed FLV or F4V in SWF and play in timeline.** This option embeds the video into the document. The video file is added to the Timeline, and the individual video frames are represented in the Timeline frames. This option should only be used for very short clips.

- **Import as mobile device video bundled in SWF.** This option is very similar to the traditional embedding option. The key difference is that a Flash Lite document is created for use on a mobile device.

● **NOTE: Already Compressed?**

If the video is already deployed to a server, you can specify its URL in the Import Video dialog.

You'll want to choose the Load external video with playback component option. Then click Continue to go to the second page of the Video Import Wizard.

○ Load external video with playback component
○ Embed FLV in SWF and play in timeline
○ Import as mobile device video bundled in SWF

Skinning the video

A common practice is to add controls to the Flash Video file to allow the end user to control playback as well as adjust volume. Flash offers more than 30 skins to quickly add controls. A skin is a collection of controls, and Flash offers multiple choices based on both technical and aesthetic considerations.

▲ **TIP: Custom Skins**

The built-in skins are a quick way to prepare interactive Flash Video. You can also use additional designs created by you or others by choosing Custom Skin URL. For more on developing custom skins, see the Flash Developer Center at www.adobe.com/devnet/flash.

1. From the Skin drop-down menu, choose SkinUnderAllNoFullNoCaption. swf to place a set of controls beneath the video.

2. Click the blue color swatch to change the color of the Flash controller. Choose the dark red from the second column (or a color of your choice).

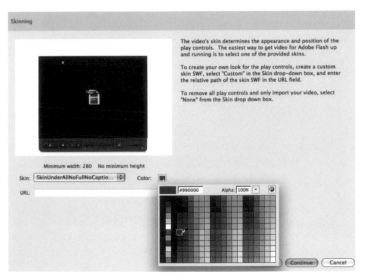

3. Click Continue to advance to the third page of the Video Import Wizard. Flash summarizes how the video file will be processed. Quickly review the details of how the video file will be used.

4. Click Finish to bundle the video file into the document for use in Flash. Flash processes the video file and adds metadata to the document. The canvas size needs to be adjusted to fit the video.

5. Choose Modify > Document. Enter a width of 640 px and a height of 400 px. Change the frame rate to 29.97 to match the frame rate of the video file. Click OK to modify the document.

6. Drag the player window so it is centered in the Flash document. Alternately, you can set the X and Y position in the Properties panel.

7. Choose File > Publish Preview > Default – (HTML) to preview the video file in a Web browser window. Your default Web browser launches and opens a temporary HTML file.

8. Experiment with the different playback controls for the file. When you're satisfied, close the browser and return to Flash.

The Flash document is ready to publish or can be further modified as desired. Close the current document.

Updating Embedded Clips After Editing

If you've already brought a video into a Flash document using an embed option, you can continue to update the file. First, select the video clip in the Library. Then, select the Properties panel. You can adjust Position and Size for the clip as needed or click the Swap button to choose a new file.

Adobe Media Encoder

To make encoding easier and more productive, Adobe developed the stand-alone Adobe Media Encoder. In previous versions of the Creative Suite, encoding of Flash Video was handled by each application. Now, in Creative Suite 4, Adobe Media Encoder is a centralized destination. Because it is meant to be used for many workflows (including Premiere Pro, Encore, and Soundbooth), the tool offers many additional formats besides Flash Video.

The Adobe Media Encoder workspace contains several tools and panels that are useful during the encoding process. Additionally, you can preprocess video, making edits and crops, as well as customize the output formats for a specific use.

Adding files to the Export Queue window

To process video with Adobe Media Encoder, you'll need to add files that you want to process. When you first open Adobe Media Encoder, only the Export Queue window is visible. This is where you add files and specify formats to encode. Let's explore how Adobe Media Encoder works.

1. If it's not already running, launch Adobe Media Encoder. Then click the Add button to add a new file to Adobe Media Encoder.

2. Navigate to the **Chapter_12 Project Files** folder, select the file **02_Bumper.mov**, and click Open.

3. From the Format drop-down menu, choose FLV|F4V.

4. From the Preset drop-down menu, choose F4V – 720p Source, Half Size. This preset matches the frame size of the original material but optimizes it by reducing the image to 640 × 360 pixels.

▲ TIP: Useful Presets

Flash offers several useful presets for encoding video, and they are made available to cover the most common usage scenarios. These presets also serve as a great starting point for compression tasks.

● NOTE: On Your Own

Adobe makes it easy to modify encoding presets, but it doesn't offer technical support for custom settings.

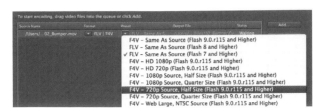

Export Settings viewing area

While Adobe Media Encoder offers several useful presets to choose from, you will still need to visit the Export Settings viewing area from time to time. Here you'll find two important tabs that allow you to toggle between Source and Output. The Source tab allows you to crop and modify the source material, whereas the Output tab lets you preview the output of a media file. You'll also find a timeline that allows for the adjustment of In and Out points and a settings area that offers precise control over the compression.

● **NOTE: Missing the Settings Button?**

If you don't see the Settings button, be sure to upgrade to the latest version of the Adobe Media Encoder. Choose Help > Updates to download the latest version of the software.

1. Make sure the item you want to compress is selected in the source name list. Then, click the Settings button in the main window to open the Export Settings viewing area.

● **NOTE: Working with Non-square Pixels?**

If you are working with video that uses non-square pixels (which is very common), be sure to click the drop-down menu in the upper-right corner of the Source tab. Choose the Aspect Ratio Corrected Preview option to display the image correctly on the television screen. You'll also need to reshape the video before exporting.

2. You can adjust the duration of the clip to be encoded using the Timeline controls. Drag the Current Time Indicator to 00;00;01;00.

3. Click the Set In Point button to adjust the start point of the clip.

4. Click the timecode display and enter 00;00;11;00.

5. Click the Set Out Point button to set the end of the clip.

6. Click the Format tab and make sure that F4V is selected. If needed, you can change the output to FLV for greater backward compatibility with Web browsers.

Pre-encoding tasks

Adobe Media Encoder allows you to complete essential processing options to your file before encoding occurs. This preprocessing allows you to more easily prepare the file for output. It is best to apply changes like cropping and deinterlacing first to produce a smaller and cleaner file.

1. In the Export Settings viewing area, select the Source tab.

2. Click the Crop button to crop the image. From the Crop Proportions menu choose 16:9 to preserve the current shape of the video.

● **NOTE: Where Are the Deinterlace Controls?**

The Adobe Media Encoder automatically deinterlaces the video before encoding. The change is applied whenever you choose to encode an interlaced source to a noninterlaced output.

3. Crop the image interactively by dragging the corner handles of the crop box around the source image.

4. Click inside the crop box to reposition it so the source image is centered inside. The following image should be slightly cropped to remove some of the image pad from the outside.

This animation was originally designed for broadcast use, so there is extra space around the outside edge (often called the action safe zone).

5. Click the Output tab to preview the cropped image.

6. Click the Filters tab to access the Gaussian Blur filter. It is common to apply a slight blur to Web video before encoding to remove any blockiness in gradiated tones. It is also a useful way to eliminate noise in video sources so they compress more cleanly. Check the box Gaussian Blur, then apply blurriness value of 2.0. Set the Blur Dimension to Vertical to soften the image slightly and to remove some of the artifacts caused by interlaced material.

Adjusting video properties

The options available in the Video tab of the Export Settings viewing area will vary depending on which format you've chosen to work with. Video settings for F4V files include the following options: Basic Video Settings, Bitrate Settings, and Advanced Settings.

1. Click the Video tab to select it. Examine the size of the video file that the Adobe Media Encoder will generate. This file should be 640 × 360.

2. Click the Frame Rate (fps) drop-down menu and set the frame rate to 15 fps to reduce the file size. The other Basic Video Settings are correct for this file.

3. Click the Bitrate Encoding drop-down menu (you may need to scroll down) and choose VBR, 2 Pass. This method analyzes the file before compressing and results in smaller, cleaner files (but does increase processing time).

4. Set the Target Bitrate (Mbps) to 1.5. Set the Maximum Bitrate (Mbps) to 2.

> ● NOTE: Take Two Passes
>
> The VBR, 2 Pass Variable bitrate option makes two passes through the file. It first analyzes the file from beginning to end and then from end to beginning. The two passes prolong the encoding process but ensure smaller files with higher quality visuals.

Adjusting audio properties

The Audio tab offers precise control over how audio is processed in the file. The options available will vary depending on the codec chosen.

1. Click the Audio tab to select it. Change the Output Channels setting to Mono to reduce file size. Set the Frequency to 44.1 kHz to use a CD-quality sample rate.

2. Set the Audio Quality to Medium to preserve a balance of file size with quality.

3. In the Bitrate Settings, change the Bitrate (kbps) to 96 to create a higher quality file.

Which AAC Is the Right AAC?

Three different AAC codecs are available to choose from. Each offers unique benefits:

- **AAC (Advanced Audio Coding).** This codec is a high-quality format supported by many mobile devices. It is the default option for the H.264 format.

- **AAC+ Version 1.** This codec uses spectral band replication (SBR) to enhance compression efficiency. It preserves low and mid frequencies, and replicates the higher frequencies. This option works well with very low bitrate compressions.

- **AAC+ Version 2.** This codec combines SBR with Parametric Stereo (PS) to enhance the compression efficiency of stereo signals. This option is commonly referred to as Joint Stereo and means that a mono file is encoded along with data for the unique information in the stereo mix. The decoder can then effectively simulate a stereo file with a smaller compression.

Saving a custom preset

After you've modified a preset, you can store it for easy access. This allows you to create highly customized presets that can be used on future projects.

1. Click the Save Preset button. A new window opens.

2. Name the preset 16_9 Output for Web. You cannot use the : symbol in a preset name.

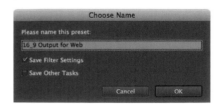

3. Select the Save Filter Settings check box to include filter settings you specified in the Filters tab. Click OK to store the preset file.

Managing Presets

You can choose to import and delete presets from within the Adobe Media Encoder. Additionally, you can manually manage the preset files to back them up or copy them. Presets are stored in the following location:

- **Windows XP.** C:\Documents and Settings\user\Application Data\Adobe\ Adobe Media Encoder\4.0\Presets

- **Windows Vista.** C:\Users\user\AppData\Roaming\Adobe\Adobe Media Encoder\4.0\Presets

- **Macintosh.** Macintosh HD/Users/user/Library/Application Support/Adobe/ Adobe Media Encoder/4.0/Presets

Starting the encode

After you've finished modifying the encoding settings, you can start the compression.

1. Click OK to close the Export Settings viewing area.

2. Click the text beneath Output File to specify an output path. The default name 02_Bumper_1.f4v is fine.

3. Target the file to write to the **Chapter_12 Project Files** folder.

4. Click the Save button to store the file path and then click the Start Queue button to begin the encoding.

▲ **TIP: Previewing the Encode**

To view the encoded F4V file, you'll need to use a different application. You can create a new Flash document and import the F4V file. Alternately, you can download and install the Adobe Media Player for viewing Flash Video files.

The After Effects Render Queue

If you are in a hurry to generate Flash content, After Effects allows you to render directly to an FLV or F4V file. While this appears to be a fast solution, we must offer a few words of caution. First, do not render only a Flash Video file. If you are dissatisfied with the output and you did not render out a high-quality AVI or QuickTime file, you have to waste time rendering again. Second, you cannot access certain advanced features, such as VBR and 2 Pass rendering, through the After Effects Render Queue.

Nonetheless, this is still a useful output method for many. The principal benefits include the ability to render and encode without having to set up additional steps. As a result, a busy user can render and walk away knowing that the animation can be processed, encoded, and even transferred via FTP to the desired location. Let's explore the After Effects process.

Adding files to the Render Queue

The most efficient way to render files in After Effects is to use the Render Queue. It gives you access to different output modules for precise control over formats and properties. Let's create an FLV file using the Render Queue (creating an F4V is a very similar process).

1. From the **Chapter_12 Project Files** folder, open the folder **03_Render_Queue**, and then double-click the file **03_Render_Queue.aep**. After Effects launches and opens the file.

2. In the Project panel, double-click the composition **01_Bumper** to open it.

3. Choose Composition > Add to Render Queue to prepare the file for rendering. The file is added to the Render Queue panel.

Specify render settings

You can adjust two types of settings in the Render Queue panel: Render Settings and Output Modules. The first, Render Settings, controls how the effects in the composition are processed, the frame rate of the file, which frames render, as well as quality options.

1. In the Render Queue panel, click the disclosure triangle next to the words Render Settings.

● NOTE: Many Choices

The Render Settings window contains many choices for output. Be sure to explore the After Effects documentation to understand the many options.

2. Click the text Best Settings to modify the Render Settings. If you've customized the Render Settings in the past, a different setting may be chosen. The Render Settings window opens.

3. Click the Time Span drop-down menu and set it to Length of Comp.

4. Lower the frame rate for Web usage by selecting Use this frame rate and entering a value of 15.

5. Click OK to store the render settings. In the Render Queue panel the Render Settings now read Based on Best Settings. These changes can be easily stored for future use.

6. Click the drop-down menu next to Render Settings and choose Make Template.

7. In the Render Setting Templates window, enter Best Flash Video 15 fps and click OK. Then click the disclosure triangle next to the words Render Queue to close it.

Specify the output module

Now that the quality of render is set, you can adjust the kind of video that is rendered. After Effects supports more than 20 different output modules. The numerous formats can serve a diverse range of audiences from Web publishers to technical engineers to feature film producers.

1. In the Render Queue panel, click the disclosure triangle next to the words Output Module.

2. Click the text Lossless to modify the output module. The Output Module Settings window opens.

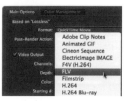

3. Click the Format drop-down menu and choose FLV. Notice that F4V files can also be chosen.

4. Click the Format Options button. From the Preset drop-down menu choose FLV – Same as Source (Flash 8 and Higher).

5. Click the Video tab to control the video properties. In the Bitrate Settings area, lower the Bitrate (kbps) to 1,000. Change the Frame Rate (fps) to 15.

▲ **TIP: Render Once Output Many**

If you need more than one file, click the plus symbol next to Output to in the Render Queue panel. This allows you to write multiple files (and formats) to disk. The majority of render time is consumed by the actual rendering of effects; adding different modules for output adds minimal time. In fact, it is a good idea to output an MOV or AVI file using the Lossless output module for backup purposes (just be sure to export your project's audio, too).

6. Click the Quality menu and choose Best (you may need to scroll down).

7. Click the Audio tab to control the audio properties. Change the Output Channels to Mono to reduce the file size. Lower the Bitrate to 96 kbps.

8. Click OK to store the settings. If you need to access them again for additional changes, just click the Format Options button.

9. Click OK to store the output module. In the Render Queue panel the Output Module Settings now read Based on Lossless. These changes can be easily stored for future use.

10. Choose Make Template from the Output Module drop-down menu.

11. In the Output Module Templates window, enter FLV for Web and click OK.

Rendering the file

Now that you've specified both the render settings and output module, the only steps remaining are to indicate an output path for the file.

1. Click the text next to Output To. A standard file navigation services window opens.

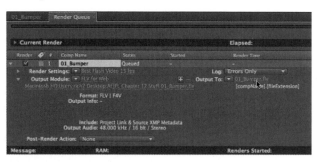

2. Navigate to the **Chapter_12 Project Files** folder, name the file Bumper.flv, and click Save.

3. Choose File > Save to capture the changes in the project file.

4. Click the Render button to process the file.

The file renders to disk. While After Effects is rendering, nothing else can be done in After Effects. You can switch to another application to work but may see reduced performance because After Effects draws heavily on RAM and system performance. It is not a good idea to attempt to run processor-intensive tasks like capturing or outputting video during a render.

What's Next?

You should now feel ready to compress video into the different Flash video formats. Knowing which options to choose is important so you can meet the technical requirements of each project. In Chapter 13, "Creating Interactive Controls" and in Chapter 14, "Making Video Accessible," you'll explore Flash video in greater depth. You'll learn ways to make video searchable and easier to index as well as how to improve the accessibility of the video for those with special needs. The easier your Flash video is to find and consume, the greater your reach and effectiveness.

▲ TIP: Save Those Settings

If you want to save a setting to your drive and load it on another system, it's a snap. Save the preset it's as you normally would by clicking the disk icon in the Export Settings viewing area. Then hold down the Option (Alt) key and click the disk icon to specify a destination like the desktop. Copy the files to the new machine, and then click the Load button to bring them in.

13 CREATING INTERACTIVE CONTROLS

Why use Flash for video? There are two reasons, one technical the other creative. The technical reason is that Flash is the leading way to display video on the Web if you want to attract the largest possible audience. More browsers have the Adobe Flash plug-in than any other technology.

That's clearly an important reason to use Flash for video, but there's a more exciting reason: Flash is an interactive, multimedia platform. By using Flash to play your video, you also gain access to Flash's other capabilities. You can enable users to interact with video in all sorts of new and exciting ways. This chapter explores just the tip of this Titanic-sinking-sized iceberg.

The Project

In this lesson you'll create a video of a news reporter sitting at his desk. It'll be used on the Get-To-Know-Our-Staff part of the news team's Web site. But you want to go beyond just showing the reporter typing on his keyboard. You want to make the video interactive. When the user clicks the reporter's phone, you want the reporter to pick up the receiver and have a phone conversation; when the user clicks the reporter's coffee cup, you want the reporter to take a sip; and so on. The goal here is to make the video allow viewer interaction (and possibly even trigger pop-up graphics or additional sounds).

● NOTE: Learn More About ActionScript

If you're intrigued and want to learn more, check out the *ActionScript 3.0 Visual Quickstart Guide* (Peachpit, 2008). You can also watch the Action-Script demo videos in this chapter's Project Files folder. More recommendations are at the end of the chapter.

You'll use a video of the reporter at his desk as your only asset: He types for a while, picks up his phone receiver, looks at a photo of his son, takes a sip of coffee, jots notes for a story, and then searches the Web. The video was shot with the camera in a locked position on a tripod, which minimized shake or jumpiness.

When the user clicks something on the desk, you'll use video cue points and ActionScript to send the video playhead to an appropriate point. ActionScript is Flash's programming language. This is not a book for programmers, so we'll just touch on the language. Even if you don't understand all the nuances, you'll appreciate the possibilities.

Prepping the Video

In this section you'll convert a QuickTime video to Flash's FLV format, one of two video formats Flash can display (the other is F4V, Flash's version of H.264). You'll add cue points to the video and add essential interactive controls.

Starting the Project

Our favorite way to prepare video for Flash is to use the Adobe Media Encoder. In the previous lesson, you learned how to run it as a stand-alone application. Another way to use it is to access it from within Flash.

1. From the book's DVD, copy the **Chapter_13 Project Files** folder to your hard drive.

2. In Flash, choose File > New and create an ActionScript 3.0 file. Save the file as reporter_01.fla in your copy of the **Chapter_13 Project Files** folder.

3. In the Properties panel, set the document to 640 × 360 pixels at 15 fps.

4. Choose File > Import > Import Video. Flash presents you with three choices as to how you want to import the video.

5. Choose "Load external video with playback component," which is the default choice.

   This option doesn't actually import the video. It leaves the video file external to the SWF but makes it appear as if it's on the SWF's Stage.

6. In the Import Video dialog, click Browse. Select the **desk.mov** file in the **Chapter_13 Project Files** folder and click Open.

7. Click OK in the error message dialog.

   Flash then prompts you to use the Adobe Media Encoder. The Creative Suite is all about seamless integration, so you can have Flash hand off the video it was using directly to the Adobe Media Encoder for optimization.

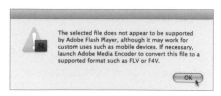

Converting the Video to Flash

When you try to import a video that is not supported by Flash Professional, it offers to convert it for you. Because Flash can't play MOV files, you'll need to convert it into an FLV or F4V file.

1. Click Launch Adobe Media Encoder at the bottom of the Import Video dialog.

● **NOTE:** F4V vs. FLV

While F4V is a newer format with several benefits, the older FLV format currently supports more interactive capabilities. Specifically, it makes working with cue points easier. (It also supports video with alpha channels, which the F4V format doesn't.) Since this chapter is about interactive video (and you'll be making heavy use of cue points), it's best to work with the FLV format.

▲ **TIP:** Using External Video

Loading an external video allows for the video's Timeline and Flash's Timeline to not be in sync. Even if Flash's Timeline runs at 5 frames per second and the video's runs at 29.97, the video will play just fine with no synching problems.

● **NOTE: Pressing Return/Enter Accidently**

If at any point you accidently press the Return/Enter key, the Adobe Media Encoder will think you're done. To return to editing the compression settings, click the hot text "Custom."

▲ **TIP: Working with F4V**

There are some complex work-arounds you can try if you want to use cue points with F4V files. You can read about them at http://theflashblog.com/?p=748.

▲ **TIP: Experiment with Distance**

The more distance between keyframes the fewer keyframes there will be. If there is not too much move-ment in the video, you'll get a smaller file. However, fewer keyframes may be imprecise. Trial and error is your friend.

2. Flash may remind you to switch back to Flash after encoding the video. If it does, click OK in the reminder dialog. Or you can click OK later when you return to Flash.

3. Switch to the Adobe Media Encoder application after it launches.

4. In the Adobe Media Encoder window, click the Preset drop-down menu and choose Edit Export Settings.

5. In the Export Settings window, choose the following options:

- Select FLV - Same As Source (Flash 8 and Higher) from the Preset menu.

- Deselect Export Audio since you're not using the audio track.

- In the Video tab:

    - Set the Frame Rate to 15 fps.

    - Set the Bitrate to 600 kbps.

    - Select Set Key Frame Distance.

    - Change the Key Frame Distance [frames] value to 3.

    You're adding more keyframes because you'll jump around in the video a lot instead of proceeding linearly from one frame to the next. To jump precisely, you need to land on a key-frame. The more frames you add, the larger the video file will be.

Now that the compression is set, let's add some cue points.

The Key to Video Keyframes

Video keyframes are completely different beasts from animation keyframes. At each video keyframe, the Adobe Media Encoder stores an entire image of that frame. On the following (nonkeyframe) frames, the encoder only stores pixels that are different from the previous keyframe. So, if the video is of a person talking and the only movement is the person's mouth, the keyframe will store the entire person; the following frames will just store the mouth. When the video plays back, it will fill in the missing pixels on nonkeyframes by grabbing them from the previous keyframe. This helps keep video files small because nonkeyframes don't need to hold copies of every pixel.

But the strategy falls apart if every frame contains a lot of movement. In such videos, nonkeyframes are so different from keyframes that few pixels will be conserved. The other problem with video keyframes is that they strain computer processors. The computer playing back the video has to keep going back to keyframes to grab pixels. We recommend testing your video on computers similar to those you are targeting.

Adding Cue Points

With cue points embedded, a video is more than just a succession of frames. Cue points add in useful metadata, which you can use to add chapter navigation and other forms of interactivity.

● NOTE: More from Cue Points

Cue points also allow you to make a video searchable and to add captions. You'll explore both in Chapter 14, "Making Video Accessible."

1. In the Cue Point area of the Export Settings window, drag the playhead to frame 00;00;06;21. You can also move to that frame by clicking the timecode, editing it directly, and pressing the Tab key (not Return/Enter) to apply the value.

   The precise frame isn't important, but you want to move to a frame that is approximately six seconds into the video—a frame in which the reporter's right hand is just barely visible.

2. Click the Add Cue Point button.

3. Double-click the cue point's default name (Cue Point) and rename it "start typing."

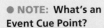

4. From the Type pop-up menu, choose Navigation.

Flash can detect Event cue points, but it can't use them as "chapter markers," for non-linear playback, Navigation cue points are best.

> **● NOTE: What's an Event Cue Point?**
>
> If you want a graphic, sound, or animation to appear next to the video when a certain point in the video is reached, use an Event cue point. You'll then need to use ActionScript to make content appear when the video reaches an Event cue point.

5. Move to frame 00;00;11;06 and add a Navigation cue point. Name this one "end typing" and press the Tab key.

6. Add the Navigation cue points found in this table.

Time	Label
00;00;23;15	start picture
00;00;29;20	end picture
00;00;59;28	start phone
00;01;23;15	end phone
00;01;43;20	start cup
00;01;56;00	end cup
00;02;23;16	start pad
00;03;01;03	end pad
00;03;17;11	start mouse
00;03;23;24	end mouse

7. Click OK in the Export Settings window.

8. Click Start Queue in the main Adobe Media Encoder window.

The Adobe Media Encoder will export an FLV version of the original MOV file. It will place the FLV in the same folder as the source video—in this case, the **Chapter_13 Project Files** folder. Wait until the video processes before switching back to Flash.

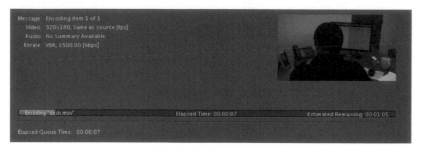

Importing the Video

Now it's time to add the video to the SWF's Stage.

1. Switch back to Flash. If necessary, dismiss the "After encoding…" message.

2. Click Browse in the Import Video dialog and open **desk.flv**. Click Continue.

3. In the Skinning screen, click the Skin pop-up menu and choose None.

4. Press Command+Return (Ctrl+Enter) to generate a test SWF. While the test is running, you'll be able to watch the video and try out the controls.

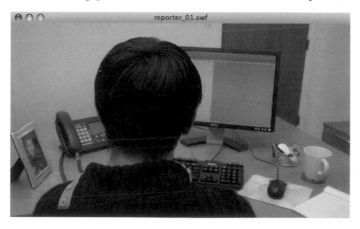

When you're ready to deploy the SWF on the Web, you'll have to upload the video file, too. If you use a skin (which we don't in this chapter), you'll need to upload three files: the SWF, the FLV, and an additional SWF that holds the skin, which Flash also stores externally to the main SWF file.

5. Close the test movie and choose File > Save.

● **NOTE: Importing in Flash? NOT!**

Although the import video process completed, the video was not actually imported into the SWF file. Instead, a reference to the external video file was imported. Flash knows to make it look as if the external file desk.flv is playing on the Stage. If you move, delete, or rename that file, Flash won't know where to find it.

● **NOTE: Remember Skins?**

You learned about using Flash's built-in skins in Chapter 12, "Professional Encoding of Flash Video." These work great, but for this exercise you'll create custom buttons.

Adding Simple Interactivity with Buttons

There are two steps to adding interactivity: indicating to Flash what action you'd like to happen and making something trigger that action. The most common trigger is a button. You'll start by adding some of these buttons. Then you'll add ActionScript code to explain what happens when the buttons are clicked.

Adding Play and Pause Buttons

▲ **TIP: Making Your Own Buttons**

In addition to using the buttons that ship with Flash, you can also create your own custom buttons. Too see how, watch the video demo in this chapter's Project Files folder called making buttons.mov.

Let's add a button to pause the video. In this case, you'll use a built-in button library that ships with Flash.

1. In the Timeline, name the video layer video.
2. Click the New Layer button.
3. Name the layer buttons (if necessary, drag it to the top of the stack).
4. Lock the video layer video and select the buttons layer.

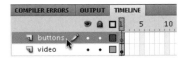

5. Choose Window > Common Libraries > Buttons.
6. Scroll down the list, and then double-click the playback rounded folder.
7. Select the rounded grey pause button and drag it to the Stage.

8. In the Properties panel, enter a width of 75 and a height of 50 for the Pause button.

9. Select the rounded grey play button and drag it to the Stage.

10. In the Properties panel, enter a width of 75 and a height of 50 for the Play button.

11. Drag the Play button so its top edge aligns with the Pause button.

12. Position the two buttons on the Stage.

13. Close the Buttons library window.

14. Choose File > Save.

Now that the buttons are added, you need to prep them to work with ActionScript.

Adding Instance Names

You're almost ready to code. If coding is new to you, it will seem very different than designing. When you're programming, your toolset shrinks. You no longer use Selection tools or Text tools. Your only tool is the keyboard. You give the computer instructions by typing commands. If you want something to happen, there has to be a name connected to that something. Your buttons and the video need names so that you can reference them in code. You also need names for the instances on Stage.

1. With the Selection tool, click the Pause button to select it. In the Properties panel, type pauseButton as the instance name.

Instance names can't contain spaces, and they must start with a letter. The rest of the name can be any mixture of letters, numbers, underscores, or dollar signs. No other sorts of characters are allowed.

2. Select the Play button and give it the instance name playButton.

3. Unlock the video layer, and then select the FLVPlayback component (click the FLV icon on the Stage). Name the instance videoPlayer.

> ● NOTE: ABC vs. abc
>
> Instance names are case sensitive. If you name an instance videoPlayer, you must type its name exactly like that in your code. VideoPlayer (with a capital "V") won't work. Always make sure your code references and instance names match. If your code doesn't work, this is the first thing you should check when you try to fix it.

Coding the Pause Button

It's time for your first foray into ActionScript. The most frustrating aspect of coding for new coders is how literal-minded computers are. The tiniest typo can cause your code to break. You may find that as you read through the rest of the chapter, you can't get your code to work. If that's the case, it's probably due to some tiny error you're not noticing.

To make it easier, we've provided the code in a TXT file. Open the file **13_Code.txt** with a plain text editor. You can then copy and paste the code. Be sure to carefully select just the required code, not the labels or other information.

● **NOTE: External ActionScript**

It's easier to keep code in the Timeline than it is to move the code to an external file, so we're using that easy method here. However, most professional ActionScript developers keep their code in external .as files. For more info, see the ActionScript demo videos in this chapter's Project Files folder.

1. Add a new layer called actionscript and drag it to the top of the stack.

   ActionScript—like everything else in Flash—needs to exist in a frame on a layer. The ActionScript program will run when the playhead hits its frame. Because you want your buttons to work immediately, you'll place your program in the first frame.

2. Select the first frame on the actionscript layer, and choose Window > Actions.

   Flash displays the ActionScript editor. This is really just a text editor with some color coding to help you see typos.

3. Click the Pin Active Script button (it looks like a thumbtack) at the bottom of the editor. This ensures that all your code goes into Frame 1. If you unpin the editor, you might accidentally insert code into another frame.

4. Type the following code into the editor:

```
import fl.video.*;
pauseButton.addEventListener(MouseEvent.CLICK, onMouseClickPause);
```

● **NOTE: Code#1**

To complete this step, you can paste the code from the Code#1 section of 13_Code.txt into the Actions panel.

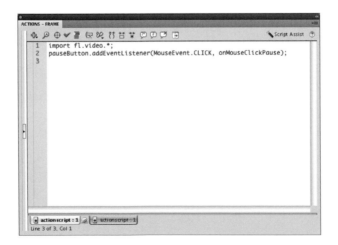

An explanation of this code follows in the next section, but first double-check the following:

- **Lowercase and uppercase letters:** ActionScript is case sensitive. Make sure your capitalization matches precisely.

- **Make sure the punctuation is correct.** In the first line of code, there are two periods, an asterisk, and a semicolon. Running from left to right in the second line the symbols are period, open parenthesis, period, comma, space, close parenthesis, and semicolon.

5. Press Return/Enter and then add the following code to line 4:

```
function onMouseClickPause(event:MouseEvent):void
{
  videoPlayer.pause();
}
```

● **NOTE: Code#2**

To complete this step, you can paste the code from Code#2 into the Actions panel.

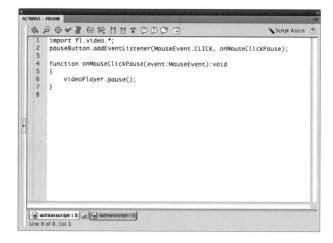

Again, make sure the letter cases (upper/lower) are correct as well as the punctuation.

Before typing videoPlayer.pause, press the Tab key to indent the line. On the line above and below are curly braces (they share real-estate space with the bracket keys on your keyboard). After videoPlayer.pause you'll see an open and close parentheses and a semicolon.

From this point forward, every nuance of the code will not be pointed out. Just be sure to double-check for typos, looking closely at case and punctuation.

What Does the Code Mean?

● NOTE: Semicolons in ActionScript

In ActionScript, semi-colons work similarly to periods in English. In English, a period marks the end of a sentence; in Action-Script, a semicolon marks the end of a statement.

ActionScript is a comprehensive language, and Flash only recognizes parts of it by default. Without help, it can't identify any commands relating to the FLVPlayback component (the official name for the video player on the Stage). That's the reason for adding the first line of code:

```
import fl.video.*;
```

This line imports a capacity to interpret video controls and cue points into the Flash file.

There are essentially two programs in the rest of the code: The first one is the line that starts "pauseButton.addEventListener..."; the second one is everything else.

Let's take a look at the second one:

```
function onMouseClickPause(event:MouseEvent):void
{
    videoPlayer.pause();
}
```

A function is like a mini computer program that performs a specific task. This function makes the video player pause. You don't want the video player to pause automatically. You only want it to pause when the user clicks the Pause button. To indicate this, the function is named onMouseClickPause. Translated into English, this program would be called "In the Event of a Mouse Click on the Pause Button."

The curly braces denote the start and end of the onMouseClickPause program. Translated into English, the code would look like this:

```
little program:
title: onMouseClickPause
start:
    pause the video player
end:
```

● NOTE: The Function of Functions

You'll find a short explanation of how functions work in the Chapter_13 Project Files folder. Simply open the PDF file 13_Function_of_Functions.pdf.

An explanation of event:MouseEvent or the word void would get pretty technical, so it's better left for a dedicated book on ActionScript. With this code, you get a taste of what ActionScript can do and an idea of how it works.

You now have a little program that pauses the video player, but how does that program know when to run? Sure, the program is called onMouseClickPause, but that's just its title. There are two buttons on the Stage. You only want this program to run when the Pause button is pressed. To ensure that, you use this line of code:

```
pauseButton.addEventListener(MouseEvent.CLICK, onMouseClickPause);
```

Recall that pauseButton was the instance name you gave the Pause button on the Stage. This code adds an Event Listener to the button. An Event Listener is an automatic process that waits (listens) for the user to do something (or in some cases for the computer to do something).

This Event Listener waits for MouseEvent.CLICK. In other words, it waits for the user to click the mouse while the cursor is over pauseButton. When the user clicks the mouse, onMouseClickPause runs.

Coding the Play Button

Since you have two buttons on the Stage, you'll also need to code the Play button. The code will seem similar to the previous code you wrote.

1. In the editor, modify the code as shown in bold, below:

```
import fl.video.*;

pauseButton.addEventListener(MouseEvent.CLICK, onMouseClickPause);
playButton.addEventListener(MouseEvent.CLICK, onMouseClickPlay);

function onMouseClickPause(event:MouseEvent):void
{
  videoPlayer.pause();
}
function onMouseClickPlay(event:MouseEvent):void
{
  videoPlayer.play();
}
```

● NOTE: **Code#3**

To complete this step, you can paste the code from Code#3 into the Actions panel.

The new lines of code are very similar to the existing lines, so copy and paste are your friends here.

2. Close the Actions panel.

3. Test the movie by pressing Command+Return (Ctrl+Enter). Try out the Pause and Play buttons.

Advanced Interactivity

Now that you've had your first experience with ActionScript, you'll venture out to the deep end. You'll add some very advanced interactivity, which was mentioned at the beginning of the chapter: When the user clicks the phone, you'll make the reporter pick up the phone; when the user clicks the cup, you'll make the reporter drink some coffee; and so on.

Once again, there is no need for you to understand every nuance of the code, we just mean to motivate you to learn ActionScript and teach you how to use the event cue points you created earlier.

Adding Invisible Buttons

How can you possibly make the phone clickable? It's not a button—it's pixels in a video. The answer is that you'll make a Flash button and position it on top of the phone. The catch is that you'll make the button invisible. Users will think they're clicking the phone when they'll actually be clicking an invisible button. Invisible buttons are very easy to make.

1. Continue with the previous file or open the file **buttons_complete.fla** from the **Chapter_13 Project Files** folder.

2. Delete the Play and Pause buttons from the Stage.

   If you want, you can also delete them from the Library by selecting them and then clicking the trash can at the bottom of the Library panel. But one nice thing about Flash is that unused Library symbols (those that aren't on the Stage) aren't exported into the final SWF, so you don't have to worry about them affecting file size.

3. Lock the video layer. Create a new layer and name it temp. Drag it immediately above the video layer. Make sure it's the selected layer.

4. Choose File > Import > Import to Stage and import the **desk.jpg** image from the **Chapter_13 Project Files** folder. Lock the temp layer.

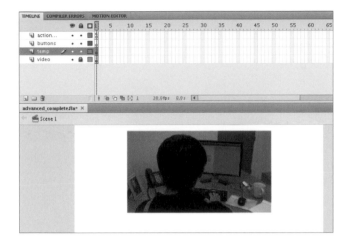

The image is a screenshot of the video playing. It will allow you to place your buttons correctly. You'll delete it when you're done.

5. On the buttons layer, draw a rectangle that covers the phone receiver. It doesn't matter what fill and stroke colors you use, because the rectangle will never be seen.

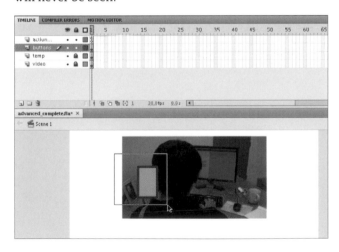

6. Select the rectangle's fill and stroke (or double-click its fill).

7. Right-click the rectangle and choose Properties from the pop-up menu. In the Convert to Symbol window name it Invisible Button. Choose Button from the Type pop-up menu and click OK.

NOTE: The Straight Dope on Buttons

Internally, button Timelines have four active frames (the rest of the frames never display): Up, Over, Down, and Hit.

For more information about buttons, watch the video in this chapter's Project Files folder, making buttons.mov.

8. Double-click Invisible Button on the Stage or in the Library. Drag the Up keyframe to the Hit frame. The button now has only a Hit image, which makes it an invisible button. You may need to try dragging more than once to get the hang of it.

9. Return to Scene 1.

The button doesn't look invisible; it looks blue. This is just Flash's way of displaying it in the authoring tool, so you can move it and resize it. If you generate a test SWF, you won't see it. But before generating a test SWF, make sure you delete the ActionScript code (see step 2 in the following section). It's leftover code from the previous section, and it will now cause errors because it refers to Play and Pause buttons that no longer exist on the Stage.

10. Select the Invisible Button on the Stage and duplicate it by pressing Command+D (Ctrl+D).

11. Place the duplicate on top of the picture of the reporter's son. Use the Free Transform tool to resize the duplicate button so that it approximately matches the dimensions of the picture.

Add more duplicates to cover the cup, the mouse, the legal pad, the computer monitor, and the keyboard. It's important that the buttons *do not* overlap.

TIP: Rotate Buttons

Using the Free Transform tool, move your mouse pointer to a corner. You can then rotate the button for better position.

12. One by one select the invisible buttons and give them the following instance names:

    • phoneButton

    • pictureButton

    • cupButton

    • mouseButton

    • padButton

- screenButton
- keyboardButton

13. Select the temp layer and click the trash icon at the bottom of the Timeline.

The Code

Now that you've hidden invisible buttons on the Stage, it's time to make them do something. As always, you need code to make a button work. In this section, you'll write code to make the video skip to specific cue points when users click the invisible buttons.

1. Keep working with your current file or open the file **invisible_buttons_ complete.fla** from the **Chapter_13 Project Files** folder.

2. Open the ActionScript editor by choosing Window > Actions. Select the code in the ActionScript editor and press Delete.

3. Add Event Listener code for the invisible phone buttons, the import statement, and the onPhoneButtonClick function:

```
import fl.video.*;

phoneButton.addEventListener(MouseEvent.CLICK, onPhoneButtonClick);

function onPhoneButtonClick(event:MouseEvent):void
{
  videoPlayer.seekToNavCuePoint("start phone");
}
```

This code tells the video player to jump to the cue point called start phone (that you created at the beginning of this chapter) when the user clicks the phone button.

The only problem now is that once the video player jumps to the start phone cue point, it will just continue playing on from that point to the end of the video. You want it to stop when it reaches the end phone cue point.

● NOTE: Code#4

To complete this step, you can paste the code from Code#4 into the Actions panel.

● NOTE: What's With the Arrows?

Some lines of Action-Script are wider than we can fit between this book's margins. In such cases, we've split the code over two lines and used arrows to show where we made the split.

4. Modify the code in the editor to read as follows:

```
import fl.video.*;

phoneButton.addEventListener(MouseEvent.CLICK, onPhoneButtonClick);
videoPlayer.addEventListener(MetadataEvent.CUE_POINT,
➥onCuePointReached);

function onPhoneButtonClick(event:MouseEvent):void
{
  videoPlayer.seekToNavCuePoint("start phone");
}

function onCuePointReached(event:MetadataEvent):void
{
  if (event.info.name == "end phone" || event.info.name == "end
➥typing")
  {
    videoPlayer.seekToNavCuePoint("start typing");
  }
}
```

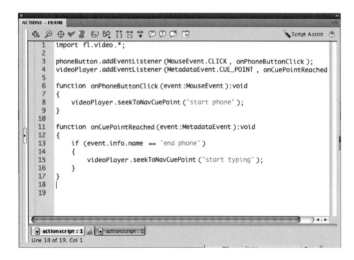

● NOTE: Seeing Double

One of ActionScript's many quirks is that equals is indicated with two equal signs instead of one, so if (event.info. ➥name == "end ➥phone") isn't a typo; it's the way the code needs to be.

The code inside the new onCuePointReached function translates into English as: "If the cue point just reached is called 'end phone,' go to the cue point called 'start typing.'" So when the reporter is done talking on the phone, he'll resume typing at his keyboard. When he's done typing, he resumes typing again, so that when the user isn't clicking any of the invisible buttons, the video loops forever between start typing and end typing.

The two vertical lines in the middle of the "if" line are pipe symbols. They share real-estate space with the Backslash key (right above the Return/Enter key) on most keyboards. In ActionScript, two pipes mean "or." So now the code translates as: "If the cue point just reached is 'end phone' or 'end typing,' return the video to 'start typing.'"

5. Generate a test movie. If you watch it for a while, you should see that the reporter is stuck in a loop of endless typing. After watching him type for a bit, click the phone receiver. The reporter should pick up the phone, have a short conversation, hang up, and then resume his typing loop.

6. Close the test movie.

Making the Code More Universal

As the code now stands, it returns to the start typing cue point when the end phone cue point is reached. But you also want it to return to start typing when end picture, end cup, end pad, and end mouse are reached. So you need to make that onCuePointReached function a bit more universal.

1. Edit the code so that it reads as follows:

```
import fl.video.*;

var endCuePoint : String;

phoneButton.addEventListener(MouseEvent.CLICK, onPhoneButtonClick);
videoPlayer.addEventListener(MetadataEvent.CUE_POINT,
➥onCuePointReached);

function onPhoneButtonClick(event:MouseEvent):void
{
  videoPlayer.seekToNavCuePoint("start phone");
  endCuePoint = "end phone";
}

function onCuePointReached(event:MetadataEvent):void
{
  if (event.info.name == endCuePoint || event.info.name == "end
➥typing")
  {
    videoPlayer.seekToNavCuePoint("start typing");
  }
}
```

● **NOTE: Code#5**

To complete this step, you can paste the code from Code#5 into the Actions panel.

```
     import fl.video.*;

     var endCuePoint : String;

     phoneButton.addEventListener (MouseEvent.CLICK , onPhoneButtonClick );
     videoPlayer.addEventListener (MetadataEvent.CUE_POINT , onCuePointReached );

     function onPhoneButtonClick (event:MouseEvent):void
     {
         videoPlayer.seekToNavCuePoint ("start phone" );
         endCuePoint = "end phone";
     }

     function onCuePointReached (event:MetadataEvent):void
     {
         if (event.info.name == endCuePoint || event.info.name == "end typing" )
         {
             videoPlayer.seekToNavCuePoint ("start typing" );
         }
     }
```

The line you added at the top,

```
var endCuePoint : String;
```

creates a variable (a var) called endCuePoint. A variable is like a temporary note pad or scratch paper (sort of like your system clipboard) where you can store information. The type of information you'll be storing there is text, which in ActionScript is called String data. So the code translates as: "Hey, computer. Give me some scratch paper with endCuePoint written at the top. I'm going to store text on it."

In the onPhoneClicked function—the program that runs when the phone is clicked—you're storing the phone sequence's end cue point on your scratch paper.

In the onCuePointReached function, you're telling the video to go back to start typing whenever the cue point on the scratch paper is reached.

2. Generate a test movie.

You shouldn't notice any difference from the previous test, but when you're coding, it's a good idea to test often. That way you can catch typos as you make them.

Coding the Other Buttons

The rest of the buttons are easy, because their code is almost the same as the code for the phone button. Each button's function tells the video to jump to its start cue point. It also stores its end cue point on the scratch paper.

(Only one piece of data can be stored on the scratch paper at once, so when a function stores something there, any previous value is erased.)

To save you some typing, you can use a text file that contains the code.

1. Open the file **13_Final_Code.txt** from the **Chapter_13 Project Files** folder using a plain text editor.

2. Copy the text to your clipboard.

3. Select the Actions panel.

4. Paste the code.

```
1   import fl.video.*;
2
3   var endCuePoint : String;
4
5   phoneButton .addEventListener (MouseEvent.CLICK , onPhoneButtonClick );
6   pictureButton .addEventListener (MouseEvent.CLICK , onPictureButtonClick );
7   cupButton .addEventListener (MouseEvent.CLICK , onCupButtonClick );
8   padButton .addEventListener (MouseEvent.CLICK , onPadButtonClick );
9   mouseButton .addEventListener (MouseEvent.CLICK , onMouseButtonClick );
10  screenButton .addEventListener (MouseEvent.CLICK , onScreenButtonClick );
11  keyboardButton .addEventListener (MouseEvent.CLICK , onKeyboardButtonClick );
12  videoPlayer .addEventListener (MetadataEvent.CUE_POINT , onCuePointReached );
13
14  function onPhoneButtonClick (event :MouseEvent ):void
15  {
16      videoPlayer .seekToNavCuePoint ("start phone" );
17      endCuePoint = "end phone" ;
18  }
19
20  function onPictureButtonClick (event :MouseEvent ):void
21  {
22      videoPlayer .seekToNavCuePoint ("start picture" );
23      endCuePoint = "end picture" ;
24  }
25
26  function onCupButtonClick (event :MouseEvent ):void
27  {
28      videoPlayer .seekToNavCuePoint ("start cup" );
29      endCuePoint = "end cup" ;
30  }
31
32  function onPadButtonClick (event :MouseEvent ):void
33  {
34      videoPlayer .seekToNavCuePoint ("start pad" );
35      endCuePoint = "end pad" ;
36  }
37
38  function onMouseButtonClick (event :MouseEvent ):void
39  {
40      videoPlayer .seekToNavCuePoint ("start mouse" );
41      endCuePoint = "end mouse" ;
42  }
43
44  function onScreenButtonClick (event :MouseEvent ):void
45  {
46      videoPlayer .seekToNavCuePoint ("start typing" );
47  }
48
49  function onKeyboardButtonClick (event :MouseEvent ):void
50  {
51      videoPlayer .seekToNavCuePoint ("start typing" );
52  }
53
54  function onCuePointReached (event :MetadataEvent ):void
55  {
56      if (event.info.name == endCuePoint || event.info.name == "end typing" )
57      {
58          videoPlayer .seekToNavCuePoint ("start typing" );
59      }
60  }
```

Script Assist

video : 1   actionscript : 1
Line 60 of 60, Col 2

Note the onScreenButtonClick and onKeyboardButtonClick functions. When the user clicks the screen or the keyboard, you'll return the video to the typing loop. You don't have to store end typing on the scratch paper, because the onCuePointReached function is already watching for end typing.

5. Test the movie. You can now click any of the invisible buttons to make the reporter interact with items on his desk.

In Flash, video is more than just video. Flash Video is a launching point for multimedia and interactive content.

One More Word About ActionScript

▲ TIP: Learn More About ActionScript

Here are a few more ActionScript resources:
- *ActionScript 3.0 for Adobe Flash CS4 Professional Classroom in a Book* (Adobe Press, 2008)
- www.lynda.com.
- *Essential Action-Script 3.0* (O'Reilly Press, 2007)
- *Foundation Action-Script 3.0* (Friends of Ed, 2007)

We know that some readers prefer to categorize themselves as designers (or motion-graphic artists). Others choose to consider themselves programmers (or developers). That's fine. The world needs both right-brained and left-brained thinkers.

Keep in mind that it's a good idea for Flash designers to understand a little ActionScript so they can collaborate with developers and tweak their scripts. This chapter has only scratched the surface of what's possible with ActionScript.

What's Next?

The next chapter explains different ways to make video more accessible. You'll learn how to harness Soundbooth to create a transcript. You'll then explore making the video searchable to find specific words. In addition, you'll use the transcript file to create open captions. This type of work has two benefits: It makes the video easier to search by a viewer, and it allows those with hearing impairments to watch the video.

14 MAKING VIDEO ACCESSIBLE

With the proliferation of video on the Web, access to information is getting easier (for most). The challenge is when an individual has an auditory impairment. The challenge with most Web video is that so much of the information is available only in the audio track. This is why there has been such a big push to make video more accessible.

There are two reasons to give everyone equal access to information: The first is simple, it's the right thing to do (and in some cases it's even the law). You need to do whatever you can to make video accessible to as many people as possible. This chapter shows you several measures you can take to greatly improve accessibility.

The second reason? Accessible video can be highly optimized for search engines. This means it's easier for people to find, and even search, your video. Video is one of the most expensive types of Web content. By getting more people to view it, you'll improve your chances of recouping your investment.

© ISTOCKPHOTO

In this chapter, you'll use Adobe's toolset for making video accessible. You'll use Adobe Soundbooth CS4 to transcribe a video's audio track, and then you'll turn that transcription into Flash Video cue points. When that's done, you'll learn how to make video searchable and how to display captions while the video is playing. Together, these features will make your video truly accessible.

First, the bad news: The key to making video accessible is to use words in the audio track to set cue points. Soundbooth exports audio transcripts in a specific XML format. Unfortunately, this is not the XML format that works best in Flash for captioning video. So you'll need to use some workarounds.

Now, the good news: By the time this book goes to press (or shortly thereafter), Adobe will likely have a solution ready for seamless cue-point integration between Soundbooth, Premiere Pro, and Flash. The developers are working on it. Check out this book's Web site at www.peachpit.com/AEFlashCS4 for the latest scoop. In the meantime, we'll offer a short-term solution.

Section 508 Compliance

In the United States, Federal agencies (and some industries) are required to make Web content (and other forms of electronic information) accessible to people with disabilities. These requirements are known as the Section 508 requirements. For more information, visit www.section508.gov.

This chapter touches the tip of the accessibility iceberg. Flash ships with many features that allow you to create accessible content, including the ability to make SWFs controllable via the keyboard and support for screen-access technologies such as the Window-Eyes screen reader from GW Micro. For more information, see the accessibility guidelines at www.adobe.com/accessibility/products/flash/author.html and http://help.adobe.com/en_US/Flash/10.0_UsingFlash/WSd60f23110762d6b883b18f10cb1fe1af6-7b34a.html (or you can search for "accessibility" in Flash's online help).

Transcribing Audio with Soundbooth

Soundbooth offers a very useful option that recognizes speech and translates it into text. The accuracy of this transcription can teeter-totter between being incredibly accurate to not very accurate. There are a few factors you can influence to improve the accuracy of the text:

- Use a professional-quality microphone to get a cleaner audio signal.
- Try to minimize or remove background noise.
- Isolate the voice from music or sound effects to make the transcription more accurate.
- Encourage the speaker to clearly pronounce words.

You will find that you'll generally have to do some cleanup after the automatic transcription process. Fortunately, Soundbooth makes cleanup easy.

1. Copy the **Chapter_14 Project Files** folder from the DVD to a local hard drive.

2. Launch Soundbooth, and then choose Window > Workspace > Edit Audio to Video to place Soundbooth in a state to work with video files.

3. Choose Window > Metadata to view the Metadata panel.

   The Metadata panel is your starting point for speech transcription. Running the transcription function takes a while, but when it's finished, all metadata for clips will be searchable from the Metadata panel. Fortunately, the process can run in the background, which means you can still edit or perform other tasks. The Metadata panel also allows you to search by any word or phrase within the clip.

4. Choose File > Open and open the file **gasPrices_original.f4v** from the **Chapter_14 Project Files** folder.

   You can open any standard type of video file in Soundbooth, such as QuickTime, AVI, F4V, or FLV.

5. Click Play to preview the file.

Become familiar with the short news story. You will optimize this clip for the Web and make it more accessible for the news channel's Web site.

● **NOTE:** Cleaning Up Audio

The clearer the audio is, the more accurate the transcription will be. If you have noise in the sound track, consider cleaning up the audio first. In Soundbooth, choose Tasks > Clean Up Audio from Soundbooth's menu. You can use the Clean Up Audio section to adjust the parameters and preview the changes until the audio sounds clean. For more information, see Soundbooth's online help.

● **NOTE:** Go for Max

Ultimately, the video you are transcribing will get recompressed as a Flash Video file. In this case, we are using a precompressed file to save space on the book's DVD. You should use the original-sized file from Premiere Pro or After Effects whenever possible.

Speech Transcription Options

To improve the accuracy of the transcription, Soundbooth needs additional information from you. Soundbooth can currently access seven different language libraries, and we expect this list to expand. You'll find that many languages offer subtle varieties, such as English offering localizations for Australia, Canada, the United Kingdom, and the United States.

1. Click the Transcribe button at the bottom of the Metadata panel.

2. Select the appropriate language. For this clip choose English - U.S.

3. Choose a Quality setting.

   Adobe offers two quality choices for the transcription. The default choice is High (Slower), which will take longer to process the files but offers significantly better translation. The second choice, Medium (Faster), should only be used when you are very tight on time. The results are less accurate but do process more quickly.

   In our tests, we used a 2.4 GHz Intel Core 2 Duo processor with 4 GB of RAM. The High method resulted in a ratio of 1.8, meaning the runtime of the clip multiplied by 1.8 equals the approximate processing time. The Medium method was nearly four times faster with a ratio of approximately .5.

   Since you have some time and it's a short clip, choose the High quality method.

4. Leave the Identify Speakers option deselected since there is only one voice in this news story.

   The transcription option can attempt to identify different speakers in a clip. In the Speech Transcription Options dialog, you can select Identify Speakers. This takes longer to process but will attempt to create separate transcripts for each person. This method can be inaccurate, so only use it if you have a long clip with multiple voices or want to export the transcript for others to view.

5. When you're ready to submit your clip, click OK.

   Depending on the speed of your computer, Soundbooth should take about three minutes to process the clip. While that's happening, let's take a look at the road ahead.

▲ **TIP: Learn Additional Languages**

To download all the additional language packs, go to www.adobe.com/products/soundbooth/speechtotext.

Cleaning Up the Transcript

When the transcript is complete, you can edit it. This means you can fix any words that you know are spelled wrong as well as add punctuation. While this involves a bit of manual labor, Soundbooth will have done 60–95 percent of the work for you.

Here is the script that the reporter read:

> *[Reporter] Despite the decreasing price of oil per barrel, gas prices at the pump continue to rise. With the onset of the economic crisis, oil companies and refineries have felt this pinch, forcing them to cut back on production. This cutback has ultimately trickled down to the consumers, causing higher prices at the pump. While commuters are grumbling about increasing gas prices, there doesn't seem to be any sign of a slowdown. Industry analysts predict prices will continue to rise for the next three months at least.*

1. Compare the preceding script to the Soundbooth transcription.

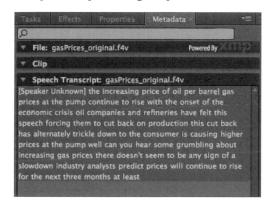

   Notice that Soundbooth was very accurate. Only two words were missed and one phrase was improperly transcribed. This is a very good start, but it's still not perfect. Some of the words are wrong, and there's no punctuation.

2. Double-click on the word increasing (in the first line). Change the word to decreasing.

3. Let's add the first punctuation mark. Double-click the word barrel (in the first line). Press the arrow key to move to the end of the word and type a comma to insert the natural pause.

Transcribe with Adobe Media Encoder

If you have several clips to transcribe, we recommend using the Adobe Media Encoder. This powerful tool is normally used to convert audio and video files to many different formats used for tasks like DVD authoring and Web distribution.

You can import an entire folder of media to transcribe. In the Adobe Media Encoder CS4 application, click the Add button in the main window. Then navigate and select multiple clips in a folder (hold down the Shift key to choose more than one clip). Next, specify Speech Transcription from the Format button. You must then specify options by clicking the word Custom (if you want to adjust multiple clips at once, Shift-click to select them all before clicking Custom). Select the Speech Params tab and set the Language, Quality, and Identify Speakers options using the aforementioned advice.

> ▲ TIP: Take Your Transcripts with You
>
> The entire transcript can be copied by selecting it all , right-clicking it, and then choosing Copy All. Additionally, you can include the transcript file in the final export if you are sending your video to the Web via Flash Video.

4. The phrase "down to the consumer is causing" has a few errors, so change the word consumer to consumers. Then, right-click the word is and choose Delete Word.

5. Continue editing the transcript, adding letters, merging or deleting words, and adding punctuation as needed. It should only take you a few minutes to clean up the text. You can reference the following text while making the fixes. The characters in red indicate a change to the transcript. You can use the Tab key from word to word in the transcript and press Return/Enter to edit:

> *[Reporter] Despite the decreasing price of oil per barrel, gas prices at the pump continue to rise. With the onset of the economic crisis, oil companies and refineries have felt this pinch, forcing them to cut back on production. This cut back has ultimately trickled down to the consumers, causing higher prices at the pump. While commuters are grumbling about increasing gas prices, there doesn't seem to be any sign of a slowdown. Industry analysts predict prices will continue to rise for the next three months at least.*

Exporting a Transcript as XML

After you've cleaned up the transcription, you can export it as an XML file. As you'll see in the next section, this XML file will become useful in several ways, notably for embedding cue points and making videos searchable.

1. From Soundbooth's menu, choose File > Export > Speech Transcription.

2. Save the file as gas.xml in the **Chapter_14 Project Files** folder. (The save is very fast; blink and you'll miss it.)

If you open the file in a text editor, it will look like this.

Importing XML Cue Points

You just exported the XML file out of Soundbooth, but now you'll bring it right back in. You can use the XML to create cue points (which Soundbooth calls "markers") on the video's Timeline. These cue points are critical because they allow Flash to associate the transcript with the video file for navigation.

1. Choose File > Import > Markers.

2. Navigate to the **Chaper_14 Project Files** folder and select the recently created gas.xml. Click Open.

   Several markers are added to the Timeline

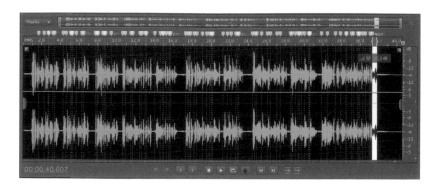

Here's Soundbooth's Timeline with the imported markers. These will become cue points in the rendered file.

Rendering an FLV

After the markers have been added, it's time to save out a file that is ready for Flash. This process is very simple.

1. Choose File > Save As. Name the file gas. Target the **Chapter_14 Project Files** folder. Choose FLV | F4V (*.f4v) form the Format pop-up menu. Click Save.

   The Export Settings window opens. You are essentially rebundling the compressed file so the markers get added into the file.

2. Choose FLV - Same As Source Flash 8 and Higher from the Preset pop-up menu.

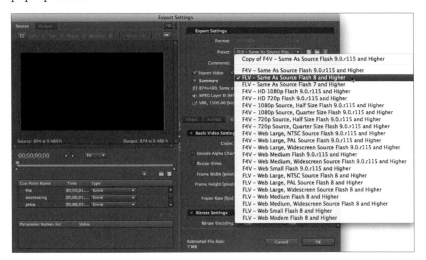

3. Change Bitrate Encoding to VBR.

4. Click OK to render out a file. This process takes a few minutes as the file re-encodes. When the process is done, quit Soundbooth.

Now that you have an XML file and an FLV file with markers, you can create accessible video.

Making Searchable Video

We've placed an HTML (Web page) application on this book's DVD. This application allows you to make your video searchable as if it was a text document. You'll need to make a couple of simple edits, and then everything will be good to go.

Loading the Assets

The HTML application looks for the XML and FLV file to be in a very specific location. You'll need to move these files into the folder for things to work.

1. Open the folder **Chapter_14 Project Files** in its own window.

2. In a second window, open the folder **VideoSearch** (which is a subfolder in the **Chapter_14 Project Files** folder).

3. Select gas.xml and gas.flv from the **Chapter_14 Project Files** folder and copy them into the **Media** folder (Chapter_14 Project Files > Video Search > Media).

4. In the **Media** folder, rename the XML file as **metadatavideo_1.xml** and the FLV file as **metadatavideo_1.flv**.

Testing the HTML

After the assets are loaded, you can simulate the searchable video. But first you'll need to get the simulation running with a few preferences tweaks.

1. Start your Web browser.

2. Open the file **SearchableVideo+Keywords.html** from the **VideoSearch** folder.

   The application won't work at first because it's running on your hard drive, not on the Web. Flash is very leery of interactions between HTML and Flash movies that run on your desktop, since they might be made by "hackers" who are trying to damage your system. In this case, the concern is unwarranted.

> ● **NOTE:** Evolving Files
>
> The provided HTML files are still in an evolving developmental stage. Check www.peachpit.com/ AEFlashCS4 for future improvements.

> ● **NOTE:** Browser Support
>
> At this time, the HTML only works with Safari and Firefox. We hope to have the code working with other browsers soon. For updates, check www.peachpit. com/AEFlashCS4

3. Right-click on the video player and choose Settings.

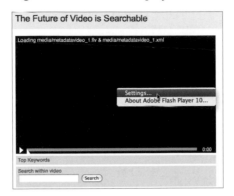

4. In the Adobe Flash Player Settings dialog, click the Advanced button.

A new window opens in the Web browser that offers links to the Settings panel. Again, to protect Flash from hackers, you'll need to manually navigate to this setting.

5. In the Settings Manager, click the Global Security Settings Panel hyperlink.

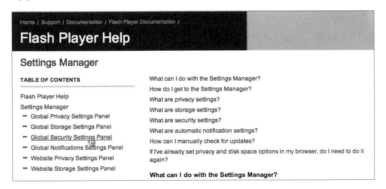

6. On the Global Security Settings tab, click the Edit Locations drop-down menu, and then choose the Add Location option.

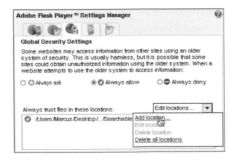

7. Add the file **video_player.swf** (Chapter_14 Project Files > Video Search > video_player.swf).

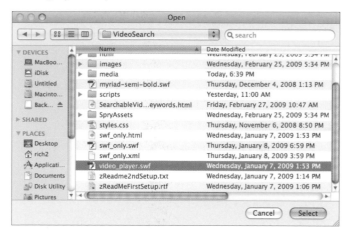

▲ **TIP: Restart Your Browser**

If you still get an error when you load the page, try closing out of your Web browser and restarting it. Then reload Searchable-Video+Keywords. html.

8. Reload the **SearchableVideo+Keywords.html** Web page.

9. Try typing gas into the search form (a word that's in the transcript), and then click the Search button.

▲ **TIP: By the Time You Read This...**

The searchable video tools have been updated. Flash is moving quickly and we have new information on searchable video. Check www.peachpit.com/ AEFlashCS4 for more details.

10. Once the video player has located cue points, click them to see the cue-point metadata.

11. Also, try clicking one of the Top Keywords to search for it in the video.

Creating Captioned Video

On its own, your XML file cannot be easily turned into captions that play alongside the video—at least not without some help from ActionScript. There's another kind of XML file—Timed-Text XML—that Flash can instantly turn into captions. Let's explore the process of creating captions and a Timed-Text XML file.

Display Captions with ActionScript

You'll use ActionScript to render captions to the Stage. This process is fairly advanced but works well.

1. Open **actionscriptCaptions.fla** from the **Captions** folder inside the **Chapter_14 Project Files** folder.

   On the Stage you'll see an FLVPlayback component and a Dynamic Text field.

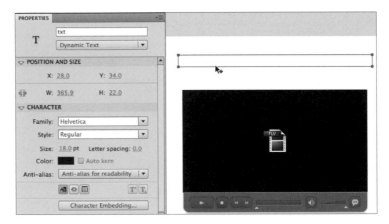

   If you want to reuse this file with your own FLV, be sure to embed cue points in it as described earlier in this chapter. Next, import the video using the steps described in Chapter 13, "Creating Interactive Controls," giving it any skin you like. Add a Dynamic Text field to the Stage. Then give the text field the instance name "txt" and the FLVPlayback component the instance name "video."

   As you can see from the Component Inspector, this instance of the FLVPlayback component is playing **gas_complete.flv**, which contains cue points created from Soundbooth's transcription.

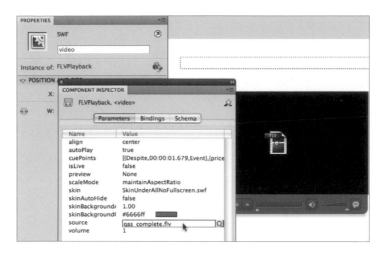

2. Select frame one of the ActionScript layer, and choose Window > Actions to reveal the code.

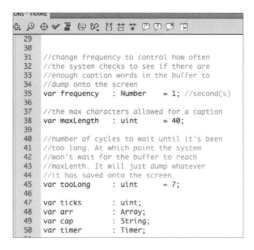

```
29
30
31    //change frequency to control how often
32    //the system checks to see if there are
33    //enough caption words in the buffer to
34    //dump onto the screen
35    var frequency   : Number   = 1; //second(s)
36
37    //the max characters allowed for a caption
38    var maxLength   : uint     = 40;
39
40    //number of cycles to wait until it's been
41    //too long. At which point the system
42    //won't wait for the buffer to reach
43    //maxLenth. It will just dump whatever
44    //it has saved onto the screen.
45    var tooLong     : uint     = 7;
46
47    var ticks       : uint;
48    var arr         : Array;
49    var cap         : String;
50    var timer       : Timer;
```

We won't describe the script here because it uses techniques covered in Chapter 13. Feel free to use it, modify it, or improve it any way you like.

3. Press Command+Return (Ctrl+Enter) to generate a test SWF.

4. Click the Caption button to view captions above the video.

crisis. Oil companies and refineries

● **NOTE: Comment Text**

In ActionScript code, any text that follows two forward slashes is a comment. It's meant for humans to read. The computer ignores it. Text surrounded by slash-asterisk and asterisk-slash (/* example */) is also comment text and is ignored by Flash.

Creating a Timed-Text XML File

If ActionScript seems like an overly complicated tool to display captions, you'll be happy to know there's an easier solution: Just drag the FLVPlayback-Captioning component from the Components panel to the Stage, and you're good to go—in theory. The problem is that the FLVPlaybackCaptioning component reads captions from an XML file that's in a very specific format: Timed-Text XML. Alas, Soundbooth doesn't export Timed-Text XML. In this screenshot, you can see Soundbooth's XML format on the left and Timed-Text XML on the right. They're very different.

● NOTE: Editing XML Files

When editing XML files, be sure to use a plain-text editor (sometimes called an ASCII editor). Sophisticated word processors, such as Microsoft Word, will add all sorts of formatting codes to the file, making it gibberish to Flash.

As of this writing, if you want to create Timed-Text XML, you have to do it by hand (in a text editor). But check this book's Web site at www.peachpit.com/AEFlashCS4 for updates. Adobe is working on a solution. As soon as we can get all the pieces working in unison, we'll post an updated solution.

In the meantime, to help you out, we've included two Timed-Text files in the **Chapter_14 Project Files** folder. In the Timed Text folder you'll find **gasPricesTimedText.xml**, which contains a transcription of the gas prices video, and **timedText.xml**, which is a template file you can use to make your own transcriptions.

In the latter file, the key section looks like this:

```
<div xml:lang="en">
  <p begin="00:00:00.00" dur="00:00:00.00" style="1">ADD CAPTION
➥TEXT HERE</p>
</div>
```

You will need to alter the line that begins with "<p" to indicate to Flash when you want the first caption to appear and disappear. You'll also have to add the caption text. For example, if the first caption is, "In 2009, paleontologists discovered that dinosaurs ate a diet of candy and pie," and you want that caption

to appear from one second into the video to three seconds into the video, you need to edit the code as follows:

```
<div xml:lang="en">
  <p begin="00:00:01.00" dur="00:00:03.00" style="1">In 2009,
➥paleontologists discovered that dinosaurs ate a diet of candy
➥and pie.</p>
</div>
```

Each caption specifies beginning and end timecodes, and each starts with "<p..." and ends with "</p>". So to make the next caption, just copy the first one and alter the copy as appropriate:

```
<div xml:lang="en">
  <p begin="00:00:01.00" dur="00:00:03.00" style="1">In 2009,
➥paleontologists discovered that dinosaurs ate a diet of candy
➥and pie.</p>
  <p begin="00:00:03.00" dur="00:00:04.00" style="1">The dinosaurs
➥were not available for comment.</p>
</div>
```

Add one "<p ... </p>" line for each caption.

FLVPlaybackCaptioning Component

Once you have a Timed-Text file you can create a captioned Flash file that is very accessible. Creating the Timed-Text file takes a little effort. But Adobe is working on a way to take the transcription file from Soundbooth and simplify this process. For this lesson, a converted file is provided.

Now for the easy part: You'll add the FLVPlaybackCaptioning component to the Stage, tell it where it's XML source file is, and that's that!

1. From the **Chapter_14 Project Files** folder, open the subfolder **Timed Text**, and then open **timedText_start.fla**.
2. Choose Window > Components to view the Components panel.
3. Click the disclosure triangle next to the Video group.

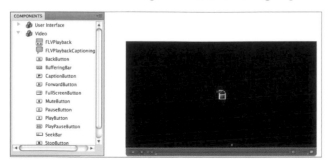

▲ **TIP: PC and Mac Text Editors Gotchas**

All computers come with plain-text editors. PCs ship with Notepad. If you use Notepad, put quotation marks around the filename when you save it for the first time (e.g., "file.xml" not file.xml). Notepad adds a .txt extension to files by default, so if you're not careful, your file will be named file.xml.txt. Wrapping the name in quotation marks, e.g. "file.xml", lets Notepad know you don't want the default extension added. (This is a general Windows tip for suppressing default extensions.)

Macs ship with TextEdit. If you use TextEdit, be sure to choose Format > Make Plain Text.

4. Drag the FLVPlaybackCaptioning component to the Stage.

You can drop it anywhere, even offstage. The FLVPlaybackCaptioning component does not show up in the exported SWF. It becomes an invisible mechanism that controls and displays captions.

5. With the component selected, choose Window > Component Inspector.

6. In the Inspector, set the source to gasPricesTimedText.xml and the path to the XML file containing the captions. You set the source by double-clicking the blank area in the Component Inspector to the right of the word "source." In this case, the source is just the XML file's filename, since the FLA and the XML file are in the same folder.

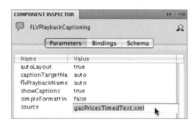

7. Generate a test SWF. Small captions appear that are superimposed over the video. In the following section, you'll format the captions so they're larger.

8. With the FLVPlaybackCaptioning component selected, change the value of showCaptions (in the Component Inspector) to false.

We chose a skin with a caption toggle button, so you don't want captions to show by default. With showCaptions set to false, captions will only appear if the user clicks the caption toggle button.

▲ **TIP:** Learn More About XMP

These features are in their infancy but should prove useful as they continue to mature. Be sure to give them a shot. For more information about XMP metadata, see www.adobe.com/go/learn_dv_tutorial_xmpcreative_en.

Changing the Look of Caption Text

You're probably having trouble reading the tiny captions Flash is currently displaying. Fortunately, caption text is easy to format. In this section, you'll edit gasPricesTimedText.xml to set styling options for the captions. You'll find a finished version of the edits in the file gasPricesTimedTextFormatted.xml in the Chapter_14 Project Files folder.

1. From the **Chapter 14 Project Files** folder, open the **Timed Text** subfolder, and then open **gasPricesTimedText.xml** in a plain text editor, such as TextEdit (Mac) or Notepad (Windows).

2. Locate the </styling> section at the top of the file.

● **NOTE:** Styling Options

For more styling options, see http://help.adobe.com/en_US/ActionScript/3.0_UsingComponentsAS3/WS5b3ccc516d4fbf351e63e3d118a9c65b32-7ee5.html.

3. Change the section so it describes the styles you want to use. In this example, centered black text on a white background was chosen with a font size of 40.

Notice that these attributes are all part of a style with the ID of 1. You can store multiple styles in a Timed-Text file. Just give each one a unique ID number. You then connect a style to a caption (or captions) as shown in the following figure.

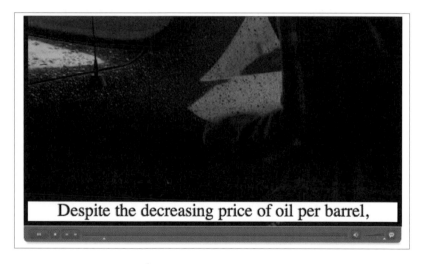

4. Save the changes to gasPricesTimedText.xml, and then generate another test SWF in Flash.

Using Your Own Text Field to Display Caption Text

If you want, you can use your own text field (created with Flash's Text tool) to display captions controlled by the FLVPlaybackCaptioning component. This is useful if you want complete control over the location and look of the caption text.

1. From the **Chapter_14 Project Files** folder, open the **Timed Text** subfolder, and then open **timedText_textfield.fla**.

2. Select the text field above the video player, and in the Properties panel, give it the instance name "caption."

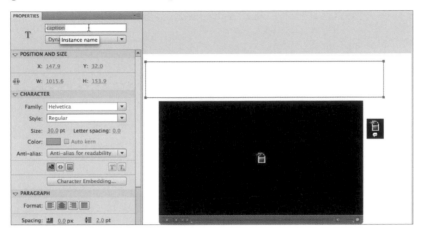

Note that the text field's type is Dynamic Text. In Flash, Dynamic Text is text that isn't set until runtime. Usually, this means text that's controlled by ActionScript. In this case, it means text that's controlled by the FLV-PlaybackCaptioning component.

3. Click the Character Embedding button in the Properties panel. In the Character Embedding dialog, click Uppercase, hold down the Shift key, click Punctuation, and then click OK.

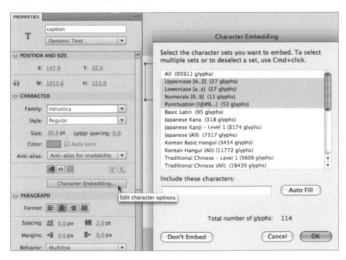

This embeds the font in the SWF, which will increase its file size by about 30K (a pretty small amount). When using Dynamic Text, it's a good idea to embed fonts, because if you don't, your viewers might not see anything if they don't have the font you're using installed on their systems.

Flash automatically embeds Static Text fonts, so you only have to worry about this with Dynamic Text (and Input Text).

4. Select the FLVPlaybackCaptioning component on the Stage, and in the Component Inspector, set autoLayout to false, captionTargetName to caption, showCaptions to true, and simpleFormatting to true.

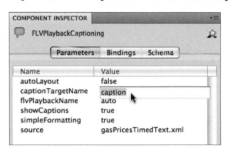

This instructs Flash to use your text field—with the instance name of "caption"—to display captions. It also forces Flash to use the text field's formatting and location instead of style instructions inside the XML file.

5. Generate a test SWF.

The captions look great and are much easier to read.

What's Next?

Well, you've reached the end of the book, so we can only offer you the end matter and the book's Web site (www.peachpit.com/AEFlashCS4). But be sure to keep an eye on the page, because we'll post updates as things continue to evolve with Flash and After Effects.

We'll also offer you some closing advice. When you boot up your computer in the morning, launch both Flash and After Effects. Log as much time as you can in each. They are two great tools that work well together. If you can command them both, you'll have a video and animation arsenal at your fingertips that is second to none.

INDEX

Get free online access to this book for 45 days!

And get access to thousands more by signing up for a free trial to Safari Books Online!

With the purchase of this book you have instant online, searchable access to it for 45 days on Safari Books Online! And while you're there, be sure to check out Safari Books Online's on-demand digital library and their free trial offer (a separate sign-up process). Safari Books Online subscribers have access to thousands of technical, creative and business books, instructional videos, and articles from the world's leading publishers.

Simply visit www.peachpit.com/safarienabled and enter code KBEUOXA to try it today.